Identifying International Financial Contagion

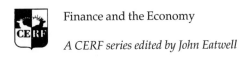

Finance and the Economy

A CERF series edited by John Eatwell

The Cambridge Endowment for Research in Finance (CERF) was founded in 2001 as an independent research center at the University of Cambridge. It is dedicated to developing an enhanced understanding of the evolution and behavior of financial markets and institutions, notably in their role as major determinants of economic behavior and performance. CERF promotes theoretical, quantitative, and historical studies, crossing conventional disciplinary boundaries to bring together research groups of economists, mathematicians, lawyers, historians, computer scientists, and market practitioners. Particular attention is paid to the analysis of the impact of financial market activity on the formulation of public policy. The CERF series of publications on Finance and the Economy embodies new research in these areas.

Global Governance of Financial Systems: The International Regulation of Systemic Risk
Kern Alexander, Rachel Dhumale, and John Eatwell

Identifying International Financial Contagion
Edited by Mardi Dungey and Demosthenes N. Tambakis

Identifying International Financial Contagion

Progress and Challenges

Edited by
Mardi Dungey
Demosthenes N. Tambakis

UNIVERSITY PRESS
2005

OXFORD
UNIVERSITY PRESS

Oxford University Press, Inc., publishes works that further
Oxford University's objective of excellence
in research, scholarship, and education.

Oxford   New York
Auckland   Cape Town   Dar es Salaam   Hong Kong   Karachi
Kuala Lumpur   Madrid   Melbourne   Mexico City   Nairobi
New Delhi   Shanghai   Taipei   Toronto

With offices in
Argentina   Austria   Brazil   Chile   Czech Republic   France   Greece
Guatemala   Hungary   Italy   Japan   Poland   Portugal   Singapore
South Korea   Switzerland   Thailand   Turkey   Ukraine   Vietnam

Published by Oxford University Press, Inc.
198 Madison Avenue, New York, New York 10016
www.oup.com

Oxford is a registered trademark of Oxford University Press

Library of Congress Cataloging-in-Publication Data
Identifying international financial contagion : progress and
challenges / Mardi Dungey, Demosthenes N. Tambakis, editors.
p. cm.
Includes bibliographical references and index.
ISBN-13 978-0-19-518-718-2
ISBN 0-19-518718-0
1. Financial crises—Prevention. 2. International finance.
I. Dungey, Mardi. II. Tambakis, Demosthenes N. (Demosthenes Nicholas), 1968–
HB3722.I34 2005
332'.042–dc22

2004027636

9 8 7 6 5 4 3 2 1

Printed in the United States of America
on acid-free paper

In memory of Dave Gardner, much loved friend
August 8, 1963–December 31, 2003   MD

To Anastasia and Nikos   DNT

Foreword

For the past three years a major theme in the research done at the Cambridge Endowment for Research in Finance (CERF) has been to develop a better understanding of the financial links between microeconomic risks and the performance of the macroeconomy. This work was stimulated by the events of 1997–98, when major financial crises emanating from the Far East and from Russia ultimately threatened the financial stability of the United States. Here was a striking case of the systemic risks familiar in national economies (via bank runs, or major shocks in asset markets) appearing on an international scale.

International financial crises have, of course, been a recurring phenomenon since the nineteenth century. But the extraordinary growth of international financial products and transactions that has been stimulated by the liberalization of international markets over the past thirty years has resulted in a qualitative change in relationships. Markets and economies are linked more closely and more rapidly than has ever been the case in the past. In relation to the size of real economies, financial flows are much larger than ever before. These factors pose immediate challenges for policymakers. The development of the current framework of international financial regulation—initially at Basel, Switzerland, and now at the International Monetary Fund and the Financial Stability Forum, too—has been the response. But that response has been predominantly reactive, patching up the international system once crises have revealed its weaknesses.

A major factor behind the limitation of policymakers to a reactive role has been the lack of an agreed, coherent theoretical understanding of the linkages among financial markets, systemic risk, and economic performance. Without a common theoretical framework, empirical work (though often providing important insights) has similarly lacked focus. An understanding of contagion is an important step toward the coherence that analysts seek and policymakers need.

That markets are "linked" has been a central element in economic analysis since Adam Smith's discussion of the division of labor in his *Wealth of Nations* of 1776. But financial contagion is clearly something different from linkages in transactions. The prices of financial assets are functions of their expected returns. Insofar as the expectations of traders in different markets are in some way related to one another, then a change in confidence in one market will spread to others. The problem is first to isolate what is meant by "in some way," and then to differentiate the proposed links from other relationships. So is the key to contagion simply "animal spirits" and "irrational exuberance," or is it embedded in the models used for financial valuation and regulatory assessment—or might it even be related to wider issues of confidence, including political factors? The use of the term *contagion* suggests that the relevant linkages, though latent, are unusual, even abnormal, or at very least a manifestation of "extreme events." And it is extreme events that are the drivers of international systemic risk. That is why an understanding of contagion is so important.

A conference held at CERF at the end of May 2003, led by Mardi Dungey and Demosthenes N. Tambakis, made significant progress in unraveling these problems and providing an intellectually satisfying framework for the understanding of contagion. The leaders of the original conference have since stimulated other researchers to join them in the endeavor, building on the earlier arguments, in particular by incorporating recent advances in measuring contagion by means of the econometric estimation of "abnormal" and unexpected linkages. The essays collected in this book represent a further important step forward.

John Eatwell
Director, CERF
Cambridge, January 2005

Acknowledgments

We are very grateful to a number of people who have encouraged and supported this project. We would like to thank our colleagues at CERF who supported the symposium from which this book began, and to all the participants at that symposium for their enthusiastic and sometimes heated discussion about what could possibly be meant by the term *contagion*. In particular, we would like to thank Bill Janeway and John Eatwell for their strong support throughout this project and Barry Eichengreen for encouraging us to collect a series of essays together in this manner. For helping with all manner of administrative tasks we are grateful to Mette Jamasb, and for enormous patience and excellence in physically compiling the text our thanks go to Edda Claus. Thanks are also due to our executive editor, Terry Vaughn at Oxford University Press, for supporting two novices in putting this book together.

We are very grateful to the American Economic Association for their permission to reprint Chapter 2, by Graciela L. Kaminsky, Carmen M. Reinhart, and Carlos A. Végh, "The Unholy Trinity of Financial Contagion," which first appeared in the *Journal of Economic Perspectives*, Fall 2003, Issue 4, pages 51–74 and to the University of Chicago Press for permission to reprint Chapter 8, by Allan Drazen, "Political Contagion in Currency Crises," which first appeared in *Currency Crises*, edited by P. Krugman, Chicago and London 2000.

Dungey acknowledges funding support for this project under Australian Research Council Grants A00001350 and DP0343418.

Canberra and Cambridge
May 31, 2005

Contents

Contributors

Shubha Chakravarty, Brookings Institution and Columbia University

Eleanor Debelle, Sydney, Australia

Allan Drazen, University of Tel Aviv, University of Maryland, College Park and NBER

Mardi Dungey, Australian National University and CERF

Luci Ellis, Reserve Bank of Australia

Renée Fry, Australian National University

Brenda González-Hermosillo, International Monetary Fund

Tim Gulden, Brookings Institution and University of Maryland

Yuko Hashimoto, Toyo University

Takatoshi Ito, University of Tokyo

Jan P. A. M. Jacobs, University of Groningen

Graciela L. Kaminsky, University of Washington and NBER

Gerard H. Kuper, University of Groningen

Lestano, University of Groningen

Vance L. Martin, University of Melbourne

Paul R. Masson, Brookings Institution and University of Toronto

Carmen M. Reinhart, University of Maryland and NBER

Demosthenes N. Tambakis, Pembroke College, Cambridge and CERF

Carlos A. Végh, UCLA and NBER

Identifying International Financial Contagion

1

International Financial Contagion

What Should We Be Looking For?

Mardi Dungey and Demosthenes N. Tambakis

1. INTRODUCTION

Use of the term *contagion* to describe the international transmission of financial crises has become fraught with controversy, to the extent that some recent authors have seen fit to avoid using the word entirely; see Favero and Giavazzi (2002) and Rigobon (2003). The term evokes an emotive response among both producers and consumers of research on international financial markets, and there is no general agreement over its use. It also implies, at least to some, that those who fall prey to financial crises do so through no fault of their own. However, this is an idea that some analysts are inclined to strongly resist: speculators appear to discriminate in choosing the countries they attack.

There are now a number of particularly good review papers on the contagion literature. The seminal paper is Dornbusch, Park, and Claessens (2000), who were the first to systematically classify this literature and provide an excellent overview of the theoretical framework and empirical work up to the turn of the century. Since that date the literature has boomed, and more recent surveys are provided by Pericoli and Sbracia (2003), Bekaert, Harvey, and Ng (2005), and Moser (2003). Pericoli and Sbracia categorize the existing literature into five broad definitions of contagion, and the empirical literature into a further five distinct, but related, approaches. They additionally provide a good description of how contagion may be related to portfolio management, particularly "rule of thumb" approaches. Bekaert and Harvey (2003) survey the literature on both crises and contagion with a focus on emerging markets. Moser has a particularly interesting focus on the policy implications of different ways of looking at contagion. Each of these papers is highly recommended reading for an overview of the existing literature.

Dungey: Australian National University and CERF, md396@cam.ac.uk; Tambakis: Pembroke College, Cambridge and CERF, dnt22@cam.ac.uk.

This chapter does not aim to provide another formal review of the literature. Rather, as a result of the existing literature it seeks to classify the types of questions that should be asked in making a reasonable assessment of existence or otherwise of contagion. Thus, the chapter proceeds to ask the following questions: First, which definition of contagion is reasonable? Second, how do we assess the empirical evidence of contagion? Third, what are the tensions between different financial market participants that may affect the international transmission of shocks and thus facilitate or hinder contagion? And fourth, what can international financial institutions such as the International Monetary Fund do about preventing contagion?

We begin with a review of what is meant by the term *contagion*. As mentioned above, there is widespread disagreement in the existing literature. When a crisis spreads from one country or market to another there may be a number of transmission channels for that spread. In the early streams of literature, the term *contagion* was often applied to all of these channels without discrimination; for example, the empirical application of Eichengreen, Rose, and Wyplosz (1995, 1996) and the theoretical models of Banerjee (1992) and Bikhchandani, Hirshleifer, and Welch (1992). However, as the debate on contagion effects intensified following the East Asian crisis of 1997–98, a number of distinctions emerged. It is now widely recognized that multiple crises across different countries and markets do not generally occur coincidentally; the probability of this is extremely low in all estimates—for example, Eichengreen and Bordo (2002) calculate the probability of a country's experiencing a financial crisis (currency, banking, or twin) at around 12 percent for 56 countries over the period 1973–97. Some obvious linkages between countries and markets that readily explain transmissions during crises include real links, such as through international trade and competitiveness effects due to exchange rate changes and macroeconomic fundamentals; and financial links created by banking structures, common creditors, and cross-market portfolio hedging and management, including liquidity effects and capital flows. These links have come to be known as fundamental links, and spawned the term *fundamentals-based* contagion, used by Dornbusch, Park, and Claessens (2000) and Kaminsky and Reinhart (2000), or *spillovers*, used by Masson (1999a,b). (However, we note that Kaminsky, Reinhart, and Végh, this volume, use the term *spillovers* alternatively to refer to the slow and gradual effects emanating from the original shock.)

In addition to vulnerabilities to crisis transmission caused by a particular country's fundamentals or structure, markets may also be affected by common shocks whereby all countries and markets respond, although not necessarily to the same extent, to a particular shock. Masson (1999a,b) distinguishes these as *monsoonal effects*. A clear example of such an event is an oil price shock. When the effects of fundamental linkages and common shocks are combined, the encompassing term for these transmissions is generally *interdependencies*, as in Forbes and Rigobon (2002); see also Pesaran, Schuermann, and Weiner (2003).

Once the channels of crisis transmission have been distinguished as fundamentals-based linkages, common shocks, or interdependencies, some observed transmissions remain unexplained. Sometimes, the extra transmissions during a crisis period relate to increased intensity in the existing fundamental channels, compared with a noncrisis period—a phenomenon captured by the term *shift-contagion;* see Pericoli and Sbracia (2003) and Forbes and Rigobon (2001). Alternatively, or perhaps additionally, there remains an unexplained residual of transmissions that do not fit into any of the previous categories. It is these residual transmissions, after controlling for fundamental links and common shocks, that have more recently become associated with "pure contagion" (Moser 2003), "true contagion" (Kaminsky and Reinhart 2000; Drazen, this volume), the "restrictive definition of contagion" according to the World Bank,[1] or purely as contagion itself differentiated from the other channels (Karolyi 2003).

In fact, Karolyi (2003) argues that the evidence for contagion is seriously tainted by the confusion in the literature over what is meant by the term. He argues for a higher bar on implementing this term to describe transmissions by excluding the use of interdependencies. In the empirical literature, Pesaran and Pick (2004) show that failing to adequately control for interdependencies leads to biased estimates of contagion.

Both Karolyi (2003) and Moser (2003) point to the importance of clarity in the source of contagion in evolving appropriate policy responses. Karolyi challenges the literature that stresses the potential role of the international financial architecture in preventing contagion, suggesting that more appropriate measurement may reveal many problems to be domestically sourced, and hence more appropriately rectified with domestic policy. If the transmission mechanisms of crises are unclear, then obtaining the appropriate policy response will be well nigh impossible (Moser).

There are a number of issues to be explored to set the scene for a more detailed exploration of financial contagion. First, contagious transmission is usually considered within the context of financial crises, so that crisis periods must be defined. The definition of crisis periods is closely related to whether contagion is characterized as a discontinuity in the data generating process, such as favored by Pericoli and Sbracia (2003). In this case, crisis dates are chosen analogously to the choice of thresholds for the proposed discontinuity. Second, appropriate fundamental controls need to be identified, either theoretically or empirically. The third issue is the appropriate capture of the characteristics of financial market data, which both theoretical and empirical models should be able to incorporate. The existing empirical evidence on contagion has led to much confusion due to the plethora of methodologies applied across different samples and data characteristics.

Having disposed of data characteristics, fundamental linkages, and thresholds, we move to consider how the views of contagion may differ from the perspective of different market participants. The policymaker and the financial market participant are likely to have different outlooks on what constitutes an important market movement based on individual portfolio placements and on views on systemic risk and common creditor risk. The heterogeneity in views has important implications for the coordination of policy responses, as amply demonstrated in the negotiations surrounding the rescue package for Long-Term Capital Management (LTCM) in September 1998. Hence, a fourth important issue is how to assess the aggregate potential of portfolio rebalancing by individual global investors to cause contagion, and how the rationality and liquidity constraints of individual investors can affect the spread of crises.

The remainder of this chapter proceeds to discuss the four issues raised above. Sections 2 and 3 discuss statistical and econometric issues arising in identifying financial contagion, and incorporated into models and tests for contagion. Section 4 reviews the literature on whether investor behavior during financial crises is driven by fundamentals or self-fulfilling beliefs (or both), and assesses the relative importance of financial and political economy constraints in analytical models of financial crises. This is followed, in section 5, by a discussion of the implications for macroeconomic and financial policy aimed at preventing contagion while maintaining international capital mobility. Finally, in section 6 we outline the structure of the book and offer some concluding remarks.

2.   DOES CONTAGION EXIST? IDENTIFICATION ISSUES

2.1   Identifying Crisis Periods and Discontinuities

To assess whether contagion truly exists, a number of requirements are raised. First, assuming that the researcher is interested in contagion as a crisis-period phenomenon, as most authors are, the crisis periods must be defined. Although theoretical models can define crisis periods, in the empirical literature this is a nontrivial exercise. The methods used depend on the asset market under consideration, and on both the span and frequency of the data available. The discussion of how to choose crisis dates is taken up in more detail for several different types of crisis in chapter 4 by Jacobs, Kuper, and Lestano. In chapter 2, Kaminsky, Reinhart, and Végh provide a chronology of crises, including their reasonings for those datings.

The historical evidence on the existence of financial crises suggests that crises are by no means a new phenomenon. Extensive overviews of the history of crises may be found in Bordo et al. (2001), Bordo and Eichengreen (1999), and Bordo and Schwartz (1999). These studies examine banking and currency crises, and their joint occurrences—so-called "twin crises"— over periods dating from as long ago as 1820 in Bordo and Schwartz.[2] Some useful generalizations as to the nature of crises result from these studies. First, there is some evidence that currency crises have grown more frequent since the collapse of Bretton-Woods, although not more severe (Bordo et al.). Second, the choice of exchange rate regime seems to matter with respect to the frequency of currency crises (Bordo and Eichengreen); and third, the cost of twin crises is much greater than that of individual crises under any regime (Bordo et al.; Bordo and Eichengreen). Bordo and Schwartz examine the successful (and otherwise) rescue attempts applied to banking and currency crises. One of their more important conclusions is that the threat of pure contagion, in the form of transmission of crisis effects to countries that have done nothing fundamentally wrong to deserve such transmission, is at least partly responsible for moral hazard problems associated with rescues in the late twentieth century. If borrowers and lenders expect to be shielded from "unfair" transmissions, then this will change their investment behavior. Bordo and Schwartz provide fascinating evidence and characterizations of successful rescue attempts, and highlight the increasingly large and unsuccessful attempts in the more recent periods, citing factors such as moral hazard, lending to insolvent as opposed to merely illiquid creditors, the involvement of taxpayers as opposed to market participants, and the relatively new role of international institutions as opposed to national solutions. Bordo and Murshid (2001) find limited evidence of contagion in either recent or past crisis events, although this evidence must be tempered by the choice of correlation tests, which it seems are likely to underreject the null hypothesis of no contagion, a point to which we return in section 3.3.

Given that crisis periods exist, there are a number of approaches to identifying and using them in the literature on contagion. In the theoretical literature, the advent of a financial crisis in one country can produce a switch in behavior, due to an ex ante rational response of global investors to the updated fundamentals leading to portfolio adjustment (as in Kodres and Pritsker 2002), or to a jump between multiple equilibria in self-fulfilling models of crisis (see Obstfeld 1995, 1996). In both cases, the switch may act as the identifying feature for the model. In the empirical literature the results may be sensitive to the choice of crisis period, although this is not often examined. Researchers must choose some date on which to start their investigation, and a number of routes are taken. The first is to follow the crisis literature and use an ad hoc approach to the dates based on chronologies or external observations by informed parties, such as the IMF or debt-monitoring agencies. This is the approach taken, for example, in Kaminsky and Schmukler (1999). An alternative approach is more data driven, letting nonlinearities in the data generating process generate the crisis dates. Observations that induce heteroskedasticity or nonnormality in the data, after controlling for interdependencies, are denoted *crisis observations* by Favero and Giavazzi (2002). Jeanne and Masson (2000) use a Markov switching mechanism.

A further approach is for the researcher to set some threshold value of the data or some constructed index of the data, and denote observations above that threshold to be periods of crisis. The use of a threshold is obvious in papers following the Eichengreen, Rose, and Wyplosz (1996) approach of a constructed exchange market pressure index, which is transformed into a binary crisis/noncrisis variable via a threshold criterion.[3]

Other examples of threshold approaches are applications considering behavior in the tails of the observed data; for example, Frankel and Rose (1996) consider annual exchange rate depreciations of 25 percent and over; Bae, Karolyi, and Stulz (2003) consider the 5 percent tails of equity market returns. Each of these approaches may make nontrivial differences to the outcomes of the tests for transmission of crises. This issue has not been systematically addressed in the literature.

2.2   Fundamental Linkages

If, as seems to be plausible in the most recent literature, the existence of contagion should be conditioned on controlling for interdependencies or fundamentals in order to identify "pure" or "true" contagion, then some means of selecting and controlling for fundamentals needs to be considered. There are, again, two distinct means of approaching this in the literature. The first is to condition on a number of observed fundamental variables, and the second is to use the characteristics of the data as a proxy for both observed and potentially unobserved relationships between markets.

The empirical evidence on controlling for observed fundamental linkages in the existing literature is canvassed in chapter 2, where the authors consider the evidence for statistically significant indicators, classified into external-sector variables, financial-sector variables, domestic real and public sector variables, and global influences. They observe that, in general, almost all variables in existing empirical work are statistically insignificant explanators of crises. This is a common finding in both the crisis and contagion literatures. Ex post rationalizations of which variables to include in identifying crises find it difficult to obtain statistical evidence to support their inclusion. And the ability of fundamentals to predict crises turns out to be woefully low, such as in the early warning indicators constructed by Goldstein, Kaminsky, and Reinhart (2000); see Berg and Pattillo (1999) and Edison (2003).

As an example, consider the paper of Sachs, Tornell, and Velasco (1996), which attempted to determine the fundamentals behind crises using the Mexican peso crisis as a case study. The evidence they present suggests a number of variables—notably, an appreciating exchange rate, a weak banking system, and low foreign exchange reserves—that do point to a propensity for crisis. Other fundamentals such as the current account position, capital inflows, and fiscal position provide more mixed evidence. However, this study particularly demonstrates the difficulties in generalizing from samples, as the counterexamples to the Latin American countries used in the paper included Indonesia, Malaysia, and Thailand—all of which were healthy "Asian Tigers" at the time of analysis but were in serious crisis shortly afterward. Similarly, Frankel and Rose (1996) find only foreign direct investment (FDI) flows, high domestic credit growth, and poor domestic output growth to be significantly associated with currency crises—from a wide range of macroeconomic and financial variables considered.

Empirical studies of contagion have also employed a wide range of fundamental control variables. Eichengreen, Rose, and Wyplosz (1995, 1996) condition on country-specific variables such as those mentioned already, and generally find that trade-related links are more likely to be significant than the others considered. Eichengreen, Rose, and Wyplosz (1995) also consider the potential importance of political links, explicitly modeled theoretically in Drazen (this volume), but find little evidence of statistical significance for these variables, particularly in isolation from economic effects.

The importance of trade linkages as a transmission mechanism for financial crises is very evident in the literature. The most often cited study is Glick and Rose (1999), who consider the association of countries in crisis (an exogenously defined variable in their study) controlling for their observed trade links. The papers of Van Rijckeghem and Weder (2001, 2003) extend the Glick and Rose methodology to linkages through the banking sector, and to a comparison of trade- and financial-sector linkages—concluding that financial-sector linkages are the more important route. This conclusion is entirely consistent with the more recent literature and the development of theoretical models such as Pavlova and Rigobon (2004), which shows how the existence of multiple asset markets can lead to contagion effects. A peculiarity of the studies based on the Glick and Rose framework is that they presuppose contagion is being identified in the transmission of crises across countries—the role of interdependence is unrecognized; see also Lowell, Neu, and Tong (1998).

The series of papers on trade-based linkages identifies an important stylized fact about financial crises, which is that they tend to be regionally clustered. Trade linkages are one potential explanation for this, as are similarities of financial systems—for example, the degree of integration of banking and equity markets in East Asia compared with Western Europe. It has also been suggested that crises spread regionally, and that transmission between regional groupings occurs through developed financial centers, such as the United States; see Kaminsky and Reinhart (2003). A number of papers suggest that the effects of financial crises beyond their own regions are relatively limited—for example, Bae, Karolyi, and Stulz (2003) for the Asian crisis, and Sachs, Tornell, and Velasco (1996) for the Tequila crisis—although in contrast the Russian crisis of 1998 spread widely (see Dungey et al. 2002). It seems likely that the importance of regionality varies both with the particular crisis and the particular asset market under consideration (Hernández and Valdés 2001), pointing to the heterogeneity of crises as discussed below.

An alternative approach to controlling for fundamentals without identifying particular control variables is to use the interdependencies between the sample data, usually modeled with a vector autoregression (VAR) of reasonably short lag length. The most direct examples of this approach are the Granger causality tests conducted by Granger, Huang, and Yang (2000) between stock and currency market pairs for particular countries, and

Sander and Kleimeier (2003) for sovereign bond markets. The VAR method of controlling for fundamental linkages is far more widespread than this, however. Forbes and Rigobon (2002) popularized a correlation-based approach to detecting contagion, examining the potential increase in correlation of the residuals from a VAR of asset returns during a crisis as evidence of contagion. The VAR prefilters for relationships between the asset returns. Debelle and Ellis in chapter 6 provide an example of correlation tests applying prefiltering with a VAR. Other papers that use the VAR to prefilter for contagion testing include Favero and Giavazzi (2002) and Bonfiglioli and Favero (2005); each of these also includes some control variables.[4]

Latent factor models also use the relationship between the sample data as a means of filtering the interdependencies from contagion. Latent factor models have an established history in the finance literature; their extension into crisis periods has been undertaken in Pericoli and Sbracia (2003), Bekaert, Harvey, and Ng (2005), and Dungey and Martin (2004), and is used as one of the comparator methods in chapter 3 by Dungey et al. In these papers the data sample is assumed to be representative of the underlying data-generating properties, and hence the observed commonalities in the sample can be used to extract the fundamental relationships between data series.

2.3   Heterogeneity in Crises

A particular problem with the empirical literature on contagion has been in our inability to draw general conclusions from the existing work. The overviews that can be drawn from a number of studies in some instances are disappointing (e.g., the insignificance of any particular macroeconomic fundamental variable across studies, as surveyed in chapter 4 by Jacobs, Kuper, and Lestano). More promisingly, as also argued in section 5, below, there now seems to be broad agreement that common lender effects do matter and that financial links are probably more important than trade links; and there is some mixed evidence on the importance of geographical proximity. The emerging consensus of the literature seems to agree with Kaminsky, Reinhart, and Végh's conditions for fast and furious contagion in chapter 2. However, there is a great deal more evidence on the heterogeneity of crises than on any agreement on generalizations.

The heterogeneity of crises themselves is demonstrated in the studies that consider contagion in particular crisis incidents. There is a substantial body of literature examining the stock market crash of 1987, the Mexican peso crisis of 1994–95 and the associated "Tequila effect," and the spread of the 1997–98 East Asian financial crisis. There is a slightly smaller literature covering the spread of the stresses in the European Exchange Rate Mechanism (ERM) during 1992; the Russian bond default in August 1998 and the subsequent near-collapse of LTCM; and the more recent crises in Latin America, focused on Argentina in 2002 and Brazil in 2001. These event studies are important in helping to draw out the similarities and differences in the transmission of crises for events that begin in markets that are at different stages of development and that involve different assets and different geographical regions.

2.3.1 Single Markets The selection of sample countries and markets is important in constructing evidence for or against contagion. The majority of existing studies consider the transmission of crises for a single asset class across national borders, either for multiple crisis periods or for a single crisis. At least four asset classes have been examined in studies of financial market contagion: currency markets, equity markets, fixed interest markets, and real estate–backed assets. Some examples of studies and results in the literature will suffice to illustrate the diversity in this field.

Currency crises have been investigated in conjunction with banking crises in the historical studies canvassed in section 1. More specific studies on particular episodes include Sachs, Tornell, and Velasco (1996) on the Mexican peso crisis; Eichengreen, Rose, and Wyplosz (1995, 1996), who cover the European ERM crisis of 1992, among other things; Dungey and Martin (2004) on four countries involved in the East Asian crisis of 1997–98; and Cerra and Saxena (2002), who investigate contagion from surrounding countries to Indonesia in the East Asian crisis. Each of these studies finds evidence of contagion, but uses different means of measuring the concept. Sachs, Tornell, and Velasco and Dungey and Martin consider contagion as a residual after having controlled for fundamentals—akin to pure contagion—but the former use observed control variables and the latter a latent factor model approach. Eichengreen, Rose, and Wyplosz consider contagion as the nonzero association of a domestic crisis with an international crisis using a probit model, and Cerra and Saxena find evidence from a two-regime Markov switching model. Currency market studies spanning longer time frames include Glick and Rose (1999), who study five different episodes of currency crises to uncover the importance of regional factors; and Fratzscher (2003) on Asian economies, finding some predictive power over the East Asian crisis.

The most fertile asset market for studies on contagion has been international equity markets. The earliest of these studies is probably that of King and Wadhwani (1990), which examines equity markets following their 1987 crash. There is a large literature around this time that examines linkages between international equity markets, without specifically identifying contagion effects—for example, Engle, Ito, and Lin (1990). The potential for contagion in equity markets across international borders has specifically been explored by Forbes and Rigobon (2002), who find little evidence for contagion between pairs of international equity markets in the U.S. equity market crash of 1987, the 1994 Mexican peso crisis, or the Hong Kong stock market crash of October 1997. This paper prompted a rash of other studies using both the correlation methodology popularized by Forbes and Rigobon and alternate methods. Most studies using the correlation method find little evidence of contagion, including Baig and Goldfajn (1999) for the East Asian crisis. However, both Wälti (2003) and Billio and Pelizzon (2003) show that alternative results may be found with different approaches; see chapter 3 of this volume. In particular, Wälti shows strong evidence of contagion for the Asian crisis sample of Forbes and Rigobon, using the methodology developed in Favero and Giavazzi (2002).

Favero and Giavazzi (2002) consider contagious transmissions in money market spreads against Germany for seven European ERM countries over a four-year period encompassing the ERM crisis of 1992. They find evidence of significant contagion effects in the sample. The Asian crisis saw relatively little volatility in fixed interest markets, but volatility in international bond markets increased markedly with the Russian bond default in August 1998. The spread of that crisis to other international bond markets is examined in Dungey et al. (2002), who find measurable contagion effects from that, and the subsequent near-collapse of LTCM, to both developing and developed countries' bond markets.

The turmoil in the East Asian financial markets following the speculative attack on the Hong Kong dollar in October 1997 transmitted directly into equity markets and markets for real estate–backed securities. While the equity market literature is relatively large, the real estate literature on contagion is currently limited. Examples include an investigation of transmissions between real estate securities markets in Hong Kong, Japan, Australia, and the United States for the Asian crisis period (Bond, Dungey, and Fry 2004), the impact of wake-up calls for physical real estate on real estate stocks (Ghosh, Guttery, and Sirmans 1998), and the role of common factors in driving higher correlations in crisis-period returns of real estate stocks (Mei and Hu 2000).[5]

2.3.2 Multiple Markets   While many of the empirical applications exploring contagion tend to focus on a single asset market, there is a growing body of evidence that the interactions between asset markets, across borders, may be an important mode of transmission. Only a few papers address this issue directly. For example, Granger, Huang, and Yang (2000) consider the relationship between equity and currency markets within countries during the Asian crisis period; Kallberg, Liu, and Pasquariello (2002) examine the hypothesis that volatility in Asian real estate markets originated with equity markets; while Mathur et al. (2002) find significant contagion effects from the Mexican peso to both Chilean equity markets and Chilean American depository receipts (ADRs) trading in the secondary market in the United States. The first two of these studies conduct Granger causality tests between pairs of assets. Mathur et al. consider the evidence from a multivariate regression, but without the capacity for endogenous links between all the asset returns examined. Asset market links within the United States are considered by Darbar and Deb (2002), who look at the bivariate linkages between U.S. equity, money, bond, and currency markets prior to and after the 1987 equity market crash. They find evidence of changes in the transmission of shocks between the pairs of assets between the two periods, from relatively small to significant transmissions during the postcrisis period.

A further complication is the potential for different asset markets to interact both within and across national borders. The potential for complex interactions in propagating transmissions is explored in an application to the Asian crisis in chapter 5 of this volume, where Ito and Hashimoto point to the statistically significant links across equity and currency markets during the Asian crisis period, both within countries and across geographical borders. This line of research has been active in the finance literature for some time in the exploration of portfolio returns during noncrisis periods, and holds substantial promise in understanding crisis periods.

The overall conclusion after examining the evidence on the studies of individual crises has to be an awareness of the great heterogeneity in the crises, and in their transmission, which leads naturally to a concern as to whether policymakers can adequately respond appropriately to such diverse events; see Karolyi (2003) and Moser (2003).

3.   GARNERING EMPIRICAL EVIDENCE

The previous section focused on the weight of the empirical evidence. However, in the collection of that evidence a number of research choices have to be made. In this section we discuss the importance and implications of choices of data frequency, empirical methodology, and assumptions about the underlying data generating process in implementing applications.

3.1   Data Frequency

Researchers' desire to control for observed macroeconomic fundamentals usually constrains the data frequency that can be examined. Most macroeconomic data are available on a relatively low frequency: monthly, quarterly, or in some cases—particularly for emerging economies—only annually. This clearly causes difficulties if the researchers believe that contagion is potentially a short-lived or high-frequency phenomenon. Some researchers do not view contagion as a high-frequency issue, rather holding the view that contagion can also be detected when it affects the real economy and that it will, in fact, be apparent only over relatively long time horizons; see, for example, Baumol (1994). Most, however, seem to view contagion as evident in relatively high-frequency data.

Consequently, three groups emerge in empirical applications. First, those who subsume their desire for high-frequency data in order to capture better measures of fundamental linkages—for example, Glick and Rose (1999), Eichengreen, Rose, and Wyplosz (1996), and Cerra and Saxena (2002). Second, those who subsume their desire for capturing fundamental linkages to the desire to have high-frequency data—for example, Ito and Hashimoto (this volume), Hashimoto and Ito (2002), and Baig and Goldfajn

(1999); although sometimes other financial market data such as interest rates are used as proxies for common shocks, as in Forbes and Rigobon (2002), Cartapanis, Dropsy, and Mametz (2002), and Connolly and Wang (2003). The third group are those who choose the potentially contagious observations in high-frequency data as being in some sense outliers, or extreme observations, and use this as the means of implicitly controlling for fundamentals. Examples of this approach are Bae, Karolyi, and Stulz (2003), who examine the tail of the distribution of equity returns, and Favero and Giavazzi (2002), who use heteroskedasticity to identify non-normal bond yields.

The importance of market microstructure issues is omitted from lower frequency applications. In particular, identifying the process of herding in the data may require access to the endogenous process of price discovery in the markets. In real time, price discovery affects the transmission of shocks, as in Farmer and Joshi (2002). To this end, a promising approach would be to examine crises using very high frequency data at an intra-day level. For example, Cohen and Shin's (2003) VAR model of tick-by-tick U.S. Treasury data finds that the sequence of market trades (order flow) and price changes may exhibit *positive* feedback in periods of market stress. That is, in addition to order flow's influencing prices as predicted by theory, there is also an important statistical relationship in the opposite direction, from price changes to order flow, highlighting the possibility of different microstructural transmission in times of turbulence. Such contagion is entirely consistent with sophisticated traders' rational decision making in the presence of binding stop-loss constraints on trading positions; it is not associated with momentum trading and other boundedly rational strategies detected in the stock market (see Grinblatt, Titman, and Wermers 1995). Thus, stop-loss constraints activated during liquidity crises may be taken to indicate the presence of time-varying risk aversion in financial markets.

In that regard, although the paper by Masson, Chakravarty, and Gulden (this volume) analyzes portfolio selection under risk aversion with endogenous asset liquidity—inversely related to the market maker's bid-ask spread—the latter is fixed within a discrete time period and so cannot adjust to sudden, large changes in market conditions. This is an inherent limitation of discrete-time modeling that can be addressed by the high-frequency literature; see Evans and Lyons (2002, 2003) for the foreign exchange market and Engle and Lange (1997) for the stock market. More generally, in modeling contagion, be it empirically or theoretically, attention should be paid as to whether the proposed methodology can reproduce the observed characteristics of the financial market data under consideration. Linear models are unlikely to capture the features of high-frequency financial market returns, which are well known to have time-varying volatility and fat-tailed distributions. We turn to this issue in the next section.

3.2 Implied Data Generating Process

The literature addresses the features of financial market data in a number of ways. A frequent approach to modeling a presumed discontinuity in the data generating process between a noncrisis and a crisis period is to adopt thresholds. These thresholds are also those used to identify crisis observations in a number of applications, discussed in section 2.1, using either an indicator, such as Eichengreen, Rose, and Wyplosz (1995, 1996); two-regime Markov switching models, such as Jeanne and Masson (2000); or a tail of distributions, as in Bae, Karolyi, and Stulz (2003). Quintos, Fan, and Phillips (2001) suggest a recursive test for distinguishing an unknown breakpoint in the behavior of the tail of distributions.

A third approach to incorporating the nonlinearities is favored by the latent factor models, where GARCH structures are included on one or more of the factors (e.g., Bekaert, Harvey, and Ng 2005; Dungey and Martin 2004). The latent factor framework is used by Corsetti, Pericoli, and Sbracia (2001) to demonstrate the reliance of the Forbes and Rigobon contagion test on a change in the ratio of the variance of country-specific and common factor volatility between the noncrisis and crisis periods. As they are at pains to point out themselves, their latent factor model was not designed to actually test for contagion, although it has been used in this fashion by Billio and Pelizzon (2003). GARCH characteristics are also incorporated in the Darbar and Deb (2002) study of conditional correlations between pairs of different asset types (bonds, money, currency, and stocks) in the United States, in the form of a multivariate GARCH model.

The challenge for both the theoretical and empirical modeler of contagion is to incorporate the known features of financial data, particularly fat tails and time-varying volatility, in a consistent manner. An example of the difficulty of this task is given in chapter 7, where Masson, Chakravarty, and Gulden explore the properties of bond data simulated from their theoretical model of the transmission process.

3.3 Empirical Methodology

A relatively large number of methodologies are currently in use in the empirical literature on financial market contagion. The major approaches are the correlation approach, associated mainly with Forbes and Rigobon (2002) due to their innovative correction for heterogeneity, although extant in the literature much earlier than that; the probability-based approaches based on bivariate indicators of crises, such as Eichengreen, Rose, and Wyplosz (1995, 1996); the VAR approach of Favero and Giavazzi (2002); and the latent factor model approach associated with Corsetti, Pericoli, and Sbracia (2001).

Each of these methods is briefly reviewed in chapter 3 by Dungey et al., who also give full step-by-step details of how each of the methods is applied. In another paper by these authors (Dungey et al. 2005), they show

how each of these methods is nested within a latent factor framework similar to that of Corsetti, Pericoli, and Sbracia (2001).

The results of contagion testing are clearly affected by the methodology applied, but as yet the literature has made little progress in comparing the properties of the individual tests, or in answering the important question of the most appropriate method in detecting and measuring contagion. The Forbes and Rigobon correlation approach has the advantage of being straightforward, but both Billio and Pelizzon (2003) and Wälti (2003) present evidence that it provides biased results, tending to underreject the hypothesis of no contagion (see also Boyer, Gibson, and Loretan 1997; Loretan and English 2000; Dungey and Zhumabekova 2001). A multivariate version of the Forbes and Rigobon test, reformulated as a Chow test which has known sample properties, is derived in Dungey et al. (2005).

The Eichengreen, Rose, and Wyplosz (1995, 1996) test is constructed around the null hypothesis of no contagion when the presence of an international financial crisis (indicated by a binary dummy variable) has no statistical effect on the presence of a domestic financial crisis (again, a binary dummy). Applications of this test usually find some evidence for contagion, although Pesaran and Pick (2004) present Monte Carlo evidence for an upward bias in results using this method. An extension of this test is given in Bae, Karolyi, and Stulz (2003), who consider the tail observations of equity returns; and in Baur and Schulze (2003), who extend this approach to deciles of the distribution of returns, finding that evidence for contagious transmissions does indeed decrease away from the extreme observations.

More recently, the approach of Favero and Giavazzi (2002) has found some favor, with applications beyond their original one (sovereign bonds) to equity markets in Bonfiglioli and Favero (2005), Wälti (2003), and chapter 3 of this volume.

In addition to these methods, there are two other growing fields of contagion tests. The first is that of Granger causality tests, such as Granger, Huang, and Yang (2000). The second is Markov switching models, such as Cerra and Saxena (2002) and Jeanne and Masson (2000), as described previously. In general, a substantial amount of work is still required in this field to consider more systematically the questions of which contagion tests are the most appropriate, of which the most pressing issues are the properties of the different contagion tests and their relationships to theoretical models of contagion.

4.   CONTAGION THROUGH THE LOOKING GLASS OF INVESTOR BEHAVIOR

4.1   Fundamentals versus Self-Fulfilling Beliefs

Although the empirical contagion literature is frequently based on time series explorations, this may not be the appropriate dimension in all instances. Understanding the origins and onset of "pure contagion"—unrelated to fundamentals—requires moving from observed financial market dynamics to individual investors' reaction functions and their underlying loss-aversion and opportunity sets. Thus, following the recent turbulence in many emerging markets, academics and policymakers have acknowledged that understanding investor behavior during times of market stress is key in assessing the potential for financial crises to spread across developing economies; for example, see the survey of Chui, Hall, and Taylor (2004).

Clearly, if herding behavior were driven by sunspots—extraneous events unrelated to fundamentals—then the contagious transmission of shocks across markets or countries would be irrational from an individual investor's ex ante perspective. Policymakers would then have no rationale for intervention, whether at the national or international level. Indeed, if a given set of fundamentals can give rise to multiple equilibria, then the phenomenon of financial crises spreading across markets and national borders would have to be explained by investors coordinating to the bad equilibrium in each country concerned—an implausible scenario.[6] At the same time, if contagion is due to investor herding behavior that is unrelated to fundamentals, this can be viewed as a rational individual in the presence of fixed costs of acquiring and processing country-specific information; see Aghion, Bacchetta, and Banerjee (2000), Caballero and Krishnamurthy (2001), Calvo and Mendoza (2000), and Chang and Velasco (2001). In equilibrium, aggregate outcomes are also sensitive to the specification of timing individual decisions during financial crises: Chari and Kehoe (2003) show that if investors move whenever they choose, rather than in a predetermined order, then herding behavior arises even when decisions are made continuous and asset prices are marked-to-market.

The speculative attack literature traces the question of fundamentals-driven models of crises versus beliefs-driven models to the issue of unique versus multiple equilibria. On fundamentals-driven models, whether real or financial, see Krugman (1979), Gerlach and Smets (1995), Glick and Rose (1999), and Kaminsky and Reinhart (2000). On beliefs-driven models see Obstfeld (1995, 1996); see also Jeanne and Masson (2000) and Masson (1999a,b). In fundamentals-based models, the crisis occurs deterministically as foreign exchange reserves run out, but there is no contagion. In contrast, beliefs-based models can admit multiple equilibria and sunspots, leading to self-fulfilling beliefs and speculative attacks. In the context of currency crises, if market participants anticipate that a successful attack on a fixed exchange rate or currency peg will alter exchange rate policy, it is *expected* future fundamentals conditional on an attack that are incompatible with the peg. In the time series domain, contagion to a country is then understood as jumps between multiple equilibria triggered by events elsewhere. In a cross-section within markets, multiplicity can also be critical for some models of contagion—for example, see the account of the 1990s U.S. high-technology stock market bubble in Shiller (2003). With complete and symmetric information there can be self-fulfilling beliefs underlying the occurrence of currency crises.

A notable consequence of the string of financial crises afflicting developing economies in the 1990s has been that the earlier sharp delineation between fundamentals-driven and beliefs-driven models is now less relevant, in two important ways. First, a consensus appears to have emerged that a unique equilibrium may be an artifact of the unrealistic treatment of expectations; see Jeanne and Masson (2000), Kehoe (1996), and Krugman (1996, 2000). One source of multiple equilibria is that investors' expectations can also be formed at the time of the financial crisis, rather than fixed beforehand. Multiplicity is also sensitive to policymakers' short-term expansionary motive. As argued by Calvo and Reinhart (2002), in the context of emerging-market economies this can be attributed to policymakers' preference for fiscal seigniorage.

The precise informational structure is also crucial over and above these timing issues. In the global games literature, associated with Morris and Shin (1998, 1999, 2000), the assumption that fundamentals are common knowledge is crucial for multiple equilibria to arise in self-fulfilling currency crisis models. If market players have higher orders of private uncertainty about other players' beliefs (i.e., everyone may know that the fundamentals are sound, but not everyone may know that everyone else knows this, and so on ad infinitum) then a unique equilibrium is obtained as a function of macroeconomic fundamentals and relevant financial state variables. Consequently, policy is reinstated because, although speculative attacks on currencies can be violent and unexpected, there is a deterministic link between economic fundamentals and market behavior.

In the original Morris-Shin framework, a necessary condition for equilibrium uniqueness in addition to the failure of common knowledge is that public and private information about the economy have independent sources (see also Rey 2001). More generally, Allen, Morris, and Shin (2003) show that market prices are biased toward the public information set. In turn, the latter is the intersection of all market participants' private information sets, hence the role for policymakers to create more common knowledge and bring observed prices closer to their true fundamentals-driven value; see also Morris and Shin (2002), Samet (1998), and Townsend (1983) on the difference between individual expectations and aggregate (market) expectations.

The second development stresses the role of balance-sheet considerations—due to maturity and currency mismatch grounded on developing economies' extensive short-term and foreign currency–denominated debt—in the financial vulnerability of countries in Southeast Asia and Latin America; see Calvo (1998a), Calvo and Reinhart (2000), Caballero and Krishnamurthy (2004), and Eichengreen, Hausmann, and Panizza (2003). At the center of this "third-generation" approach to modeling crises lie rapid reversals in capital flows to developing countries, with adverse short-term balance-sheet consequences. In that respect, the paper by Kaminsky, Reinhart, and Végh (this volume) argues that that the presence of leveraged common creditors is a necessary condition—part of the "unholy trinity" proposition—for *fast and furious* contagion to emerge; that is, for financial crises to spread across national borders with immediate adverse consequences. Under incomplete and asymmetric information, financial linkages coupled with liquidity or capital constraints imply that a country-specific decline in asset prices may spread across emerging-market economies; on the two types of constraints see Calvo (1998a,b) and Peek and Rosengren (1997, 2000). Moreover, the evidence suggests that these outflows have commonly been triggered by currency and banking crises, so their abrupt nature is the consequence of unanticipated announcements and changes in the macroeconomic background—the second pillar of financial contagion's "unholy trinity."

Therefore, the relevant policy question is not whether capital outflows in the original country are triggered by fundamentals—this is answered in the affirmative (e.g., Thailand in July 1997)—but whether the subsequent capital outflows in other countries are justified by their respective fundamentals. The informational assumptions that researchers adopt are crucial in that respect. Following the spread of the "Asian flu" from Thailand to other East Asian countries in 1997–98, Goldstein (1998) stressed that a crisis in one country may cause global investors to "wake up" to similar fundamental problems elsewhere that they had previously underestimated or ignored altogether. Along the same lines, asymmetrically informed global investors may extract different signals from the original country-specific shock, which may lead them to underestimate or overestimate its potential effects on other countries; see King and Wadhwani (1990) and Pritsker (2001). Thus, in the case of overestimation, some shocks may be propagated that would not have been in a situation of full information. Asymmetric information channels may also lead to contagion if they result in global investors revising their expectations of future IMF-led bailouts in a particular country following a crisis elsewhere. In that case, the probability distributions of future fundamentals are conditional on the availability and scale of an international rescue package because the latter generally induces sovereign moral hazard; see Dooley (2000).

In the context of contagious currency crises, Drazen's model of political contagion in chapter 8 of this volume offers another channel of transmission based on investors' incomplete information about the authorities' incentive to devalue. This notion of contagion is inherently political because speculative pressure would not extend to other member-countries in the absence of the political objective. In particular, policymakers in "clubs" or groups of countries that have joined a fixed exchange rate mechanism may subsequently optimally realign their political and economic incentives to adhere to the agreement when faced with devaluation by one "club member." Effectively, the cost of breaking the agreement is not exogenously fixed, but a function of each government's time-varying trade-off between its political and macroeconomic goals. Membership contagion then occurs as several countries reevaluate their individual incentives and opt to devalue their currencies against mounting speculative pressure. Fundamental uncertainty over the potentially conflicting nature of policymakers' economic and political objectives may result in financial market participants' using Bayes rule to update their devaluation expectations; see also Drazen and Masson (1994) and Drazen (2000).

This approach has been particularly fruitful for understanding the unraveling of the European ERM in the currency crises of 1992–93. It may also offer fresh insight into the political economy of developing free-trade zones and international zones of economic integration. However, it may not be as applicable to developing countries for which devaluation is frequently not a political choice but a forced capitulation to foreign exchange market pressure. Moreover, the devaluations in most East Asian and Latin American countries in recent years were immediately followed by sharp recessions, thus contradicting the basic premise of Drazen's model that there are short-term economic gains from giving up "club membership."[7]

4.2 Financial Channels for Contagion: The Role of Liquidity

The role of bank liquidity (and the lack of it) is a key driving factor underlying investor action that may trigger financial crises and facilitate or hinder their contagion across asset markets or national borders. At the aggregate level, balance-sheet weakness, including maturity mismatch and extensive liability dollarization, can generate "twin crises" rippling from the currency to the banking and corporate sectors and resulting in sharp declines in real output; see Chang and Velasco (2000a,b), Eichengreen, Hausmann, and Panizza (2003), and Kaminsky and Reinhart (1999). In particular, Eichengreen, Hausmann, and Panizza argue that developing countries' financial vulnerability resulting from extensive liability dollarization (i.e., those countries' inability to borrow internationally in their own currencies and at long maturities domestically—referred to as their international and domestic "original sin," respectively) constrains their macroeconomic policies in normal periods and limits their access to international liquidity in crisis episodes.

In an influential set of papers, Allen and Gale (1998, 2000, 2004) have traced the aggregate effects of crises at the microeconomic level. These authors define *contagion* as the disproportionately amplified effect of liquidity shocks hitting one sector to many other sectors, leading to economywide financial crisis. This definition is closely related to that of *financial fragility:* disproportionate aggregate damage caused to a financial system by a small shock in one of its components, with the potential for real consequences.

The Allen and Gale framework significantly extends the domestic banking crisis model of Diamond and Dybvig (1983) and Diamond (1991) by making the existence of incomplete markets the raison d'être for contagion.[8] While aggregate demand for liquidity is constant, there are incomplete markets for interregional bank claims, implying that if an aggregate short-run liquidity shock is big enough, then certain sectors—and, by extension, geographical regions or countries—are intrinsically unable to manage the mismatch of long-dated assets and short-dated liabilities by obtaining insurance from neighboring sectors. They may then be forced to liquidate their long asset, which is very costly, and the resulting decline in value in one sector can thus propagate to others and generate a run on the whole banking system. Contagion in this framework is pervasive and *rational* because it is anticipated in any equilibrium of the model. Despite the fact that it is originally restricted to liquidity crises with no currency component, the Allen-Gale framework places incomplete capital market interconnectedness and aggregate liquidity firmly at the center of developing-country financial crises;[9] see also Tirole (2002).

Furthermore, capital market imperfections can explain financial contagion if, in response to a country-specific liquidity shock, global investors rebalance their portfolios by lowering their exposure to other countries. This is the key insight of Kodres and Pritsker (2002), who show that such rebalancing is rational even in the absence of fundamental links between countries, provided the global investors' risk-adjusted positions are exposed to the same macroeconomic country-specific risk factors. These authors show that contagion can arise in a rational expectations equilibrium if investors engage in cross-market hedging of the shared macroeconomic risk factors in their portfolio. The severity of contagion then depends on different markets' sensitivities to the shared macroeconomic risks, as well as on the degree of information asymmetry in each market. As cross-market hedging normally requires moderate to high correlation between countries' financial markets, the implication is that higher co-movement between asset returns makes contagion *more* likely; see also Kyle and Xiong (2001).

The issues of rationality and liquidity constraints of individual investors are addressed by Masson, Chakravarty, and Gulden in chapter 7. The assumption of rational expectations is relaxed and heterogeneity introduced, whereby individual investors form expectations based on a combination of experience and imitating others. With appropriate model calibration they show the impact of endogenous bid-ask spreads on emerging-market bond investors' portfolio rebalancing. Illiquidity can result in fat tails and pure contagion.

5. WHAT SHOULD POLICYMAKERS DO ABOUT EXTERNAL VULNERABILITY?

At any time horizon the loss functions of individual market participants and policymakers are likely to be different, making a uniform assessment of contagion difficult. From a market participant's individual perspective, *any* trading day can be a "crisis" if an incorrect positioning or trading decision has been taken. In that sense, the individual's loss function can be thought of as being symmetric.[10] In contrast, in the case of the policymaker the loss function is likely to be asymmetric. Ceteris paribus, relatively more weight will be placed on avoiding a precipitous financial market downturn in order to avoid systemic risk.[11]

The fact that the onset of contagion is rationally anticipated generates a role for the central bank as a lender of last resort whose mission is to complete markets.[12] In that regard, the conventional view that the benefits of more international capital market integration outweigh the costs (Rogoff 1999) has been questioned following the recent financial crises in the developing world; see Obstfeld and Taylor (2004) and Prasad et al. (2003). Recent work has queried this by highlighting the adverse side effects of more interconnectedness, including the common-lender issue highlighted in the chapter by Kaminsky, Reinhart, and Végh in this volume.

Although policymakers generally wish to reduce the probability of extreme market movements, they are asymmetrically concerned with avoiding extreme negative outcomes. Examples of public policy actions to limit the risk of systemic failure are the adoption of electronic program–driven "stops" in equity market trading, and the Federal Reserve's decision to act as a coordinator of the private-sector bailout of the LTCM investment fund in September 1998. The potential for crises may raise the ex ante real interest rate on financial assets and thus impose real economic costs; see Greenspan (1999).

Early academic work on financial crises and contagion was motivated by the question of whether other countries were suffering unnecessarily for crimes they did not commit. This line of reasoning has been applied by Sachs, Tornell, and Velasco (1996) following the Mexican currency and debt crisis, and by Radelet and Sachs (1998) on the deep and protracted recession in Indonesia following the Asian crisis.

There has recently been a spate of proposals for market-driven measures to enhance international financial stability and prevent contagion. These often involve creating new financial instruments: Eichengreen, Hausmann, and Panizza (2003) propose creating a synthetic unit of account, putting together many emerging-market currencies to overcome international original sin; while Borensztein and Mauro (2004) argue that issuing GDP growth-indexed bonds can reduce the likelihood of sovereign default; see also Caballero (2003) and Shiller (2003). The challenge is how to make markets for these new traded instruments liquid.

In the same spirit, Allen and Gale (2004) suggest that credit derivatives can function as a market-based solution to incomplete markets. This would involve the development of credit derivative instruments to provide financial institutions with liquidity insurance against unforeseen, but well-specified, credit events. The sovereign credit risk transfer market is growing fast following the implementation of the International Swaps and Derivatives Association (ISDA) standardized definitions of credit events in 1999, and the Argentine default in 2001 provided a useful test case; see also Packer and Suthiphongchai (2003), Ranciere (2002), and World Bank (2003). Alternatively, Allen and Gale propose that the monetary authorities can step in as a lender of last resort to provide liquidity to the troubled sector or region. Indeed, the fact that the onset of contagion is rationally anticipated generates a role for the central bank as a lender of last resort whose mission is to complete markets.

In the event of a sovereign liquidity crisis, collective action clauses (CACs) offer a market-driven mechanism for improving the resolution of the debt-restructuring process. CACs written in the sovereign debt contract stipulate that a certain threshold proportion (e.g., 75 percent) of creditors can collectively decide to reject a debt-restructuring offer from the debtor.[13] The potential to disrupt orderly debt restructurings meant such clauses were considered to be suboptimal to unanimity bonds, and until recently de facto unavailable under New York law. However, recent analytical work by Haldane et al. (2003, 2004) has shown that a debt issuer's optimal choice of threshold can reveal information to the market about their risk aversion and creditworthiness. Risk-neutral (risk-averse) debtors will thus set higher (respectively, lower) thresholds because the ex ante benefits of lower interest rates and consequent smaller default likelihood outweigh the ex post costs of a lower offer in the event of a debt restructuring. Moreover, lower-rated debtors will generally set higher thresholds, ceteris paribus, to compensate for the higher default-risk compensation required by creditors. Bonds containing CACs have been gaining in popularity with sovereign debtors since Mexico's original issue in March 2003.

6. STRUCTURE OF THE BOOK AND CONCLUDING REMARKS

Following the discussions above, a number of major themes are apparent in assessing the importance of international financial contagion effects in financial crises. We first asked which definition of contagion was most tenable. We then asked a series of questions on how to identify contagion, particularly empirically. The third question considers how contagion may be affected by the tensions between different financial market participants, and finally what international financial institutions can do about preventing contagion. The chapters in this book are designed to address a number of these questions.

Each of the chapters addresses the definition of contagion in some way. Most agree that fundamental controls are important, and so consider pure contagion. Chapter 2, by Kaminsky, Reinhart, and Végh, most directly addresses the question of what is meant by contagion, and sets out three conditions—"the unholy trinity"—for what they dub "fast and furious" contagion.

The empirical evidence on contagion is much confused, not least because of the plethora of different methods and samples in use. Dungey, Fry, González-Hermosillo, and Martin attempt to throw some light on this in chapter 3, by conducting five different contagion tests using the same sample of three crises. Although the tests tend to agree at a general level, there is much divergence when it comes to contagion in specific pairs of countries.

In conducting such tests it is usually necessary to define both the crisis period and, for tests of pure contagion, the fundamental control variables.

Jacobs, Kuper, and Lestano directly address the existing literature on these issues in chapter 4. They survey the different methods of identifying crisis periods in banking, currency, and debt crises, and the relative lack of success of different types of fundamentals as significant explanators of any of these types of crisis.

Identifying financial market contagion has usually proceeded across national borders for a single asset market. In chapter 5, Ito and Hashimoto demonstrate the potential importance of incorporating cross-market, cross-border links. This is one of the very few chapters taking this into account in the current literature, and it emphasizes that these linkages are potentially very important to our understanding of crisis transmission.

Understanding crisis transmission is vitally important to producing sensible policy outcomes. To that end it is also imperative to study instances where crises are unexpectedly *not* transmitted. In chapter 6, Debelle and Ellis examine the cases of Australian and New Zealand financial markets during the East Asian and Russian/LTCM crises. They conclude that shock transmission to these countries from East Asia was actually *reduced* during the crisis period, compared with previous experience. Australia and New Zealand suffered *less* than expected, indicating that the nonlinear transmission process associated with crises can work in reverse.

The chapter in chapter 7, by Masson, Chakravarty, and Gulden, is an important step in the research agenda on contagion. Here, the authors attempt to develop a theoretical model that is also consistent with the empirically observed characteristics of financial market data, in this case bonds. They illustrate the difficulties of this research agenda, while making progress using a heterogeneous investor model. In the model, liquidity problems are intrinsic in achieving the observed features of the financial data. The important role of liquidity is consistent with the literature on financial crises and contagion at a more aggregate level, such as in the arguments of Kaminsky, Reinhart, and Végh in chapter 2.

The final chapter in this book, chapter 8 by Drazen, addresses more directly the problems facing policymakers in responding to financial market problems. Drazen raises the idea of "membership contagion," whereby in any potentially cooperative group, if one breaks the membership rules, this may act to weaken the incentive on all members to cooperate. This is illustrated with an example from the European Monetary Union, but clearly represents problems associated with any attempt to coordinate international financial markets at political and institutional levels, where incentives are not perfectly aligned.

To summarize and conclude, three key insights are obtained from our introductory chapter. First, in most cases more information is a good thing. In that sense information transparency and timely disclosure promoted by the IMF are welcome, as they reduce information asymmetries.[14] It may at least partially remove one of the three pillars of the "unholy trinity" of financial contagion, namely the unanticipated nature of the shocks. However, this must be tempered by an assessment of whether the propogation of shocks is fundamentals or (self-fulfilling) beliefs driven. It is only in the second case that more information will reduce contagion; in the first case, informational transparency may not eliminate contagion (Chang and Majnoni 2001, 2002).

The second insight relates to assessing the role of fundamentals or beliefs. Although empirical evidence finds it difficult to identify significant fundamental channels, it seems prudent that policymakers keep a watchful eye on buildup of capital inflows and related evidence of "irrational exuberance" in normal times, regardless of the underlying fundamentals. Capital inflows are necessary in order to experience reversals, and so lay the ground for potential contagion. Modeling individual investor preferences asymmetrically in good and bad times may offer useful insights.

The third point relates to the evidence on whether contagion is really an international phenomenon or is more related to national policies. To some extent we agree with Karolyi (2003) that perhaps more emphasis is needed on sound national policies and prudential supervision. More research is needed into the relative source of contagion effects, particularly cross-border and cross-market links.

Overall, containing the likelihood of contagious financial crises is a pressing policy issue at both national and international levels. As yet, there is no professional consensus on the appropriate definitions of what constitutes contagion, despite substantial research progress toward these goals. We know that financial crises and contagion are intrinsically linked, and that contagious effects arise when crises are propagated across countries or markets after controlling for fundamental linkages and interdependencies. We also know that these transmissions may spread further through mechanisms such as cross-market hedging.

New models will undoubtedly be required with the advent of new crises, as they seem to be intrinsically heterogeneous. However, some of the salient aspects outlined in this chapter are likely to recur. These include the need to identify and capture the appropriate fundamental controls; the means of transmission across countries and asset classes; the statistical properties of the data; the simultaneous identification of contagion, interdependency, and herding; and the endogenous identification of crisis and noncrisis periods from sample data. Each of these issues is extremely important for assessing the appropriate policy response to prevent crises and for adequately managing those that occur.

The challenge for researchers and policymakers remains to produce models that incorporate financial contagion and that are both theoretically coherent and empirically consistent in order to better understand these interactions. We should be looking for heterogeneous-agent models with investor behavior inducing cross-country portfolio rebalancing, that are able to incorporate cross-country and cross-market interactions. The implications for both portfolio management and international financial regulation of capturing these aspects of financial market links during financial crises are enormous.

NOTES

1. See http://www1.worldbank.org/economicpolicy/managing%20volatility/contagion/ for the World Bank's Web site on contagion in financial crises.

2. Bordo and Eichengreen (1999) provide a particularly useful description of crises in the late nineteenth century in their appendix.

3. An interesting aspect of this approach is that a set of secondary rules is required to reduce the number of observed crisis periods, notably windows such that crises cannot last more than two periods, for example.

4. Forbes and Rigobon (2002) and Favero and Giavazzi (2002) both condition on U.S. interest rates in testing for contagion in equity markets and sovereign bonds, respectively. Bonfiglioli and Favero (2005) consider U.S. and German equity markets, and condition on forecast earnings and ten-year bond yields in both countries.

5. The literature on portfolio diversification in real estate markets parallels that in the finance literature more generally (see Bond, Karolyi, and Sanders 2003 for a recent example) so that many of the same extensions to crisis-period applications could be made.

6. A model where this is not the case is Chang and Majnoni (2002), where contagion arises even when the equilibrium-selection mechanisms ("sunspots") are independent in different countries and over time.

7. On these points see also Reinhart (2000).

8. For international extensions of the Diamond-Dybvig bank-run model see Garber and Grilli (1989) and Valdés (1997).

9. In a similar vein, Kiyotaki and Moore (2002) show that firm-specific liquidity shocks can generate balance-sheet contagion when firms are credit-constrained and there are long chains of credit across sectors.

10. In practice, the application of institution-specific thresholds is likely to introduce asymmetries.

11. In closed-economy monetary policy models, such asymmetries may stem from central banks' disliking recessions more than booms. This provides a rationale for "opportunistic" loss functions introduced by Aksoy, Y. et al. (2003) and studied by Tambakis (2002), among others.

12. On lender-of-last-resort issues see also Fischer (1999) and Gale and Vives (2002) and Goodhart and Illing (2003).

13. The original CAC proposal was made by Eichengreen and Portes (1995). On the related catalytic-finance approach to IMF lending see Eichengreen and Mody (2001), Eichengreen and Ruhl (2001), and Morris and Shin (2003).

14. Examples of information transparency programs are Financial Sector Assessment Program, as well as the Joint IMF/World Bank/Bank for International Settlements/Organization for Economic Cooperation and Development Data Initiative on emerging-market economies' external debt.

REFERENCES

Aghion, P., P. Bacchetta, and A. Banerjee, 2000, A Simple Model of Monetary Policy and Currency Crises, *European Economic Review* 44, 728–738.

Aksoy, Y., A. Orphanides, D. H. Small, D. W. Wilcox, and V. Wieland, 2003, A quantitative exploration of the opportunistic approach to disinflation. CEPR Discussion Paper no. 4073.

Allen, F., and D. Gale, 1998, Optimal Financial Crises, *Journal of Finance* 53, 1245–1284.

———, 2000, Financial Contagion, *Journal of Political Economy* 108, 1–33.

———, 2004a, Financial Fragility, Liquidity and Asset Prices, *Journal of the European Economic Association* 2, 1015–1042.

———, 2004b, Financial Intermediaries and Markets, *Econometrica* 72, 1023–1061.

Allen, F., S. Morris, and H. S. Shin, 2003, Beauty Contests, Bubbles and Iterated Expectations in Asset Markets, *University of Pennsylvania, Wharton Financial Institutions Center Working Paper* 03-06.

Bae, K.-H., G. A. Karolyi, and R. M. Stulz, 2003, A New Approach to Measuring Financial Contagion, *Review of Financial Studies* 16, 717–763.

Baig, T., and I. Goldfajn, 1999, Financial Market Contagion in the Asian Crisis, *International Monetary Fund Staff Papers* 46, 167–195.

Banerjee, A. V., 1992, A Simple Model of Herd Behavior, *Quarterly Journal of Economics* 107, 797–817.

Baumol, W. J., 1994, Multivariate Growth Patterns: Contagion and Common Forces as Possible Sources of Convergence, in W. J. Baumol, R. R. Nelson, and E. N. Wolff, eds., *Convergence of Productivity: Cross-National Studies and Historical Evidence* (Oxford University Press, Oxford).

Baur, D., and N. Schulze, 2003, Coexceedances in Financial Markets: A Quantile Regression Analysis of Contagion, *University of Tuebingen Economics Discussion Paper* 253.

Bekaert, G., and C. R. Harvey, 2003, Emerging Markets Finance, *Journal of Empirical Finance* 10, 3–55.

Bekaert, G., C. R. Harvey, and A. Ng, 2005, Market Integration and Contagion, *Journal of Business*, forthcoming.

Berg, A., and C. Pattillo, 1999, Predicting Currency Crises: The Indicators Approach and an Alternative, *Journal of International Money and Finance* 18, 561–586.

Bikhchandani, S., D. Hirshleifer, and I. Welch, 1992, A Theory of Fads, Fashion, Custom, and Cultural-Change as Informational Cascades, *Journal of Political Economy* 100, 992–1026.

Billio, M., and L. Pelizzon, 2003, Contagion and Interdependence in Stock Markets: Have They Been Misdiagnosed? *Journal of Economics and Business* 55, 405–426.

Bond, S., M. Dungey, and R. Fry, 2004, A Web of Shocks: Crises across Asian Real Estate Markets, *CAMA Working Paper* 2.

Bond, S. A., G. A. Karolyi, and A. B. Sanders, 2003, International Real Estate Returns: A Multifactor, Multicountry Approach, *Real Estate Economics* 31, 481–500.

Bonfiglioli, A., and C. A. Favero, 2004, Explaining Co-Movements between Stock Markets: The Case of U.S. and Germany, *Journal of International Money and Finance* forthcoming.

Bordo, M., and B. Eichengreen, 1999, Is Our Current International Economic Environment Unusually Crisis Prone? in D. Gruen and L. Gower, eds., *Reserve Bank of Australia 1999 Conference, Capital Flows and the International Financial System* (Reserve Bank of Australia, Sydney).

Bordo, M. D., B. Eichengreen, D. Klingebiel, M. S. Martinez-Peria, and A. K. Rose, 2001, Is the Crisis Problem Growing More Severe? *Economic Policy* 16, 51–82.

Bordo, M. D., and A. P. Murshid, 2001, Are Financial Crises Becoming More Contagious? What Is the Historical Evidence on Contagion? in S. Claessens and K. J. Forbes, eds., *International Financial Contagion* (Kluwer Academic Publishers, Boston).

Bordo, M. D., and A. J. Schwartz, 1999, Under What Circumstances, Past and Present, Have International Rescues of Countries in Financial Distress Been Successful? *Journal of International Money and Finance* 18, 683–708.

Borensztein, E., and P. Mauro, 2004, The Case for GDP-Indexed Bonds, *Economic Policy* 19, 165–216.

Boyer, B. H., M. S. Gibson, and M. Loretan, 1997, Pitfalls in Tests for Changes in Correlations, *Board of Governors of the Federal Reserve System, International Finance Discussion Paper* 597.

Caballero, R. J., 2003, The Future of the IMF, *American Economic Review* 93, 31–38.

Caballero, R. J., and A. Krishnamurthy, 2001, International and Domestic Collateral Constraints in a Model of Emerging Market Crises, *Journal of Monetary Economics* 48, 513–548.

———, 2004, Smoothing Sudden Stops, *Journal of Economic Theory, 119* (1), 104–127.

Calvo, G. A., 1998a, Capital Flows and Capital-Market Crises: The Simple Economics of Sudden Stops, *Journal of Applied Economics* 1, 35–54.

———, 1998b, Understanding the Russian Virus, with Special Reference to Latin America, *unpublished manuscript.*

Calvo, G. A., and E. G. Mendoza, 2000, Rational Contagion and the Globalization of Securities Markets, *Journal of International Economics* 51, 79–113.

Calvo, G. A., and C. M. Reinhart, 2000, When Capital Inflows Come to a Sudden Stop: Consequences and Policy Options, in P. Kenen and A. Swoboda, eds., *Reforming the International Monetary and Financial System* (International Monetary Fund, Washington, DC).

———, 2002, Fear of Floating, *Quarterly Journal of Economics* 117, 379–408.

Cartapanis, A., V. Dropsy, and S. Mametz, 2002, The Asian Currency Crises: Vulnerability, Contagion, or Unsustainability. *Review of International Economics* 10, 79–91.

Cerra, V., and S. C. Saxena, 2002, Contagion, Monsoons, and Domestic Turmoil in Indonesia's Currency Crisis, *Review of International Economics* 10, 36–44.

Chang, R., and G. Majnoni, 2001, International Contagion: Implications for Policy, in S. Claessens and K. J. Forbes, eds., *International Financial Contagion* (Kluwer Academic Publishers, Boston).

———, 2002, Fundamentals, Beliefs, and Financial Contagion, *European Economic Review* 46, 801–808.

Chang, R., and A. Velasco, 2000a, Banks, Debt Maturity and Financial Crises, *Journal of International Economics* 51, 169–194.

———, 2000b, Financial Fragility and the Exchange Rate Regime, *Journal of Economic Theory* 92, 1–34.

———, 2001, A Model of Financial Crises in Emerging Markets, *Quarterly Journal of Economics* 116, 489–517.

Chari, V. V., and P. J. Kehoe, 2003, Financial Crises as Herds: Overturning the Critiques, *National Bureau of Economic Research Working Paper* 9658.

Chui, M., S. Hall, and A. Taylor, 2004, Crisis Spillovers in Emerging Market Economies: Interlinkages, Vulnerabilities and Investor Behaviour, *Bank of England Working Paper* 212.

Cohen, B. H., and H. S. Shin, 2003, Positive Feedback Trading under Stress: Evidence from the U.S. Treasury Securities Market, *Bank for International Settlements Working Paper* 122.

Connolly, R. A., and F. A. Wang, 2003, International Equity Market Comovements: Economic Fundamentals or Contagion? *Pacific Basin Finance Journal* 11, 23–43.

Corsetti, G., M. Pericoli, and M. Sbracia, 2001, Correlation Analysis of Financial Contagion: What One Should Know before Running a Test, *Yale University, Economic Growth Center Discussion Paper* 822.

Darbar, S. M., and P. Deb, 2002, Cross-Market Correlations and Transmission of Information, *Journal of Futures Markets* 22, 1059–1082.

Diamond, D. W., 1991, Debt Maturity Structure and Liquidity Risk, *Quarterly Journal of Economics* 106, 709–737.

Diamond, D. W., and P. H. Dybvig, 1983, Bank Runs, Deposit Insurance, and Liquidity, *Journal of Political Economy* 91, 401–419.

Dooley, M. P., 2000, A Model of Crises in Emerging Markets, *Economic Journal* 110, 256–272.

Dornbusch, R., Y. C. Park, and S. Claessens, 2000, Contagion: Understanding How It Spreads, *World Bank Research Observer* 15, 177–197.

Drazen, A., 2000, Interest-Rate and Borrowing Defense against Speculative Attack, *Carnegie-Rochester Conference Series on Public Policy* 53, 303–348.

Drazen, A., and P. R. Masson, 1994, Credibility of Policies versus Credibility of Policy-Makers, *Quarterly Journal of Economics* 109, 735–754.

Dungey, M., R. Fry, B. González-Hermosillo, and V. L. Martin, 2002, International Contagion Effects from the Russian Crisis and the LTCM Near-Collapse, *International Monetary Fund Working Paper* 02/74.

———, 2005, Empirical Modelling of Contagion: A Review of Methodologies, *Quantitative Finance*, forthcoming.

Dungey, M., and V. L. Martin, 2004, A Multifactor Model of Exchange Rates with Unanticipated Shocks: Measuring Contagion in the East Asian Currency Market, *Journal of Emerging Markets Finance*, 3, 305–330.

Dungey, M., and D. Zhumabekova, 2001, Testing for Contagion Using Correlations: Some Words of Caution, *Federal Reserve Bank of San Francisco, Pacific Basin Working Paper* PB01-09.

Edison, H. J., 2003, Do Indicators of Financial Crises Work? An Evaluation of an Early Warning System, *International Journal of Finance and Economics* 8, 11–53.

Eichengreen, B., and M. D. Bordo, 2002, Crises Now and Then: What Lessons from the Last Era of Financial Globalization, *National Bureau of Economic Research Working Paper* 8716.

Eichengreen, B., R. Hausmann, and U. Panizza, 2003, The Pain of Original Sin, in B. Eichengreen and R. Hausmann, eds., *Debt Denomination and Financial Instability in Emerging Market Economies* (University of Chicago Press, Chicago).

Eichengreen, B., and A. Mody, 2001, Bail-ins, Bailouts, and Borrowing Costs, *International Monetary Fund Staff Papers* 47, 155–187.

Eichengreen, B., and R. Portes, 1995, *Crisis? What Crisis? Orderly Workouts for Sovereign Debtors* (Centre for Economic Policy Research, London).

Eichengreen, B., A. K. Rose, and C. Wyplosz, 1995, Exchange Market Mayhem: The Antecedents and Aftermath of Speculative Attacks, *Economic Policy: A European Forum* 21, 249–296.

———, 1996, Contagious Currency Crisis, *National Bureau of Economic Research Working Paper* 5681.

Eichengreen, B., and C. Ruhl, 2001, The Bail-in Problem: Systematic Goals, Ad Hoc Means, *Economic Systems* 25, 3–32.

Engle, R. F., T. Ito, and W. L. Lin, 1990, Meteor-Showers or Heat Waves: Heteroskedastic Intradaily Volatility in the Foreign-Exchange Market, *Econometrica* 58, 525–542.

Engle, R. F., and J. Lange, 1997, Measuring, Forecasting and Explaining Time Varying Liquidity in the Stock Market, *National Bureau of Economic Research Working
Paper* 6129.

Evans, M. D. D., and R. K. Lyons, 2002, Order Flow and Exchange Rate Dynamics,
Journal of Political Economy 110, 170–180.

———, 2003, How Is Macro News Transmitted to Exchange Rates? *National Bureau
of Economic Research Working Paper* 9433.

Farmer, J. D., and S. Joshi, 2002, The Price Dynamics of Common Trading Strategies,
Journal of Economic Behavior and Organization 49, 149–171.

Favero, C. A., and F. Giavazzi, 2002, Is the International Propagation of Financial
Shocks Non-Linear? Evidence from the ERM, *Journal of International Economics*
57, 231–246.

Fischer, S., 1999, On the Need for an International Lender of Last Resort, *Journal of
Economic Perspectives* 13, 85–104.

Forbes, K. J., and R. Rigobon, 2001, Measuring Contagion: Conceptual and Empirical Issues, in S. Claessens and K. J. Forbes, eds., *International Financial Contagion*
(Kluwer Academic Publishers, Boston).

———, 2002, No Contagion, Only Interdependence: Measuring Stock Market Co-
movements, *Journal of Finance* 57, 2223–2261.

Frankel, J. A., and A. K. Rose, 1996, Currency Crashes in Emerging Markets: An
Empirical Treatment, *Journal of International Economics* 41, 351–366.

Fratzscher, M., 2003, On Currency Crises and Contagion, *International Journal of Finance and Economics* 8, 109–129.

Gale, D., and X. Vives, 2002, Dollarization, Bailouts, and the Stability of the Banking System, *Quarterly Journal of Economics* 117, 467–502.

Garber, P. M., and V. U. Grilli, 1989, Bank Runs in Open Economies and the International Transmission of Panics, *Journal of International Economics* 27, 165–175.

Gerlach, S., and F. Smets, 1995, Contagious Speculative Attacks, *European Journal of
Political Economy* 11, 45–63.

Ghosh, C., R. S. Guttery, and C. F. Sirmans, 1998, Contagion and REIT Stock Prices,
Journal of Real Estate Research 16, 389–400.

Glick, R., and A. K. Rose, 1999, Contagion and Trade: Why Are Currency Crises
Regional? *Journal of International Money and Finance* 18, 603–617.

Goldstein, M., 1998, The Asian Financial Crisis: Causes, Cures, and Systemic Implications, in *Policy Analyses in International Economics* (Institute for International
Economics, Washington, DC).

Goldstein, M., G. L. Kaminsky, and C. M. Reinhart, 2000. *Assessing Financial Vulnerability: An Early Warning System for Emerging Markets* (Institute for International
Economics, Washington, D.C.).

Goodhart, C., and G. Illing, 2003. *Financial Crises, Contagion and the Lender of Last
Resort: A Reader* (Oxford University Press, Oxford).

Granger, C. W. J., B.-N. Huang, and C.-W. Yang, 2000, A Bivariate Causality between Stock Prices and Exchange Rates: Evidence from Recent Asian Flu, *Quarterly Review of Economics and Finance* 40, 337–54.

Greenspan, A., 1999, Risk, Liquidity and the Economic Outlook, *Business Economics*
34, 20–24.

Grinblatt, M., S. Titman, and R. Wermers, 1995, Momentum Investment Strategies,
Portfolio Performance, and Herding: A Study of Mutual Fund Behavior, *American Economic Review* 85, 1088–1105.

Haldane, A. G., A. Penalver, V. Saporta, and H. S. Shin, 2003, Analytics of Sovereign Debt Restructuring, *Bank of England Working Paper 203*.

———, 2004, Optimal Collective Action Clause Thresholds, *unpublished manuscript*.

Hashimoto, Y., and T. Ito, 2002, High Frequency Contagion of Currency Crises in Asia, *National Bureau of Economic Research Working Paper 9376*.

Hernández, L. F., and R. O. Valdés, 2001, What Drives Contagion: Trade, Neighborhood, or Financial Links? *International Review of Financial Analysis* 10, 203–218.

Jeanne, O., and P. Masson, 2000, Currency Crises, Sunspots and Markov-Switching Regimes, *Journal of International Economics* 50, 327–350.

Kallberg, J. G., C. H. Liu, and P. Pasquariello, 2002, Regime Shifts in Asian Equity and Real Estate Markets, *Real Estate Economics* 30, 263–291.

Kaminsky, G. L., and C. M. Reinhart, 1999, The Twin Crises: The Causes of Banking and Balance-of-Payments Problems, *American Economic Review* 89, 473–500.

———, 2000, On Crises, Contagion, and Confusion, *Journal of International Economics* 51, 145–168.

———, 2003, The Center and the Periphery: The Globalization of Financial Turmoil, *National Bureau of Economic Research Working Paper 9479*.

Kaminsky, G. L., and S. L. Schmukler, 1999, What Triggers Market Jitters? A Chronicle of the Asian Crisis, *Journal of International Money and Finance* 18, 537–560.

Karolyi, G. A., 2003, Does International Financial Contagion Really Exist? *International Finance* 6, 179–199.

Kehoe, T. J., 1996, Comments on P. Krugman: Are Currency Crises Self-Fulfilling? in B. S. Bernanke and J. J. Rotemberg, eds., *National Bureau of Economic Research Macroeconomics Annual* (MIT Press, Cambridge).

King, M. A., and S. Wadhwani, 1990, Transmission of Volatility between Stock Markets, *Review of Financial Studies* 3, 5–35.

Kiyotaki, N., and J. Moore, 2002, Balance-Sheet Contagion, *American Economic Review* 92, 46–50.

Kodres, L. E., and M. Pritsker, 2002, A Rational Expectations Model of Financial Contagion, *Journal of Finance* 57, 769–799.

Krugman, P., 1979, Model of Balance-of-Payments Crises, *Journal of Money Credit and Banking* 11, 311–325.

———, 1996, Are Currency Crises Self-Fulfilling? *National Bureau of Economic Research Macroeconomics Annual* 345–378.

———, ed., 2000. *Currency Crises* (University of Chicago Press, Chicago).

Kyle, A. S., and W. Xiong, 2001, Contagion as a Wealth Effect, *Journal of Finance* 56, 1401–1440.

Loretan, M., and W. B. English, 2000, Evaluating "Correlation Breakdowns" during Periods of Market Volatility, *Board of Governors of the Federal Reserve System, International Finance Discussion Paper 658*.

Lowell, J., C. R. Neu, and D. Tong, 1998, Financial Crises and Contagion in Emerging Market Countries, *RAND Working Paper MR-962*.

Masson, P. R., 1999a, Contagion: Macroeconomic Models with Multiple Equilibria, *Journal of International Money and Finance* 18, 587–602.

———, 1999b, Contagion: Monsoonal Effects, Spillovers and Jumps between Multiple Equilibria, in P.-R. Agénor, M. Miller, D. Vines, and A. Weber, eds., *The Asian Financial Crisis: Causes, Contagion and Consequences* (Cambridge University Press, Cambridge).

Mathur, I., K. C. Gleason, S. Dibooglu, and M. Singh, 2002, Contagion Effects from the 1994 Mexican Peso Crisis: Evidence from Chilean Stocks, *The Financial Review* 37, 17–37.

Mei, J. P., and J. W. Hu, 2000, Conditional Risk Premiums of Asian Real Estate Stocks, *Journal of Real Estate Finance and Economics* 21, 297–313.

Morris, S., and H. S. Shin, 1998, Unique Equilibrium in a Model of Self-Fulfilling Currency Attacks, *American Economic Review* 88, 587–597.

———, 1999, A Theory of the Onset of Currency Attacks, in P.-R. Agénor, M. Miller, D. Vines, and A. Weber, eds., *The Asian Financial Crisis: Causes, Contagion and Consequences* (Cambridge University Press, Cambridge).

———, 2000, Global Games: Theory and Applications, in M. Dewatripont, L. P. Hansen, and S. J. Turnovsky, eds., *Advances in Economics and Econometrics, Theory and Applications, Eighth World Congress, Volume 3*.

———, 2002, Social Value of Public Information, *American Economic Review* 92, 1521–1534.

———, 2003, Catalytic Finance: When Does It Work? *Cowles Foundation Discussion Paper* 1400.

Moser, T., 2003, What Is International Financial Contagion? *International Finance* 6, 157–178.

Obstfeld, M., 1995, The Logic of Currency Crises, in B. Eichengreen, J. Frieden, and J. von Hagen, eds., *Monetary and Fiscal Policy in an Integrated Europe* (Springer, Heidelberg, Germany).

———, 1996, Models of Currency Crises with Self-Fulfilling Features, *European Economic Review* 40, 1037–1047.

Obstfeld, M., and A. M. Taylor, 2004. *Global Capital Markets: Integration, Crisis, and Growth* (Cambridge University Press, Cambridge).

Packer, F., and C. Suthiphongchai, 2003, Sovereign Credit Default Swaps, *Bank for International Settlements Quarterly Review* December, 79–88.

Pavlova, A., and R. Rigobon, 2004, Asset Prices and Exchange Rates, MIT Sloan Working Paper No. 4322-03.

Peek, J., and E. S. Rosengren, 1997, The International Transmission of Financial Shocks: The Case of Japan, *American Economic Review* 87, 495–505.

———, 2000, Collateral Damage: Effects of the Japanese Bank Crisis on Real Activity in the United States, *American Economic Review* 90, 30–45.

Pericoli, M., and M. Sbracia, 2003, A Primer on Financial Contagion, *Journal of Economic Surveys* 17, 571–608.

Pesaran, H., and A. Pick, 2004, Econometric Issues in the Analysis of Contagion, CESito Working Paper 1176.

Pesaran, M. H., T. Schuermann, and S. M. Weiner, 2004, Modelling Regional Interdependencies Using a Global Error-Correcting Macroeconometric Model, *Journal of Business Economics and Statistics*, 22 (2), 129–162.

Prasad, E., K. S. Rogoff, S.-J. Wei, and M. A. Kose, 2003, *Effects of Financial Globalization on Developing Countries: Some Empirical Evidence* (International Monetary Fund, Washington, DC).

Pritsker, M., 2001, The Channels for Financial Contagion, in S. Claessens and K. J. Forbes, eds., *International Financial Contagion* (Kluwer Academic, Boston).

Quintos, C., Z. H. Fan, and P. C. B. Phillips, 2001, Structural Change Tests in Tail Behaviour and the Asian Crisis, *Review of Economic Studies* 68, 633–663.

Radelet, S., and J. D. Sachs, 1998, The East Asian Financial Crisis: Diagnosis, Remedies, Prospects, *Brookings Papers on Economic Activity* 1998, 1–90.

Ranciere, R. G., 2002, Credit Derivatives in Emerging Markets, *International Monetary Fund Policy Discussion Paper.*

Reinhart, C. M., 2000, Comments on P. Krugman: Political Contagion in Currency Crises, in P. Krugman, ed., *Currency Crises* (University of Chicago Press, Chicago).

Rey, H., 2001, Rethinking Multiple Equilibria in Macroeconomic Modeling: Comment, *National Bureau of Economic Research Macroeconomics Annual 2000,* 171–178.

Rigobon, R., 2003, On the Measurement of the International Propagation of Shocks: Is the Transmission Stable? *Journal of International Economics* 61, 261–283.

Rogoff, K. S., 1999, International Institutions for Reducing Global Financial Instability, *Journal of Economic Perspectives* 13, 21–42.

Sachs, J. D., A. Tornell, and A. Velasco, 1996, Financial Crises in Emerging Markets: The Lessons from 1995, *Brookings Papers on Economic Activity* 1996, 147–215.

Samet, D., 1998, Iterated Expectations and Common Priors, *Games and Economic Behavior* 24, 131–141.

Sander, H., and S. Kleimeier, 2003, Contagion and Causality: An Empirical Investigation of Four Asian Crisis Episodes, *Journal of International Financial Markets, Institutions and Money* 13, 171–186.

Shiller, R. J., 2003, *The New Financial Order: Risk in the Twenty-First Century* (Princeton University Press, Princeton, NJ).

Tambakis, D. N., 2002, Expected Social Welfare under a Convex Phillips Curve and Asymmetric Policy Preferences, *Journal of Money Credit and Banking* 34, 434–449.

Tirole, J., 2002, *Financial Crises, Liquidity, and the International Monetary System* (Princeton University Press, Princeton, NJ).

Townsend, R. M., 1983, Forecasting the Forecasts of Others, *Journal of Political Economy* 91, 546–588.

Valdés, R. O., 1997, Emerging Markets Contagion: Evidence and Theory, *Central Bank of Chile Working Paper* 007.

Van Rijckeghem, C., and B. Weder, 2001, Sources of Contagion: Is It Finance or Trade? *Journal of International Economics* 54, 293–308.

———, 2003, Spillovers through Banking Centers: A Panel Data Analysis of Bank Flows, *Journal of International Money and Finance* 22, 483–509.

Wälti, S., 2003, Testing for Contagion in International Financial Markets: Which Way to Go? *HEI Working Paper* 04/2003.

World Bank, 2003. *Global Development Finance 2003—Striving for Stability in Development Finance* (World Bank Group, Washington, DC).

2

The Unholy Trinity of Financial Contagion

Graciela L. Kaminsky, Carmen M. Reinhart, and Carlos A. Végh

1. INTRODUCTION

For reasons that are not always evident at the time, some financial events, such as the devaluation of a currency or an announcement of default on sovereign debt obligations, trigger an immediate and startling adverse chain reaction among countries within a region and in some cases across regions. This phenomenon, which we dub "fast and furious" contagion, was manifest after the floatation of the Thai baht on 2 July 1997, as it quickly triggered financial turmoil across East Asia. Indonesia, Korea, Malaysia, and the Philippines were hit the hardest—by December 1997, their currencies had depreciated (on average) by about 75 percent. Similarly, when Russia defaulted on its sovereign bonds on 18 August 1998, the effects were felt not only in several of the former Soviet republics, but also in Hong Kong, Brazil, Mexico, many other emerging markets, and the riskier segments of developed markets.[1] The economic impact of these shocks on the countries unfortunate enough to be affected included declines in equity prices, spikes in the cost of borrowing, scarcity in the availability of international capital, and declines in the value of their currencies and in output.

Table 1 presents summary material for recent contagion episodes. The first column lists the country, the date that marks the beginning of the episode, the nature of the shock, and currency market developments in the crisis country, while the remaining columns include information on the existence and nature of common external shocks, the suspected main mechanism for propagation across national borders, and the countries that were most affected.

The challenge for economic researchers is to explain why the number of financial crises that did not have significant international consequences is far

Kaminsky: University of Washington and NBER, graciela@gwu.edu; Reinhart: University of Maryland and NBER, creinhart@umd.edu; Végh: UCLA and NBER, cvegh@ucla.edu. Reprinted from *Journal of Economic Perspectives*, Fall 2003. With permission from the American Economic Association. The authors wish to thank Laura Kodres, Vincent Reinhart, and Miguel Savastano for very useful comments and suggestions, and Kenichi Kashiwase for excellent research assistance.

Table 1. Financial Crises with Immediate International Repercussions: 1980–2000

Origin of the shock, country and date	Nature of common external shock, if any	Contagion mechanisms	Countries affected
On August 1982 Mexico defaults on its external bank debt. By December, the peso had depreciated by 100 percent.	Between 1980 and 1985, commodity prices fell by about 31 percent. US short term interest rates rise to about 7 percent, the highest levels since the Depression.	U.S. banks, heavily exposed to Mexico, retrenched from emerging markets	With the exception of Chile, Colombia and Costa Rica all countries in Latin America defaulted.
On September 8, 1992 the Finnish markka is floated and the ERM crisis unfolds.	High interest rates in Germany. Rejection by Danish voters of the Maastricht treaty.	Hedge funds.	All the countries in the European Monetary System except Germany.
On December 20, 1994 Mexico announced a 15 percent devaluation of the peso. It sparked a confidence crisis and by March 1995 the peso's value had declined by about 100 percent.	From January 1994 to December, the Federal Reserve raised the federal funds rate by 2 1/2 percentage points.	Mutual funds sell off other Latin American countries, notably Argentina and Brazil. Massive bank runs and capital flight in Argentina.	Argentina suffered the most, losing about 20 percent of deposits in early 1995. Brazil was next, while losses in other countries in the region limited to declines in equity prices.
On July 2 1997, Thailand announces that the baht will be allowed to float. By January 1998 the baht had depreciated by about 113 percent.	The yen depreciated by about 51% against the US dollar during April 1995 and April 1997. Given the Asian currencies link to the US dollar, this translated into a significant appreciation for their currencies as well.	Japanese banks, exposed to Thailand, retrenched from emerging Asia. As Korea is affected, European banks also withdraw.	Indonesia, Korea, Malaysia, and the Philippines were hit hardest. Financial markets in Singapore and Hong Kong also experienced some turbulence.

continued

Table 1. (continued)

Origin of the shock, country and date	Nature of common external shock, if any	Contagion mechanisms	Countries affected
On August 17, 1998, Russia defaults on its domestic bond debt. Between July 1998 and January 1999, the ruble depreciated by 262 percent. On September 2, 1998, it became public knowledge that LTCM had gone bankrupt.	With heavy exposure to Russia and other high-yield instruments, Long Term Capital Management (LTCM) is revealed to be bankrupt.	Margin calls and leveraged hedge funds fueled the sell off in other emerging and high yield markets. It is difficult to distinguish contagion from Russia and fear of another LTCM.	Apart from several of the former Soviet republics, Hong Kong, Brazil, and Mexico were hit hardest. But most emerging and developed markets were affected.

Sources: International Monetary Fund) *International Financial Statistics,* dates of the default or restructurings are taken from Beim, D. and C. Calomiris (2001), Standard and Poor's *Credit Week* and *Debt Cycles in the World Economy* (1992).

greater than those that did. It is no surprise that a domestic crisis (no matter how deep) in countries that are approximately autarkic (either voluntarily or otherwise) will not likely have immediate repercussions in world capital markets. The countries may be large (China or India) or comparatively small (Bolivia and Guinea-Bissau). More intriguing cases of "contagion that never happened" are those where the crisis country is relatively large (at least by emerging market standards) and is reasonably well integrated to the rest of the world through trade or finance. Along with the fast and furious contagion episodes, these are the cases we focus on in this chapter.

Some recent examples of financial crises with limited *immediate* consequences include Brazil's devaluation of the real on 13 January 1999 and eventual flotation on February 1, the Argentine default and abandonment of the Convertibility Plan in December 2001, and Turkey's devaluation of the lira on 22 February 2001. Given that Brazil, Turkey, and Argentina are relatively large emerging markets, these episodes could have been—at least potentially—as highly "contagious" as the Thai and Russian crises. Nonetheless, financial markets shrugged off these events, despite the fact that it was evident at the time that some of these shocks would have trade and real sector repercussions on neighboring countries over the medium term.[2] Table 2 presents some summary material for these episodes, in a format parallel to table 1.

This chapter seeks to address the central question of why financial contagion across borders occurs in some cases but not others.[3] Throughout the chapter, we stress that there are three key elements—an abrupt reversal in capital inflows, surprise announcements, and a leveraged common

Table 2. Selected Financial Crises without Immediate International Repercussions: 1999–2001

Origin of the shock: country and date	Background on the run-up to the shock	Spillover mechanisms	Countries affected
On January 13, 1999 Brazil devalues the real and eventually floats on February 1. Between early January and end-February the real depreciates by 70 percent.	The crawling peg exchange rate policy (the Real Plan) that was adopted in July 1994 to stabilize inflation is abandoned.	There is an increase in volatility in some of larger equity markets and Argentina spreads widened. Equity markets in Argentina and Chile rallied. These effects lasted only a few days.	Significant and protracted effect on Argentina, as Brazil is Argentina's largest trading partner.
Turkey, February 22, 2001 Devaluation and floatation of the lira.	Facing substantial external financing needs, in late November 2000, rumors of the withdrawal of external credit lines to Turkish banks triggered a foreign exchange outflows and overnight rates soared to close to 2,000 percent.		There has been some conjecture that the Turkish crisis may have exacerbated the withdrawal of investors from Argentina but given the weakness in Argentina's fundamentals at the time, it is difficult to suggest developments owed to contagion.
On December 23, 2001, the president of Argentina announces intentions to default.	Following several waves of capital flight, on December 1st capital controls are introduced.	Bank deposits fall by more than 30 percent in Uruguay, as Argentines withdraw deposits from Uruguayan banks. Significant effects on economic (trade and tourism) activity in Uruguay.	Uruguay and, to a much lesser extent, Brazil

Sources: See table 1.

creditor (the unholy trinity)—that distinguish the cases where contagion occurs from those where it does not.

First, contagion usually followed on the heels of a surge in inflows of international capital and, more often than not, the initial shock or announcement pricked the capital flow bubble, at least temporarily. The capacity for a swift and drastic reversal of capital flows—the so-called sudden stop problem—played a significant role.[4]

Second, the announcements that set off the chain reactions came as a surprise to financial markets. The distinction between anticipated and unanticipated events appears critical, as forewarning allows investors to adjust their portfolios in anticipation of the event.

Third, in all cases where there were significant immediate international repercussions, a leveraged common creditor was involved—be it commercial banks, hedge funds, mutual funds, or individual bondholders—who helped to propagate the contagion across national borders.

Before turning to the question of what elements distinguish the cases where contagion occurs from those where it does not, however, we provide a brief tour of the main theoretical explanations for contagion and the most salient empirical findings on the channels of propagation.

2. WHAT IS CONTAGION?

Since the term "contagion" has been used liberally and taken on multiple meanings, it is useful to clarify how it will be used in this chapter. We refer to contagion as an episode in which there are significant *immediate* effects in a number of countries following an event—that is, when the consequences are *fast and furious* and evolve over a matter of hours or days. This "fast and furious" reaction is a contrast to cases in which the initial international reaction to the news is muted. The latter cases do not preclude the emergence of gradual and protracted effects that may cumulatively have major economic consequences. We refer to these gradual deaths by a thousand cuts cases as *spillovers.* Common external shocks, such as changes in international interest rates or oil prices, are also not automatically included in our working definition of contagion. Only if there is "excess comovement" in financial and economic variables across countries in response to a common shock do we consider it contagion.

2.1 Theories of Contagion

Through what channels does a financial crisis in one country spread across international borders? Some models have emphasized investor behavior that gives rise to the possibility of herding and fads. It is no doubt possible (if not appealing to many economists) that such "irrational exuberance," to quote Federal Reserve Chairman Alan Greenspan,[5] influences the behavior of capital flows and financial markets and exacerbate the booms as well as the busts. Other models stress economic linkages through trade or finance. This section provides a selective discussion of theories of contagion. The main message conveyed here—consistent with our unholy trinity proposition—is that financial linkages (i.e., cross border capital flows and common creditors) and investor behavior figure the most prominently in the theoretical explanations of contagion.

2.1.1 Herding   Bikhchandani, Hirshleifer, and Welch (1992) model the fragility of mass behavior as a consequence of informational cascades.[6] An information cascade occurs when it is optimal for an individual, after observing the actions of those ahead, to follow the behavior of the preceding individual without regard to their own information. Under relatively mild conditions, cascades will almost surely start, and often they will be wrong. In those circumstances, a few early individuals can have a disproportionate effect. Changes in the underlying value of alternative decisions can lead to "fads," that is drastic and seemingly whimsical swings in mass behavior without obvious external stimulus.

Banerjee (1992) also develops a model to examine the implications of decisions that are influenced by what others are doing. The decisions of others may reflect potentially important information in their possession that is not in the public domain. With sequential decision making, people paying attention to what others are doing before them end up doing what everyone else is doing (i.e., herding behavior), even when one's own private information suggests doing something different. The herd externality is of the positive feedback type: If we join the crowd, we induce others to do the same. The signals perceived by the first few decision makers—random and not necessarily correct—determine where the first crowd forms, and from then on, everybody joins the crowd. This characteristic of the model captures (to some extent) the phenomena of "excess volatility" in asset markets, or the frequent and unpredictable changes in fashions.

Another story suggests that the channels of transmission arise from the global diversification of financial portfolios in the presence of information asymmetries. Calvo and Mendoza (2000), for instance, present a model where the fixed costs of gathering and processing country-specific information give rise to herding behavior, even when investors are rational. Because of information costs, there are equilibria in which the marginal cost exceeds the marginal gain of gathering information. In such instances, it is rational for investors to mimic market portfolios. When a rumor favors a different portfolio, all investors "follow the herd."

2.1.2 Trade Linkages   Some recent models have revived Nurkse's (1944) classic story of competitive devaluations (Gerlach and Smets 1995). Nurkse argued that since a devaluation in a one country makes its goods cheaper internationally, it will pressure other countries that have lost competitiveness to devalue as well. In this setting, a devaluation in a second country is a *policy* decision whose effect on output is expected to be salutary, as it induces expenditure-switching (i.e., reduces imports, increases exports, and improves the current account). An empirical implication of this type of model is that we should observe a high volume of trade among the "synchronized" devaluers. As a story of *voluntary* contagion, this explanation does not square with the fact that central banks often go to great lengths to avoid a devaluation in the first place (often by engaging in an active interest rate defense of the existing exchange rate, as in Lahiri and Végh (2003) or by enduring massive losses of foreign exchange reserves nor that devaluations have often been contractionary.

2.1.3   Financial Linkages   Other studies have emphasized the important role of common creditors and financial linkages. The "type" of the common creditor may differ across models but the story tends to remain consistent.

In Shleifer and Vishny (1997), arbitrage is conducted by relatively few specialized and leveraged investors, who combine their knowledge with resources that come from outside investors to take large positions. Funds under management become responsive to past performance. The authors call this Performance Based Arbitrage (PBA). In extreme circumstances, when prices are significantly out of line and arbitrageurs are fully invested, PBA is particularly ineffective. In these instances, arbitrageurs might bail out of the market when their participation is most needed. That is, arbitrageurs face fund withdrawals, and are not very effective in betting against the mispricing. Risk averse arbitrageurs might choose to liquidate, even when they do not have to, for fear that a possible further adverse price movement may cause a drastic outflow of funds later on. While the model is not explicitly focused on contagion, one could see how an adverse shock that lowers returns (say, like the Mexican peso crisis) may lead arbitrageurs to liquidate their positions in other countries that are part of their portfolio (Argentina, Brazil, etc.), as they fear future withdrawals.

Similarly, Calvo (1998) has stressed the role of liquidity. A leveraged investor facing margin calls needs to sell asset holdings. Because of the information asymmetries, a "lemons problem" arises and the asset can only be sold at a firesale price. For this reason, the strategy will be not to sell the asset whose price has already collapsed, but other assets in the portfolio. In doing so, however, other asset prices fall and the original disturbance spreads across markets.

Kodres and Pritsker (2002) develop a rational expectations model of asset prices to explain financial market contagion. In their model, assets' long run values are determined by macroeconomic risk factors, which are shared across countries, and by country-specific factors. Contagion occurs when "informed" investors respond to private information on a country-specific factor, by optimally rebalancing their portfolio's exposures to the shared macroeconomic risk factors in other countries' markets. When there is asymmetric information in the countries hit by the rebalancing, "uninformed" investors cannot fully identify the source of the change in asset demand; they therefore respond as if the rebalancing is related to information on their own country (even though it is not). As a result, an idiosyncratic shock generates excess co-movement—contagion—across countries' asset markets. A key insight from the model is that contagion can occur between two countries even when contagion via correlated information shocks, correlated liquidity shocks, and via wealth effects are ruled out by assumption, and even when the countries do not share common macroeconomic factors, provided that both share at least one underlying macroeconomic risk factor with a third country, through which portfolio rebalancing can take place. Their model, like the rational herding model of Calvo and Mendoza (2000), has the empirical implication that countries with more internationally-traded financial assets and more liquid markets should be more vulnerable to contagion. Small, highly illiquid markets are likely to be underrepresented in international portfolios to begin with and, as such, shielded from this type of contagion.

Kaminsky and Reinhart (2000) focus on the role of commercial banks in spreading the initial shock. The behavior of foreign banks can exacerbate the original crisis by calling loans and drying up credit lines, but can also propagate crises by calling loans elsewhere. The need to rebalance the overall risk of the bank's asset portfolio and to recapitalize following the initial losses can lead to a marked reversal in commercial bank credit across markets where the bank has exposure.

2.1.4 Other Explanations   The so-called wake-up call hypothesis (a term coined by Goldstein 1998) relies on either investor irrationality or a fixed cost in acquiring information about emerging markets. In this story, once investors "wake up" to the weaknesses that were revealed in the crisis country, they will proceed to avoid and move out of countries that share some characteristics with the crisis country. So, for instance, if the original crisis country had a large current account deficit and a relatively "rigid" exchange rate, then other countries showing similar features will be vulnerable to similar pressures (see Basu 1998 for a formal model).

2.2   Channels of Propagation: The Empirical Evidence

As discussed, some theoretical models emphasized trade linkages as a channel for the cross-border propagation of shocks, while most models have looked to financial markets for an explanation.

Perhaps because trade in goods and services has a longer history in the post–World War II period than trade in financial assets, or because of far better data availability, trade links have received the most attention in the empirical literature on channels of contagion. Eichengreen, Rose, and Wyplosz (1996) find evidence that trade links help explain the pattern of contagion in 20 industrial countries over 1959–1993. Glick and Rose (1999), who examine this issue for a sample of 161 countries, come to the same conclusion. Glick and Rose (1999) and Kaminsky and Reinhart (2000) also study trade linkages, which involve competition in a common third market. While sharing a third party is a necessary condition for the competitive devaluation story, Kaminsky and Reinhart (2000) argue it is clearly not a *sufficient* one. If a country that exports wool to the United States devalues, it is not obvious why this would have any detrimental effect on a country that exports semiconductors to the United States. Their study shows that third-party trade links is a plausible transmission channel in some cases but not for the majority of countries recently battered by contagion. For example, at the time of the Asian crisis, Thailand exported many of the same goods to the same third parties as Malaysia. This, however, does not explain all the other Asian crisis countries. Bilateral or third-party trade also does not appear to carry any weight in explaining the effects of Mexico (1994) on Argentina and Brazil. At the time of Mexico's 1994 devaluation, only about 2 percent of Argentina's and Brazil's total exports went to Mexico. Similarly, Brazil hardly trades with Russia, as only 0.2 percent of its exports are destined for Russian markets; yet in the weeks following the Russian default Brazil's interest rate spreads doubled and Brazil's equity prices fell by more than 20 percent.

Kaminsky and Reinhart (2000) compare countries clustered along the lines of trade links versus countries with common bank creditors, and conclude that common financial linkages better explains the observed pattern of contagion. Mody and Taylor (2003), who seek to explain the comovement in an exchange market pressures index by bilateral and third-party trade and other factors, also cast doubt on the importance of trade linkages in explaining the propagation of shocks.

Conversely, in many cases of crises without contagion, there are strong trade links. About 30 percent of Argentina's exports are destined for Brazil, yet in the week following Brazil's devaluation, the Argentine equity market increases 12 percent. Similarly, nearly 13 percent of Uruguay's exports are bound for the Argentine market. Yet, the main reason why the crisis in Argentina ultimately affected Uruguay was the tight financial linkages between the two countries. Uruguayan banks have (for many years) been host to Argentinean depositors, who thought their deposits safer when these were denominated in U.S. dollars and kept across the Río de la Plata. At first, as the crisis deepened in Argentina, many deposits fled from Argentine banks and found their way to Uruguay. But when the Argentine authorities declared a freeze on bank deposits in December 2001, Argentine firms and households began to draw down the deposits they kept at Uruguayan banks. The withdrawals escalated and became a run on deposits amid fears that the Uruguayan central bank would either run out of international reserves or (like Argentina) confiscate the deposits.

Other studies focused primarily on financial channels of transmission. Frankel and Schmukler (1998) and Kaminsky, Lyons, and Schmukler (2000) show evidence to support the idea that U.S.-based mutual funds have played an important role in spreading shocks throughout Latin America by selling assets from one country when prices fall in another—with Mexico's 1994 crisis being a prime example. Caramazza, Ricci, and Salgado (2000), Kaminsky and Reinhart (2000), and Van Rijckeghem and Weder (1999) focus on the role played by commercial banks in spreading shocks and inducing a sudden stop in capital flows in the form of bank lending, especially in the debt crisis of 1982 and the crisis in Asia in 1997. Mody and Taylor (2003) link contagion to developments in the U.S. high yield or "junk" bond market. The common thread in these papers is that, without the financial sector linkages, contagion of the fast and furious variety would be unlikely.

2.2.1 Summing Up   Table 3 summarizes some of the arguments about propagation of contagion among the five fast and furious cases emphasized earlier: Mexico in 1982, the European Exchange Rate Mechanism crises of 1992, Mexico's currency devaluation in 1994, Thailand's devaluation in 1997, and Russia's devaluation in 1998.[7] In each case, we consider the possible trade channel, whether the affected countries shared similar characteristics with the crisis country and with each other, and whether a common creditor was present with the possible financial channel. Indeed, table 3 lays the foundation for our unholy trinity of financial contagion proposition, which the next section discusses in greater detail.

Several features summarized in table 3 are worth highlighting. In all five cases, a common leveraged creditor was present, making it consistent with the explanations offered by Shleifer and Vishny (1997), Calvo (1998), and discussed in Kaminsky and Reinhart (2000). In three of the five cases, the scope for propagation via trade links is virtually nonexistent and in one of the two remaining cases (Thailand) the extent of third-party competition is with Malaysia, not the other affected Asian countries. Last, with the exception of the countries that suffered most from the Russia/Long-Term Capital Management (LTCM) fallout, the affected countries tended to have large capital inflows and relatively fixed exchange rates.

3. THE UNHOLY TRINITY: CAPITAL INFLOWS, SURPRISES, AND COMMON CREDITORS

Having summarized some of the key findings of the literature on contagion, we now return to our central question of why contagion occurs in some instances but not in others.

3.1 The Capital Flow Cycle

Fast and furious contagion episodes are typically preceded by a surge in capital inflows which, more often than not, come to an abrupt halt or sudden stop in the wake of a crisis. The inflow of capital may come from banks, other financial institutions, or boldholders. The debt contracts typically have short maturities, which means that the investors and financial institutions will have to make decisions about rolling over their debts—or not doing so. With fast and furious contagion, investors and financial institutions are exposed to the crisis country and often highly leveraged. Thus, the investors can be viewed as halfway through the door, ready to back out on short notice.

This rising financial exposure to emerging markets is not present to nearly the same extent in the crises without major external consequences.

Table 3. Propagation Mechanisms in Episodes of Contagion

Episode	Trade	Common characteristic across affected countries	Common creditor
Mexico, August 1982	As the entire region was affected, trade links are significant, even though there are low levels of bilateral trade among most of the affected countries.	Large fiscal deficits, weak banking sectors, dependence on commodity prices and heavy external borrowing.	U.S. commercial banks.
Finland, September 8, 1992—ERM crisis	While bilateral exports to Finland from the affected countries are small, there are substantial trade links among all the affected countries.	Large capital inflows, common exchange rate policy as part of the EMS.	Hedge funds.
Mexico, December 21, 1994	No significant trade links. Bilateral trade with Argentina and Brazil was minimal. Only 2 percent of Argentina's and Brazil's exports were destined to Mexico. Little scope for third party trade story. Mexico's exports to the United States were very different from Argentine and Brazilian exports.	Exchange rate based inflation stabilization plans. Significant real appreciation of the exchange rate and concerns about overvaluation. Large capital inflows in the run-up to the crisis.	Primarily U.S. bondholders, including mutual funds.

Financial crises that have not set off major international dominos have usually unfolded against low volumes of international capital flows. Given lower levels of exposure, investors and institutions in the financial sector have a much lower need to adjust their portfolios when the shock occurs. In many instances, because the shock is anticipated, portfolios were adjusted prior to the event.

In all five of the examples from table 1, the capital flow cycle has also played a key role in determining whether the effects of a crisis have significant international ramifications. For example, in the late 1970s, soaring commodity prices, low and sometimes negative real interest rates (as late as 1978 real interest rates oscillated between −2 percent and zero), and weak loan demand in the United States made it very attractive for U.S. banks to lend to Latin America and other emerging markets—and lend

Table 3. (continued)

Episode	Trade	Common characteristic across affected countries	Common creditor
Thailand, July 2, 1997	Bilateral trade with other affected countries was very limited. Malaysia exported similar products to some of the same third markets.	Heavily managed exchange rates and large increase in the stock of short-term foreign currency debt.	European and Japanese commercial banks lending to Thailand, Korea, Indonesia, and Malaysia. Mutual Funds sell off in Hong Kong and Singapore.
Russia/ LTCM, August 17, 1998	Virtually no trade with the most affected countries (bilateral or third party). Exports from, Brazil, Mexico and Hong Kong to Russia accounted for 1 percent or less of total exports for these countries.	The most liquid emerging markets, Brazil, Hong Kong and Mexico were most affected. These three countries accounted for the largest shares of mutual fund holdings.	Mutual funds and hedge funds

Sources: See table 1.

they did. Capital flows, by way of bank lending, surged during this period, as shown in figure 1. By the early 1980s, the prospects for repayment had significantly changed for the worse. U.S. short-term interest rates had risen markedly in nominal terms (the federal funds rate went from below 7 percent in mid 1978 to a peak of about 20 percent in mid-1981) and in real terms (by mid-1981 real short-term interest rates were around 10 percent, the highest level since the 1930s). Since most of the loans made had either short maturities or variable interest rates, the effects were passed on to the borrower relatively quickly. Commodity prices had fallen almost 30 percent between 1980 and 1982, and many governments in Latin America were engaged in spending sprees that would seal their fate and render them incapable of repaying their debts. In 1981, Argentina's public sector deficit as a percent of GDP was about 13 percent while Mexico's was 14 percent; during 1979–80 Brazil's deficit was of a comparable order of magnitude. Prior to Mexico's default in August 1982, one after another of these countries had already experienced currency crises, banking crises, or both. When Mexico ultimately defaulted, the highly exposed and leveraged banks retrenched from emerging markets in general and Latin America in particular.

During the decade that followed, there were numerous crises in Latin America, including some severe hyperinflations (Bolivia in 1985; Peru,

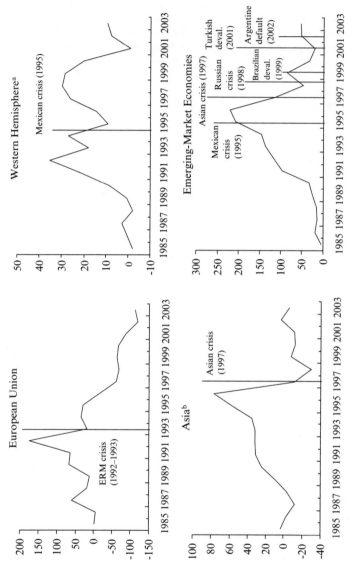

Fig. 1. Net private capital flows, 1985–2003 (U.S.$ billions)
Source: IMF *World Economic Outlook* (various issues).
Note: If the crisis occurred in the second half of the year, the vertical line is inserted in the following year.
[a]Includes Argentina and Mexico
[b]Includes Indonesia, Malaysia, the Philippines, South Korea, and Thailand.

Argentina, and Brazil in 1990) and other defaults. Yet, these crises had minimal international repercussions, as most of the region was shut out of international capital markets. The drought in capital flows lasted until 1990.

Figure 1 shows net private capital flows for the contagion episodes of the 1990s, while table 4 provides complementary information on capital flows and capital flight for the crisis country and those affected by it.

Again, notice the common pattern of a run-up in borrowing followed by a crash at the time of the initial shock and much inflow of capital thereafter. Net private capital flows to Europe had risen markedly and peaked in 1992 before coming to a sudden stop after the collapse of the Exchange Rate Mechanism crisis, in which the attempt to hold exchange rates within pre-set bands fell apart under pressure from international arbitrageurs. The crisis in the European Monetary System in 1992–93 showed that emerging markets do not have a monopoly on vulnerability to contagion, although they certainly tend to be more crisis prone.

In the case of Mexico, as the devaluation of the peso loomed close late in 1994, capital flows were close to their 1992 peak after surging considerably. (As late as 1989, Mexico had recorded net large capital outflows.) The rise in capital flows to Indonesia, Korea, Malaysia, the Philippines and Thailand (shown in figure 1) was no less dramatic—especially after 1995, when Japanese and European bank lending to emerging Asia escalates.

The bottom right panel of figure 1 shows the evolution of capital flows to all emerging markets and the progression of crises. The halcyon days of capital flows to emerging markets took place during the first half of the 1990s and held up at least for a short time after the Mexican crisis and its contagious effects on Argentina. But the East Asian crisis brings another wave of contagion along the marked decline in capital flows in 1997. The Russian crisis of August 1998 delivers another blow from which emerging market flows never fully recover in the 1990s. As shown in the bottom right panel of figure 1, this crisis is associated with the second major leg of decline in private capital flows to emerging markets. Since figure 1 is based on annual capital flow data, it significantly blurs the stark differences in capital flows during the pre- and post-Russia crisis. Figure 2 plots weekly data on emerging market bond issuance before (negative numbers) and after (positive numbers) the Russian default (dashed line) and, for contrast, the Brazilian devaluation on January 1999 (solid line). The vertical line marks the week of the crisis. It is evident that bond issuance collapses following the Russian crisis and remains for over two months following the event; by contrast, the Brazilian devaluation has no discernible impact on issuance, which actually increases following the devaluation.

As figure 1 highlights, the next three crises—the Brazilian devaluation of January 1999, the Turkish devaluation of February 2001, and the Argentine default at the end of 2001—take place during the downturn of the cycle and at levels of net capital inflows that were barely above the levels of the 1980s drought. Indeed, the estimates of capital flows to emerging markets

Table 4. **Capital Flows and Capital Flight on the Eve of Crises (U.S. dollars)**

Episode	Capital flow background in crisis country	Capital flow background in other relevant countries[1]
Fast and furious episodes		
Exchange Rate Mechanism Crisis: Finland September 8, 1992	Net capital flows to Finland had risen from less than $2 billion in 1988 to $9 billion at their peak in 1990. Portfolio flows, which were about $3 billion in 1988, however, hit their peak prior to the crisis in 1992 at $8 billion.	In 1989 private net capital flows to the European Union (EU) were about $11 billion in 1992, on the eve of the crisis these had risen to $174 billion.
Tequila Crisis: Mexico, December 21, 1994	In 1990 private net capital flows were less than $10 billion by 1993 flows had risen to $35 billion. Estimates of capital flight showed a repatriation through 1994.	Net flows to the other major Latin American countries had also risen sharply, for Western Hemisphere as a whole it went from net outflows in 1989 to inflows of $47 billion in 1994.
Asian Crisis: Thailand, July 2, 1997	From 1993 to 1996 net capital flows to Thailand doubled to about $20 billion. In 1997 capital outflows amounted about $14 billion.	Flows to emerging Asia had risen from less than $10 billion to almost $80 billion in 1996.
Russian Crisis: August 18, 1998	While total flows into Russia peaked in 1996, foreign direct investment peaked in 1998, rising from about $0.1 billion in 1992 to $2.2 billion in 1998.	Excluding Asia, which witnessed a sharp capital flow reversal in 1997, capital flows to other emerging markets remained buoyant through 1997 and early 1998, having risen from about $9 billion in 1990 to $125 billion in 1997.

in recent years shown in figure 1, indeed, may actually be overstated because total net flows include foreign direct investment, which held up better than portfolio bond and equity flows.

3.2 Surprise Crises and Anticipated Catastrophes

Fast and furious crises and contagion cases have a high degree of surprise associated with them while their quieter counterparts are more broadly anticipated. This distinction appears to be critical when "potentially affected

Table 4. (continued)

Episode	Capital flow background in crisis country	Capital flow background in other relevant countries[1]
Cases without immediate international consequences		
Brazil Devalues and Floats: February 1, 1999	Repatriation of capital flight amounted to about 3 percent of GDP in 1996. By early 1998 it had reversed into capital flight. Yet net capital flows did not change much between 1997 and 1999, currency crisis notwithstanding.	At about $54 billion in 1999, capital flows to Western Hemisphere well below their peak ($85 billion) in 1997.
Turkey floats the lira February 22, 2001	While repatriation amounted to about 2 percent of GDP during 1997–1999, capital flight began in earnest in 2000.	Following the successive crises in Asia (1997) and Russia (1998) private capital flows to emerging markets had all but dried up by 2001. At a meager $20 billion in 2001, flows were $200 billion off their peak in 1996.
Argentina Defaults: December 23, 2001	Until 1998, capital abroad was being repatriated. By 1999, however, capital flight amounted to 5 percent of GDP. After several waves of bank runs, capital flight was estimated at 6 percent of GDP in 2001.	(see Turkey commentary)

Sources: See table 1.

countries" have a common lender. If the common lender is surprised by the shock in the initial crisis country, there is no time ahead of the impending crisis to rebalance portfolios and scale back from the affected country. In contrast, if the crisis is anticipated, investors have time to limit the damage by scaling back exposure or hedging their positions.

Evidence that quieter episodes were more anticipated than the fast and furious cases is presented in table 5. Standard and Poor's credit ratings had remained unchanged during the twelve months prior to the Mexican and Thai currency crises. In the case of Russia, the credit rating is actually upgraded as late as June 1998, when the broader definition that includes Credit Watch (CW) status is used. The CW lists the names of credits whose Moody's ratings have a likelihood of changing. These names are actively under review because of developing trends or events which warrant a

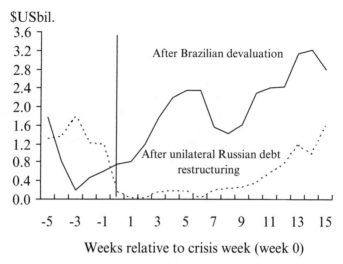

$USbil.

Weeks relative to crisis week (week 0)

Fig. 2. Emerging market: Bond market issuance around crises (U.S.$ billions;
weekly data, centered three-week moving average)
Source: IMF staff calculations based on data from Capital Data.
Note: Data prior to Russian default exclude the July 1998 debt exchange.

more extensive examination. Two downgrades eventually take place prior
to the crises on 13 August 1998 and again on 17 August, the day before the
default. By contrast, Argentina has a string (five) of downgrades as it
marches toward default, with the first one taking place in October 2000,
over a year before the eventual default. Likewise, Brazil and Turkey suffered downgrades well before the eventual currency crisis.

As further evidence that markets anticipated some of the shocks and not
others, figure 3 plots of the domestic-international interest rate differential
for the Emerging Market Bond Index (EMBI) and the EMBI+ for two of the
contagious episodes (Mexico and Russia, top panels) and for two crises
without immediate international repercussions (Argentina and Brazil, bottom panels).[8] The patterns shown in these four panels are representative of
the behavior of spreads ahead of anticipated and unanticipated crises.
(The vertical axis is measured in basis points, so a measure of 1,000 means
a gap of 10 percentage points between the domestic borrowing rate and the
international benchmark.) If bad things are expected to happen, risk increases and spreads should widen. The overall message is that fast and furious episodes are accompanied by sharp spikes in yield differentials—reflecting the unanticipated nature of the news—whereas other episodes
have tended to be anticipated by financial markets.

The top left panel of figure 3, which shows the evolution of Mexico's
spread in the pre-crisis period is striking. In Mexico, spreads are stable at
around 500 basis points in the months and weeks prior to the 21 December
1994 devaluation. Indeed Mexico's spreads remained below 1,000 until the
week of 6 January 1995. Russian spreads, illustrated in the top right panel

Table 5. Expected and Unexpected Crises: Standard and Poor's Sovereign Credit Ratings Before and After Crises

Country	Crisis Date	Change in Rating (including Credit Watch) 12 months prior to the crisis	Change in rating after the crisis
Fast and furious contagion episodes			
Mexico	December 21, 1994	None	Downgraded two days after the crisis December 23, 1994
Thailand	July 2, 1997	None	Downgraded in August
Russia	August 18, 1998	1 upgrade and 2 downgrades (on the week of the crisis)	1 further downgrade
Crises with limited external consequences			
Brazil	February 1, 1999	2 downgrades	No immediate change
Turkey	February 22, 2001	1 upgrade and two downgrades	1 further downgrade the day after the crisis
Argentina	December 23, 2001	5 downgrades between October 2000 and July 2001	

Source: Standard and Poor's.

of figure 3, show remarkable stability until a couple of weeks prior to the announcement and default. In the case of Russia, the devaluation of the rouble appears to have been widely expected by the markets, as evident on the spreads on ruble-denominated debt. One can conjecture that it was either the actual default or the absence of an IMF bailout (following on the heels of historically large bail-out packages for Mexico and Korea) that took markets by surprise.

The data presented in figure 3 bottom panel illustrates the fact that markets foreshadowed turbulence in the cases of Argentina (2001) and Brazil (1999). The bottom left panel of figure 3 presents evidence for interest rate spreads for Argentina and shows that the cost of borrowing began to rise steadily and markedly well before its default on December 23, 2001. In effect, since the week of 22 April, spreads began to settle above 1,000 and since 20 July never fell below 1,500. The bottom right panel of figure 3 shows Brazilian spreads. There is a run-up in spreads well before Brazil floats the real on 1 February 1999. This chart also reveals that Brazil—more so than Argentina—was quickly and markedly affected by the Russian crisis.

In sum, we have provided suggestive evidence that anticipated crises are preceded by credit ratings downgrades and widening interest spreads before the crisis while for unanticipated crises the downgrades and widening of spreads come during the crisis or after the fact.

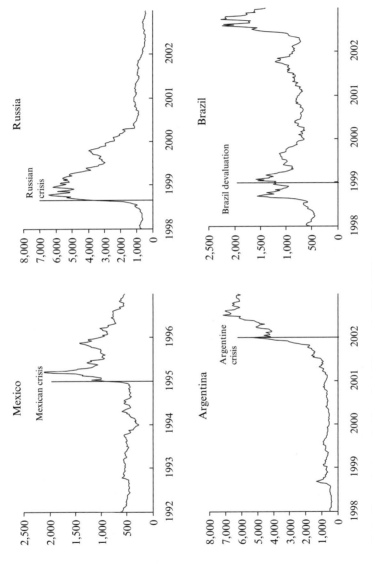

Fig. 3. Emerging-market bond yield spreads 1992–2002

Source: JP Morgan Chase.

Note: Emerging Market Bond Index Plus (EMBI+) spreads are plotted.

3.3   Common Creditors

As noted, international banks played an important role in the transmission of some of the crises of the 1980s and the 1990s. In the 1980s it was US banks lending heavily to Latin America while in the 1990s it was European and Japanese bank lending to Asia, the transition economies and, in the case of Spanish banks, Latin America. In the remainder of this section, we discuss the role that commercial banks and mutual and hedge funds have played in the recent contagion episodes.

International bank lending to the Asian crisis countries grew at a 25 per-cent annual rate from 1994 to 1997 (or at a pace of about US$40 billion inflow per year). At the onset of the crisis, European and Japanese banks' lending to Asia was at its peak at US$165 and US$124 billion, respectively, while the exposure of US banks was much more limited. Japanese banks had the highest exposure to Thailand, which also accounted for 26 percent of their total lending to emerging markets (the largest representation of any emerging market country in their portfolio). Collectively, the Asian crisis countries (excluding the Philippines, which did not borrow much from Japanese banks), accounted for 65 percent of the emerging market loan portfolio of Japanese banks. For European banks, the comparable share was 23 percent. Following the floatation of the Thai baht on 2 July 1997, the exposed banks retrenched quickly and cut credit lines to emerging Asia. The bank inflows quickly became outflows of about US$47 billion.

As with Asia, lending to transition economies had accelerated in the mid-1990s. In the three years before the Russian crisis, international bank lending to the region grew at 14 percent per annum. German banks were more heavily exposed to Russia, with lending to Russia averaging about 20 percent of all their lending to emerging economies. As with earlier fast and furious contagion episodes, bank flows to the region, which oscillated around US$28 billion per year in the years before the crisis, turned into a US$14 billion dollar outflow in the year following the crisis. This retrench-ment in lending helps explain why other transition economies were af-fected by the Russian crisis. However, it fails to explain why Brazil, Hong Kong, and Mexico come under significant pressures at this time. To under-stand these and other cases, we need to turn our attention to non-bank common creditors.

Equity and bond flows also declined sharply in the aftermath of the fast and furious crises of the 1990s. For example, US-based mutual funds spe-cialized in Latin America withdrew massively from the region following the Mexican crisis in 1994. As discussed in Kaminsky, Lyons, and Schmuk-ler (2002), withdrawals from Latin America oscillated around 40 percent in the immediate aftermath of the crisis. The countries most affected were Ar-gentina, Brazil, and (of course) Mexico, which were the countries where the mutual funds were most heavily exposed in Latin America at the time of the crisis. For example, if one examines the Latin American portfolio of mu-tual funds specialized in emerging markets at around the time of the crisis,

Brazil, Mexico, and Argentina account for 37, 26, and 14 percent of their portfolio, respectively (i.e., three countries accounted for 77 percent of the Latin American portfolio)!

The Thai crisis in 1997 also triggered equity outflows through mutual funds from Asia. As discussed in Kaminsky, Lyons, and Schmukler (2002), the countries most affected by abnormal withdrawals were Hong Kong, Singapore, and Taiwan, the countries with the most liquid financial markets in the region. As was the case of the Mexican crisis, these were the countries to which mutual funds were heavily exposed. Of the portfolio allocated to Asia, 30 percent was directed to Hong Kong, 7 percent to Singapore, and 13 percent to Taiwan. They estimate that abnormal withdrawals (relative to the mean flow during the whole sample) oscillated at around 10 percent for the three economies.

Similarly, highly leveraged funds seem to have had an important role in the speculative attack against Hong Kong dollar in August 1998, following the Russian crisis (See Corsetti, Pesenti, and Roubini (2001)). According to the Financial Stability Forum (2000) Report of the Working Group on Highly Leveraged Institutions, large macro hedge funds appear to have detected fundamental weaknesses early and started to build large short positions against the Hong Kong dollar. According to available estimates, hedge funds' short positions in the HK$ market were close to U.S.$10 billion (6 percent of Hong Kong's GDP), but some observers believe that the correct figure was much higher. Several large hedge funds also took very large short positions in the equity markets, and these positions were correlated over time. As reported in the FSF study, among those taking short positions in the equity market were four large hedge funds, whose futures and options positions were equivalent to around 40 percent of all outstanding equity futures contracts as of early August prior to Hong Kong Monetary Authority (HKMA) intervention. Position data suggest a correlation, albeit far from perfect, in the timing of the establishment of the short positions. Two hedge funds substantially increased their positions during the period of the HKMA intervention. At end August, four hedged funds accounted for 50,500 contracts or 49 percent of the total open interest/net delta position; one fund accounted for one third. The group's meetings suggested that some large highly leveraged institutions had large short positions in both the equity and currency markets.

4. CONCLUDING REFLECTIONS

To date, what has distinguished the contagion episodes that *happened* from those that *could have happened* seems to have had little to do with more "judicious" and "discriminating" investors—nor with any improvements to boast of in the state of the international financial architecture. If investors behaved in a more discriminating manner in the recent crises where contagion could have happened but did not, it is because: (i) those crises tended to unfold in slow motion and were thus widely anticipated; and (ii) the capital flow bubble had been pricked at an earlier stage, when those same investors were more "exuberant" and (iii) hence, the "common creditor" we have stressed in our discussion was less leveraged in these episodes. When looking back into history, one is struck by an overwhelming sense of déjà vu. It certainly seems a mystery why episodes of financial crises and contagion recur, in spite of the major costs associated with crises (this would seem to provide a sufficient motivation for avoiding them). But based on historical experience, there appears to be little hope that during the good times future generations of sovereign borrowers or investors will remember that the four most expensive words in financial history are "this time it is different."

If history is any guide, financial crises will not be eliminated—as Kindleberger noted, they are hardy perennials. But it should be possible, based on the understanding of what causes contagion and what does not, for countries to take steps to reduce their vulnerability to international contagion.

Contagion appears to be linked to a substantial inflow of capital to a country. Of course, the prospect of financial autarky as a way of avoiding fast and furious contagion is not particularly attractive as a long run solution. In fact, it may not even be feasible when countries have already liberalized the financial sector and the capital account. But before turning to the issue of capital account restrictions, it is critical to remember that in many crises (most of those discussed here and many others), the lead and largest borrower in international capital markets during the boom periods are the sovereign governments themselves. As Reinhart, Rogoff, and Savastano (2003) observe, it is the most debt intolerant countries with a history of serial default that can least afford to borrow that usually borrow the most. Often the outcome is default.

So, as a first important step, the risk of contagion would be reduced if policymakers in countries that are integrated with world capital markets remember that a surge in capital inflows often ends in a *sudden stop*— whether owing to home-grown problems or contagion from abroad. As a consequence, prudent policymaking would *at a minimum* ensure that the government does not overspend and overborrow when international capital markets are all too willing to lend, as most of those episodes end in tears. In contrast, fiscal policy in emerging markets currently tends to be markedly procyclical, with countries engaging in expansionary fiscal policy in good times and contractionary fiscal policy in bad times (Talvi and Végh 2000). Fiscal reforms aimed at designing institutional mechanisms that would discourage such procyclical behavior (particularly on the part of "provinces" or other autonomous entities) appear as an essential ingredient in preventing future crises from building up. Such consistent self discipline, however, on the part of governments has historically proved elusive.

As regards to curbing private borrowing from abroad, the issues are even more complex. The best case for restrictions on international financial inflows would seem to focus on debt contracts with short maturities that are denominated in a foreign currency—which have been the trigger in many modern contagion episodes. But although such policies may help in tilting the composition of capital flows toward longer maturities, their overall long-term effectiveness is unclear. Curbing capital outflows, once contagion and the ensuing sudden stop have occurred, is even more problematic. Experience has shown that capital flight has been an endemic problem for countries that have tried to turn the clock back and reintroduce tight capital account and financial restrictions amidst economic turmoil. More fundamentally, pervasive capital controls hardly seem likely to be the solution in the medium and long run to the contagion and sudden stop problem.

As to new mechanisms in financial centers that could curb these periodic bouts of lending and "irrational exuberance" and lessen the likelihood of unpleasant future surprises, we remain very skeptical that there are easy or obvious solutions. Access to more information may not lessen surprises when borrowers and lenders have often shown themselves willing to downplay worrisome fundamentals that are in the public domain in the late 1990s under the guise of having superior information. The economic historian Max Winkler wrote:

> The over-abundance of funds, together with the difficulty of finding the most profitable employment therefore at home has contributed greatly to the pronounced demand for and the ready absorption of large foreign issues, irrespective of quality . . . While high yield on a foreign bond does not necessarily indicate inferior quality, great care must be exercised in the selection of foreign bonds, especially today, when anything foreign seems to find a ready market . . . Promiscuous buying, however, is destined to prove disastrous. (*The New York Tribune,* 17 March 1927)

In 1929 a wave of currency crises swept through Latin America; it was quickly followed by a string of defaults on sovereign external debt obligations. At the time of this writing, with investors searching for high yields quickly snapping up emerging market bonds, Winkler's warning rings as true now as it did then.

NOTES

1. The international financial turmoil that followed Russia's default was compounded in a significant manner by another negative surprise announcement: On 2 September 1998 it became public knowledge that Long Term Capital Management (LTCM), owing to its large exposure to Russia and other high-yield assets, had gone bankrupt.

2. As Brazil is Argentina's largest trading partner, the sharp depreciation of the real (about 70 percent between January and end February) left the Argentine peso overvalued. Similarly, through its extensive financial and trade links, Uruguay's economy (as it has through history) would be whiplashed by the Argentine crisis.

3. Of course, there are historical examples of fast and furious contagion before the last few decades. Commonly cited examples of contagion include the first Latin American debt crisis—which began with Peru's default in April 1826—and the international financial crisis of 1873. Going back even further in time, Neal and Weidenmier (2002) also discuss the "contagion" dimension of the Tulip Mania of the 1630s and the Mississippi and South Sea Bubbles of 1719–20. Two leading examples of financial crises that did not lead to contagion include the well-documented Argentina-Baring crisis of 1890, and the United States financial crisis of 1907. For detailed accounts of historical episodes of financial crises, see Bordo and Eichengreen (1999), Bordo and Murshid (2001), Kindleberger (2000), and Neal and Weidenmier (2002).

4. See Calvo and Reinhart (2000) for an empirical analysis of sudden stop episodes and Caballero and Krishnamurthy (2004) for a model that traces out the economic consequences of sudden stops.

5. Greenspan (1996).

6. See Bikhchandani, Hirshleifer, and Welch (1998) for a thoughtful discussion of this literature.

7. For a detailed discussion of the evolution of these contagion episodes, the interested reader is referred to International Monetary Fund World Economic Outlook (January 1993) for the ERM crisis, International Monetary Fund International Capital Markets Developments, Prospects, and Key Policy Issues (August 1995) for the more recent Mexican crisis; Nouriel Roubini's home page http://pages.stern.nyu.edu/~nroubini/ for an excellent chronology of the Asian crisis; and IMF World Economic Outlook and International Capital Markets Interim Assessment (December 1998) for Russia's default and LTCM crisis. Diaz-Alejandro (1984) provides a compelling discussion of the debt crisis of the early 1980s.

8. The Emerging Market Bond Index Plus (EMBI+) tracks total returns for traded external debt instruments in the emerging markets. While the EMBI covers only Brady bonds, the EMBI+ expands upon the EMBI, covering three additional markets: (1) Eurobonds, (2) U.S. dollar local markets, and (3) loans. The country coverage of the EMBI+ varies over time, currently including 19 members. Current members are: Argentina, Brazil, Bulgaria, Colombia, Ecuador, Egypt, Mexico, Malaysia, Morocco, Nigeria, Panama, Peru, Philippines, Poland, Russia, Turkey, Ukraine, Venezuela, and South Africa. The selection of countries and instruments follow four eligibility criteria imposed by JP Morgan Chase: (1) a minimum balance in outstanding, (2) rating, (3) remaining maturity, and (4) ability for international settlement. In order to construct the index of a specific country, a daily total return of each instrument is first computed, and then aggregated by market-capitalization-weight.

REFERENCES

Banerjee, A. V., 1992, A Simple Model of Herd Behavior, *Quarterly Journal of Economics* 107, 797–817.

Basu, R., 1998, Contagion Crises: The Investor's Logic, *unpublished manuscript*.

Bikhchandani, S., D. Hirshleifer, and I. Welch, 1992, A Theory of Fads, Fashion, Custom, and Cultural-Change As Informational Cascades, *Journal of Political Economy* 100, 992–1026.

———, 1998, Learning from the Behavior of Others: Conformity, Fads, and Informational Cascades, *Journal of Economic Perspectives* 12, 151–170.

Bordo, M., and B. Eichengreen, 1999, Is Our Current International Economic Environment Unusually Crisis Prone?, in D. Gruen and L. Gower, eds., *Reserve Bank of Australia 1999 Conference, Capital Flows and the International Financial System* (Reserve Bank of Australia, Sydney).

Bordo, M. D., and A. P. Murshid, 2001, Are Financial Crises Becoming More Contagious?: What Is the Historical Evidence on Contagion?, in S. Claessens, and K. J. Forbes, eds., *International Financial Contagion* (Kluwer Academic Publishers, Boston, MA).

Caballero, R. J., and A. Krishnamurthy, 2004, Smoothing Sudden Stops, *Journal of Economic Theory* forthcoming.

Calvo, G. A., 1998, Capital Market Contagion and Recession: An Explanation of the Russian Virus, *unpublished manuscript*.

Calvo, G. A., and E. G. Mendoza, 2000, Rational Contagion and the Globalization of Securities Markets, *Journal of International Economics* 51, 79–113.

Calvo, G. A., and C. M. Reinhart, 2000, When Capital Inflows Come to a Sudden Stop: Consequences and Policy Options, in P. Kenen, and A. Swoboda, eds., *Reforming the International Monetary and Financial System* (International Monetary Fund, Washington, DC).

Caramazza, F., L. Ricci, and R. Salgado, 2000, Trade and Financial Contagion in Currency Crises, *International Monetary Fund Working Paper* 00/55.

Corsetti, G., P. Pesenti, and N. Roubini, 2001, The Role of Large Players in Currency Crises, *National Bureau of Economic Research Working Paper* 8303.

Diaz-Alejandro, C. F., 1984, Latin American Debt: I Don't Think We Are in Kansas Anymore, *Brookings Papers on Economic Activity* 2, 335–389.

Eichengreen, B., A. K. Rose, and C. Wyplosz, 1996, Contagious Currency Crises: First Tests, *Scandinavian Journal of Economics* 98, 463–484.

Financial Stability Forum, 2000, *Report of the Working Group on Highly Leveraged Institutions* (Financial Stability Forum, Basel).

Frankel, J. A., and S. L. Schmukler, 1998, Crisis, Contagion, and Country Funds: Effects on East Asia and Latin America, in R. Glick, ed., *Managing Capital Flows and Exchange Rates: Perspectives from the Pacific Basin* (Cambridge University Press, Cambridge).

Gerlach, S., and F. Smets, 1995, Contagious Speculative Attacks, *European Journal of Political Economy* 11, 45–63.

Glick, R., and A. K. Rose, 1999, Contagion and Trade—Why Are Currency Crises Regional?, *Journal of International Money and Finance* 18, 603–617.

Goldstein, M., 1998, The Asian Financial Crisis: Causes, Cures, and Systemic Implications, in *Policy Analyses in International Economics* (Institute for International Economics, Washington, DC).

Greenspan, A., 1996, The Challenge of Central Banking in a Democratic Society, *Remarks by Chairman Alan Greenspan at the Annual Dinner and Francis Boyer Lecture of the American Enterprise Institute for Public Policy Research, Washington, D.C., December 5, 1996* (http://www.federalreserve.gov/boarddocs/speeches/1996/19961205.htm).

International Monetary Fund, *International Capital Markets Developments, Prospects, and Key Policy Issues,* International Capital Markets Developments, Prospects, and Key Policy Issues (International Monetary Fund, various issues, Washington, DC).

———, *World Economic Outlook,* World Economic Outlook (International Monetary Fund, various issues, Washington, DC).

Kaminsky, G. L., R. K. Lyons, and S. L. Schmukler, 2000, Managers, Investors, and Crises: Mutual Fund Strategies in Emerging Markets, *National Bureau of Economic Research Working Paper* 7855.

————, 2002, Liquidity, Fragility, and Risk: The Behavior of Mutual Funds during Crises, *unpublished manuscript*.

Kaminsky, G. L., and C. M. Reinhart, 2000, On Crises, Contagion, and Confusion, *Journal of International Economics* 51, 145–168.

Kindleberger, C. P., 2000. *Manias, Panics and Crashes: A History of Financial Crises* (John Wiley & Sons, 4th edition, Indianapolis, IN).

Kodres, L. E., and M. Pritsker, 2002, A Rational Expectations Model of Financial Contagion, *Journal of Finance* 57, 769–799.

Lahiri, A., and C. A. Végh, 2003, Delaying the Inevitable: Interest Rate Defense and Balance of Payments Crises, *Journal of Political Economy* 111, 404–424.

Mody, A., and M. P. Taylor, 2003, Common Vulnerabilities, *Centre for Economic Policy Research Discussion Paper* 3759.

Neal, L., and M. Weidenmier, 2002, Crises in the Global Economy from Tulips to Today: Contagion and Consequences, *National Bureau of Economic Research Working Paper* 9147.

Nurkse, R., 1944, *International Currency Experience: Lessons of the Inter-War Period* (League of Nations, Geneva).

Reinhart, C. M., K. S. Rogoff, and M. A. Savastano, 2003, Debt Intolerance, *Brookings Papers on Economic Activity* 1, 1–62.

Shleifer, A., and R. W. Vishny, 1997, The Limits of Arbitrage, *Journal of Finance* 52, 35–55.

Talvi, E., and C. A. Végh, 2000, Tax Base Variability and Procyclical Fiscal Policy, *National Bureau of Economic Research Working Paper* 7499.

Van Rijckeghem, C., and B. Weder, 1999, Financial Contagion: Spillovers through Banking Centers, *Center for Financial Studies Working Paper* 1999/17.

3

A Comparison of Alternative Tests of Contagion with Applications

Mardi Dungey, Renée Fry, Brenda González-Hermosillo, and Vance L. Martin

1. INTRODUCTION

A common characteristic of asset markets during periods of crisis is that asset returns exhibit greater volatility than they do during noncrisis periods. One suggested mechanism to account for the increased volatility is transmissions due to contagion, and a number of empirical tests have been developed to try to identify this effect.

Forming a consensus on the empirical evidence for contagion in the existing literature is complicated by applications that differ by methodology, common factor specification, sample period selection, and asset market choice; see, for example, the overviews in Dornbusch, Park, and Claessens (2000) and Pericoli and Sbracia (2003). This chapter investigates these issues by making a comparison of four tests of contagion applied to common data sets and sample periods for three specific incidences of crisis in financial markets. The tests examined are the latent factor model of Dungey, Fry, González-Hermosillo, and Martin (2002, 2005; the *DFGM test*), the correlation approach of Forbes and Rigobon (2002; the *FR test*), the dummy-variable approach of Favero and Giavazzi (2002; the *FG test*), and the probability-based measure of Bae, Karolyi, and Stulz (2003; the *BKS test*).

The DFGM test is based on a linear latent factor model, where the parameters are identified by the change in volatility structure of returns

Dungey: Australian National University and CERF, mardi.dungey@anu.edu.au; Fry: Australian National University, renee.fry@anu.edu.au; González-Hermosillo; International Monetary Fund, bgonzalez@imf.org; Martin, vance@unimelb.edu.au. This project was funded under ARC large grant A00001350. We are grateful to Stuart Gourley for research assistance. This chapter was partly written while Mardi Dungey was a Visiting Fellow at CERF, and she thanks them for their hospitality. The views expressed in this chapter are those of the authors and do not necessarily represent those of the IMF or IMF policy.

under the two regimes, noncrisis and crisis periods. The FR test is based on comparing the correlation of returns between assets across regimes. This test is initially presented as a bivariate test, but can be extended to a multivariate setting by embedding the approach into a regime model augmented by dummy variables, and simply performing a Chow test (Dungey et al. 2005). The FG test is based on the exceedances (outliers) in one country to represent crisis periods, and testing the significance of these dummies in the return equations of other countries to test for contagion. The BKS approach is related to the FG approach, with the main difference being that the explanatory variable is transformed to a polychotomous dummy variable to represent the number of countries experiencing a crisis.

The various tests of contagion can be viewed as alternative ways of testing the statistical significance of changes in the volatility of asset returns between noncrisis and crisis periods, having conditioned on common and idiosyncratic factors (Dungey et al. 2005). The key distinguishing feature of these tests, however, is the way that information is filtered during crisis periods to identify potentially contagious linkages. An important aim of this chapter is to determine whether these alternative filtering methods result in different conclusions by using a range of common data sets. The tests are applied to equity markets during the Mexican peso crisis of 1994–95 (Tequila effect), the Hong Kong speculative attack in October 1997 (Asian flu), and the Argentine crisis of 2001–02. In each case a sample of three countries is chosen. Three hypotheses are tested. The first (hypothesis 1) is an overall test of contagion allowing for linkages among all countries during a crisis period. Hypothesis 2 tests for contagion from one country (the host country) to both of the other countries in the sample. Hypothesis 3 tests for contagion between two individual countries. For the first two hypotheses, the results show that there is broad agreement for evidence of contagion among all test statistics. For the third hypothesis the evidence is more mixed.

The chapter is organized as follows. Section 2 outlines the four methods of testing for contagion. A number of empirical issues in implementing these tests are discussed in section 3, while section 4 sets out the steps for the practical application of each test. The tests are then applied in section 5. Concluding comments are given in section 6.

2.   EMPIRICAL TESTS OF CONTAGION

A relatively common means of representing asset returns in the finance literature is as a two-factor model. Let the return on the ith asset in a noncrisis period be represented by $x_{i,t}$, while the corresponding return on the asset during a crisis period is given by $y_{i,t}$. The durations of the noncrisis and crisis samples are, respectively, T_x and T_y. During periods of calm a standard two-factor model is assumed, in that the return in each market is a linear function of a set of common shocks (w_t), which affect all asset markets, and an idiosyncratic shock $(u_{i,t})$. For a set of N asset markets, this relationship is represented as

$$x_{i,t} = \lambda_i w_t + \delta_i u_{i,t}, \quad i = 1, 2 \dots N, \tag{1}$$

where λ_i and δ_i are the loadings on the common factor and the idiosyncratic factor, respectively. For certain classes of models the common shocks represent the market fundamentals while the idiosyncratic shocks correspond to periods where actual returns deviate from the market fundamental values.

Crisis periods are commonly characterized as periods of increased volatility in asset returns, whereby the variance of $y_{i,t}$ is greater than the variance of $x_{i,t}$. This may be due to increased volatility in either the common shocks or the idiosyncratic shocks, or the result of additional channels that may arise only during crisis periods. It is this last channel which is commonly referred to as *contagion* (e.g., Kaminsky, Reinhart, and Végh, this volume; Masson 1999; Forbes and Rigobon 2002). That is, in the measurement of contagion any increases in volatility would necessarily exclude increases in either the volatility of the common shocks w_t, or increases in the volatility of the idiosyncratic shocks $u_{i,t}$, or both. To allow for potentially contagious transmission mechanisms during financial crises, it is necessary to augment equation (1) by including additional contagion variables when modeling returns in crisis period $y_{i,t}$.

2.1   The DFGM Test

The Dungey, Fry, González-Hermosillo, and Martin (2002, 2005) contagion test (DFGM) is based on modeling contagion as the transmission of idiosyncratic shocks across asset markets. This involves extending the noncrisis-period asset returns equation in (1) to

$$y_{i,t} = \lambda_i w_t + \delta_i u_{i,t} + \sum_{j=1, j \neq i}^{N} \gamma_{i,j} u_{j,t}, \quad i = 1, 2 \dots N, \tag{2}$$

where the $x_{i,t}$ is replaced by $y_{i,t}$ as the model is defined for the crisis period. The term $\gamma_{i,j} u_{j,t}$ represents the effect of a shock in asset j at time t transmitted to the returns of asset i. To test the null hypothesis of no contagion in all asset markets amounts to a joint test of $\gamma_{i,j} = 0$ for all $i, j, i \neq j$.

In performing the DFGM test, the world shocks are treated as a latent factor. The simplest representation is given by specifying w_t to be independently and identically distributed with zero mean and unit variance

$$w_t \sim \text{i.i.d. } (0,1). \tag{3}$$

To complete the specification of the model, the idiosyncratic shocks are also assumed to be

$$u_{i,t} \sim \text{i.i.d. } (0,1). \tag{4}$$

The assumptions on the factors mean that the difference in the volatility of the ith asset return between crisis and noncrisis periods is solely due to contagion, where

$$E[y_{i,t}^2] - E[x_{i,t}^2] = \sum_{j=1, j \neq i}^{N} \gamma_{i,j}^2. \qquad (5)$$

A more general specification is to let the common factor exhibit auto-correlation and a GARCH volatility structure; see Dungey and Martin (2004). This property is particularly important when using high-frequency asset returns data as the conditional volatility structures of asset returns tend to exhibit common features that can be parsimoniously modeled within a latent factor structure (Dungey et al. 2002).

The DFGM test is implemented by equating the theoretical moments as derived from equations (1) to (4) with the empirical moments from the sample data. The estimation is based on Generalized Method of Moments (GMM). For example, when the number of assets $N = 3$, the number of un-known loading parameters in equations (1) and (2) is 12. These parameters can be uniquely identified from the variance-covariance matrix of the asset returns in the precrisis and crisis periods, as both matrices contain six unique moments, yielding a total of twelve empirical moments. For this model a test of contagion amounts to testing the overidentifying restrictions arising from setting the relevant $\gamma_{i,j}$ parameters in equation (2) to zero.

2.2 The FR Test

The Forbes and Rigobon (2002) test is based on testing the (unconditional) correlations between pairs of asset returns in the crisis and noncrisis periods. The common shocks w_t in equation (2) are modeled using a vector autoregression (VAR), augmented by additional control variables, with the residuals representing the idiosyncratic factors. In computing the unconditional correlation in the crisis period, an adjustment factor is introduced to allow for any increases in asset return volatility arising from increases in the volatility of the factors in equation (1).

To test for contagion from one asset market, the host market, to another asset market using the FR test, the FR test statistic is

$$FR = \frac{\frac{1}{2} \ln\left(\frac{1 + v_y}{1 - v_y}\right) - \frac{1}{2} \ln\left(\frac{1 + \rho_x}{1 - \rho_x}\right)}{\sqrt{\frac{1}{T_y - 3} + \frac{1}{T_x - 3}}}, \qquad (6)$$

where ρ_x is the correlation coefficient between the two asset returns in the noncrisis period. Forbes and Rigobon (2002) define the noncrisis period as the total sample. The unconditional correlation coefficient in the crisis period, v_y, is adjusted to account for the higher volatility in that period using

$$v_y = \frac{\rho_y}{\sqrt{1 + \left(\frac{\sigma_{y,i}^2 - \sigma_{x,i}^2}{\sigma_{x,i}^2}\right)(1 - \rho_y^2)}}, \qquad (7)$$

where ρ_y is the correlation between two asset returns in the crisis period, and $\sigma_{x,i}^2$ and $\sigma_{y,i}^2$ are, respectively, the variances of the asset returns in the noncrisis and crisis periods of the ith (host) asset returns.[1]

An alternative way to represent the FR test is to express it as a Chow test (Dungey et al. 2005). This has the advantage that it provides a natural framework in which to generalize the FR test to allow for multivariate versions of the test as well as correcting for endogeneity bias. For the bivariate problem, the approach is based on the following regression equation:

$$\left(\frac{z_{2,t}}{\sigma_{x,2}}\right) = \gamma_0 + \gamma_1 d_t + \gamma_2 \left(\frac{z_{1,t}}{\sigma_{x,1}}\right) + \gamma_3 \left(\frac{z_{1,t}}{\sigma_{x,1}}\right) d_t + \eta_t, \tag{8}$$

where

$$z_i = (x_{i,1}, x_{i,2}, \ldots x_{i,T_x} \quad y_{i,1}, y_{i,2}, \ldots y_{i,T_y})', \quad i = 1, 2 \tag{9}$$

represents the $(T_x + T_y) \times 2$ scaled pooled data set by stacking the precrisis and crisis scaled data with T_x and T_y observations, respectively. The dummy variable, d_t, is defined as

$$d_t = \begin{cases} 1: & t > T_x \\ 0: & \text{otherwise,} \end{cases} \tag{10}$$

and $\sigma_{x,i}$ is the standard deviation of the ith asset returns during the noncrisis period and η_t is an error term. The test of contagion is based on testing $\gamma_3 = 0$ in equation (8). Rewriting the FR test as in equation (8) shows that contagion is modeled by the additional contemporaneous effects of $y_{1,t}$ on $y_{2,t}$ in the crisis period.

2.3 The FG Test

The Favero and Giavazzi (2002) test of contagion is based on modeling increases in volatility during the crisis period in one asset market by the extreme movements in the asset returns of other markets. To highlight the approach, consider a bivariate version ($N = 2$) of the crisis period model in equation (2):

$$y_{i,t} = \lambda_i w_t + \delta_i u_{i,t}, \tag{11}$$

$$y_{j,t} = \lambda_j w_t + \delta_j u_{j,t} + \gamma u_{i,t}, \tag{12}$$

where a test of contagion is given by the impact of $u_{i,t}$ on $y_{j,t}$ a test of $\gamma = 0$. The FG approach is to replace the $u_{i,t}$ in equation (12) by a set of dummy variables representing points in time when an asset market experiences an extreme movement, as follows:

$$y_{i,t} = \lambda_i w_t + \delta_i u_{i,t}, \tag{13}$$

$$y_{j,t} = \lambda_j w_t + \delta_j u_{j,t} + \sum_{k=1}^{K} \gamma_{i,k} d_{i,k,t}, \tag{14}$$

where $d_{i,k,t}$ represent the K extreme observations associated with $y_{i,t}$, defined as

$$d_{i,k,t} = \begin{cases} 1: & |e_{i,t}| > \text{THRESH}_i \\ 0: & \text{otherwise,} \end{cases} \tag{15}$$

where $e_{i,t}$ is taken as the residuals from a VAR containing all variables in the system. THRESH_i is set equal to $3\sigma_i$, where σ_i is the pertinent residual standard deviation of equation i of the VAR. The dummy variables are also commonly referred to as *exceedances*.

The FG test contrasts with the DFGM and FR tests where the latter tests use all information during the crisis period, not just the extreme values, to test for contagion. The test of contagion is a test of the parameter $\gamma_{i,k}$. FG, in defining w_t, include the exceedances of all other countries. Further, the FG test requires specifying the common factor as consisting of own lagged returns and contemporaneous returns on the other assets. This choice is partly governed by identification issues. For a bivariate system the model is just identified with estimation based on an instrumental variables (IV) procedure. However, as asset returns exhibit very little autocorrelation, identification of the model may be problematic. This may manifest itself into a weak instrument problem resulting in the moments of the sampling distribution being undefined and in inflated standard errors. These identification issues do not arise for the DFGM test, as the common factor is modeled explicitly as a latent factor that is identified by information on the returns in all asset markets. In contrast, endogeneity issues are not taken into account in the FR test in equation (6), which suggests that this test statistic is likely to be affected by endogeneity bias.

2.4 The BKS Test

As with the Favero and Giavazzi (2002) contagion test, Bae, Karolyi, and Stulz (2003) focus on the effects of extreme shocks in one asset market on another asset market using exceedances. The exceedance in asset market i in their approach is defined as

$$d_{i,t} = \begin{cases} 1: & |y_{i,t}| > \text{THRESH}_i \\ 0: & \text{otherwise,} \end{cases} \tag{16}$$

where THRESH_i is set to capture the 5 percent tail of large positive and negative values. Baur and Schulze (2003) extend this to consider a number of different thresholds endogenously. Unlike the FG test, there is only a single exceedance variable for each asset market. Once the exceedances have been identified, the co-exceedances between shocks originating from asset i and asset j are constructed when

$$d_{i,t}d_{j,t} = 1. \tag{17}$$

For N asset markets, categorizing asset returns into coexceedances yields a polychotomous variable that gives the number of coexceedances occurring at each point in time. A multinomial logit framework is then used to model the coexceedances as

$$P_{j,t} = \frac{\exp(\beta_j x_{j,t})}{\sum\limits_{k=0}^{N} \exp(\beta_k x_{k,t})}, \quad j = 0, 1, 2, \ldots N, \tag{18}$$

where $P_{j,t}$ is the probability that there are j co-exceedances occurring at time t, and $x_{j,t}$ represents a set of explanatory variables used to explain asset returns and hence the co-exceedances. The model is normalized by setting $\beta_0 \equiv 0$, which corresponds to the case of no exceedances (i.e., no outliers).

The BKS contagion test consists of specifying the exceedances/co-exceedances of other sets of countries in the set of explanatory variables, given by $x_{j,t}$ in equation (18), and testing the joint significance of the corresponding parameters. To test for contagion within a region of three countries, for example, the co-exceedance variable is initially constructed for a pair of countries (the jth and kth) with the polychotomous variable consisting of the values 0, 1, 2. The exceedance of the remaining country (the ith) is then constructed and included in the set of explanatory variables. The BKS contagion test is then a test of the significance of the ith exceedance variable in explaining the jth and kth co-exceedances.

A special case of the BKS contagion test is the approach of the Eichengreen, Rose, and Wyplosz (1995, 1996), who test for significant correlations between extreme movements in asset returns by creating a binary variable for the presence or otherwise of domestic and international crises as left- and right-hand-side variables, respectively. As noted above, the BKS and FG tests are similar in that both tests amount to testing the significance of the effects of extreme observations in one market, or set of markets, on another asset market. One obvious difference between the two approaches is that the BKS test uses information on co-exceedances in measuring contagion, whereas the FG test uses co-exceedances as conditioning information. Part of the reason for this is the way in which Favero and Giavazzi (2002) construct their exceedance variables—namely, assigning a separate dummy variable to each extreme observation.

3. ADDITIONAL EMPIRICAL ISSUES

3.1 Identifying Crisis Periods

A particularly difficult problem in the financial contagion literature is the choice of sample period; see, for example, Kaminsky and Schmukler (1999) and Jacobs, Kuper, and Lestano (this volume). Most authors wish to identify the period during which the financial markets are in crisis, and in some cases compare the crisis period with a clear noncrisis period. The literature on early warning systems (see Goldstein, Kaminsky, and Reinhart 2000) attempts to predict vulnerability to crises, although such indicators do not have a strong record in correctly predicting crisis events (Edison 2003; Berg and Pattillo 1999). Ideally, a systematic means of choosing crisis dates would result in a consistent set of dating conventions. In practice, however, this does not occur.

The choice of both crisis and noncrisis periods is almost always ad hoc, although often the sample selection is based on ex post rationalizations, making it difficult to compare studies, even those apparently conducted on the same crisis. This complicates comparisons across different studies, as variations in the outcomes are jointly determined by methodological and sample differences. Examples of ad hoc, ex post rationalizations of period choice are found in Forbes and Rigobon (2002) and Dungey et al. (2002). Glick and Rose (1999) and Van Rijckeghem and Weder (2001) use judgments based on newspaper and International Monetary Fund (IMF) staff views to determine whether contagion exists. Kaminsky and Schmukler (1999) also use news-based data to determine the dating of crises.

The alternate course taken in the literature is to use the sample data to identify the crisis periods compared with tranquil periods. This is most commonly through some form of threshold approach, such as found in Eichengreen, Rose, and Wyplosz (1995, 1996); Lowell, Neu, and Tong (1998); Favero and Giavazzi (2002); and Bae, Karolyi, and Stulz (2003).[2]

To further compound the difficulties in dating crises consistently, there are several obstacles to overcome. First, crises are typically quite short in duration. Second, there are a number of periods when multiple crises occur in quick succession—for example, the Russian bond default in mid-1998 and the Long-Term Capital Management (LTCM) near-collapse in August-September 1998. Third, the starting point of a crisis is often associated with a large shock, such as the float of the Thai baht in July 1997, but the endpoint of the crisis is far more difficult to determine.

Productive future work would be to find a more objective procedure for dating crises in high-frequency data based on the data characteristics. However, any of the frameworks discussed above for testing contagion could in theory be extended to allow for endogenous breaks; see Dungey et al. (2005).

3.2 Data Frequency, Missing Observations, and Time Zone Issues

Most studies of contagion aim to control for the influence of fundamentals. Data for many of the fundamental variables are available only at relatively low frequency; for example, Eichengreen, Rose, and Wyplosz (1995, 1996). For this reason there are two distinct streams in the literature. The first contains those that consider relatively low-frequency data, including Glick and Rose (1999) and Van Rijckeghem and Weder (2001), which have the advantage of directly incorporating fundamental variables, such as trade and banking flows. The second involves high-frequency data, and represents the majority of the empirical work, including the correlation studies, most of the threshold models, and the latent factor models. An important difference between the two streams is that the high-frequency studies tend to consider contagion as a relatively short-lived feature, whose extremes would not be captured in lower frequency applications.

In moving to higher frequency observations, two common problems emerge: missing observations and time zone alignment. Missing observations cause problems in tracking volatility across markets at time t. This can be dealt with in the following ways: replacing the missing observation with the previous market observation, interpolating between observations, or removing that data point from the investigation. In practice, only the first and last of these is considered, as interpolating volatile data would defeat the point of tracking the changes. The advantage of simple replacement is that it maintains a longer data series, but with the downside of changing the way in which shocks are presumed to track through the different countries. The alternative of simply deleting the missing observations may reduce information on the dynamics of that process. In practice, most researchers seem to adopt a strategy of deleting missing observations, and this is the strategy adopted in the empirical application of this chapter.

The time zone alignment problem occurs because, although markets are open on nominally the same date, there may be no actual trading-time overlap, such as occurs for Argentina and Indonesia. Events in Indonesia at observed date t can be processed by Argentinean markets on date t also. However, events occurring on date t in Argentina cannot be absorbed by Indonesian markets until date $t + 1$. This problem is most severe for equity markets where local trade-closing data are often used; see, for example, the contemporaneous and day-after correlations between equity market returns provided in Kaminsky and Reinhart (2003).

There are a number of ways to deal with time zone problems. One approach is to control for differences in time zones by using moving averages of returns (e.g., Forbes and Rigobon 2002). A drawback of this strategy is that it may mask some of the movements in asset prices, and potentially introduce spurious dynamics into the relationships among asset returns via the moving-average filter. Kaminsky and Reinhart (2003) test the significance of dummy variables that reflect time zone differences and show there are discernible differences. Bae, Karolyi, and Stulz (2003) choose different lags depending on the time zone and causal patterns studied. For the more general case where the timing of domestic market trading times overlap, simulation methods may be a useful approach.[3] The importance of correctly matching the timing of financial market data is highlighted by Taylor (1987) and more recently by Knif and Pynnonen (1999).

4. NUMERICAL PROCEDURES

In this section, numerical procedures for implementing contagion tests are presented. In each application there are $N = 3$ countries. All programs are written in GAUSS v.5.0.1, with computer codes available from the first author's Web site.

Before implementing the DFGM, FR, and BKS tests, the returns are filtered by estimating a VAR with one lag, with U.S. returns as a control variable. The residuals represent the filtered returns in the calculations that follow for these tests. This filtering is not conducted for the FG test, to be commensurate with their methodology. For the Tequila crisis and Argentine crisis, U.S. returns at time t are used. For the Asian flu, the U.S. returns are dated at time $t - 1$ to allow for time zone effects.

4.1 The DFGM Test

Step 1: Estimate the following unconstrained system of equations by GMM:

$$x_{i,t} = \lambda_i w_t + \delta_i u_{i,t}, \quad i = 1, 2, 3,$$

$$y_{i,t} = \lambda_i w_t + \delta_i u_{i,t} + \sum_{j=1, j \neq i}^{3} \gamma_{i,j} u_{j,t}, \quad i = 1, 2, 3.$$

The system is just identified as there are twelve empirical moments based on the variances and covariances for the noncrisis and crisis periods, and twelve unknown parameters ($\lambda_1, \lambda_2, \lambda_3, \delta_1, \delta_2, \delta_3, \gamma_{1,2}, \gamma_{1,3}, \gamma_{2,1}, \gamma_{2,3}, \gamma_{3,1},$ and $\gamma_{3,2}$).

Step 2: Contagion tests are performed by using a Wald test on the contagion parameters ($\gamma_{i,j}$).

4.2 The FR Test

4.2.1 Bivariate FR Test

Step 1: Compute the unconditional correlation between two returns over the precrisis period (ρ_x).

Step 2: Compute the unconditional correlation (v_y) between two returns over the total period based on equation (7).

Step 3: Compute the FR test statistic given in equation (6).

Step 4: Perform a one-sided test of the null hypothesis $v_y = \rho_x$ against the null of $v_y > \rho_x$, indicating contagion.

4.2.2 Multivariate FR Test

Step 1: Construct the dummy variable (d_t) in equation (10).

Step 2: Estimate the following system of equations:

$$\left(\frac{z_{1,t}}{\sigma_{x,1}}\right) = \gamma_{1,0} + \gamma_{1,1}d_t + \gamma_{1,2}\left(\frac{z_{2,t}}{\sigma_{x,2}}\right) + \gamma_{1,3}\left(\frac{z_{3,t}}{\sigma_{x,3}}\right) + \gamma_{1,4}\left(\frac{z_{2,t}}{\sigma_{x,2}}\right)d_t$$
$$+ \gamma_{1,5}\left(\frac{z_{3,t}}{\sigma_{x,3}}\right)d_t + \eta_{1,t}$$

$$\left(\frac{z_{2,t}}{\sigma_{x,2}}\right) = \gamma_{2,0} + \gamma_{2,1}d_t + \gamma_{2,2}\left(\frac{z_{1,t}}{\sigma_{x,1}}\right) + \gamma_{2,3}\left(\frac{z_{3,t}}{\sigma_{x,3}}\right) + \gamma_{2,4}\left(\frac{z_{1,t}}{\sigma_{x,1}}\right)d_t$$
$$+ \gamma_{2,5}\left(\frac{z_{3,t}}{\sigma_{x,3}}\right)d_t + \eta_{2,t}$$

$$\left(\frac{z_{3,t}}{\sigma_{x,3}}\right) = \gamma_{3,0} + \gamma_{3,1}d_t + \gamma_{3,2}\left(\frac{z_{1,t}}{\sigma_{x,1}}\right) + \gamma_{3,3}\left(\frac{z_{2,t}}{\sigma_{x,2}}\right) + \gamma_{3,4}\left(\frac{z_{1,t}}{\sigma_{x,1}}\right)d_t$$

$$+ \gamma_{3,5}\left(\frac{z_{2,t}}{\sigma_{x,2}}\right)d_t + \eta_{3,t}$$

Step 3: Perform Wald tests for contagion on the parameters $\gamma_{i,4}$ and $\gamma_{i,5}$.

4.3 The FG Test

Step 1: Estimate a VAR on returns over the total period and identify dummy variables corresponding to outliers in the residuals based on equation (15).

Step 2: Classify local shocks for each asset return ($d_{1,j,t}$, $d_{2,j,t}$, $d_{3,j,t}$; i.e., where there is an outlier that is unique to that asset return at a point in time). Let the number of local shocks for each asset return be M, N, and P, respectively.

Step 3: Classify dummy variables into K global shocks, $d_{c,k,t}$, where the c subscript denotes common shocks (i.e., where there is an outlier in at least two asset returns at time t).

Step 4: Estimate the following structural model by instrumental variables:

$$y_{1,t} = \alpha_{1t} + \beta_1 y_{1,t-1} + \delta_{1,1}y_{2,t} + \delta_{1,2}y_{3,t} + \sum_{k=1}^{K}\gamma_{1,k}d_{c,k,t} + \sum_{j=1}^{M}\gamma_{1,1,j}d_{1,j,t}$$
$$+ \sum_{j=1}^{N}\gamma_{1,2,j}d_{2,j,t} + \sum_{j=1}^{P}\gamma_{1,3,j}d_{3,j,t} + e_{1,t'}$$

$$y_{2,t} = \alpha_{2t} + \beta_2 y_{2,t-1} + \delta_{2,1}y_{1,t} + \delta_{2,2}y_{3,t} + \sum_{k=1}^{K}\gamma_{2,k}d_{c,k,t} + \sum_{j=1}^{M}\gamma_{2,1,j}d_{1,j,t}$$
$$+ \sum_{j=1}^{N}\gamma_{2,2,j}d_{2,j,t} + \sum_{j=1}^{P}\gamma_{2,3,j}d_{3,j,t} + e_{2,t'}$$

$$y_{3,t} = \alpha_{3t} + \beta_3 y_{3,t-1} + \delta_{3,1}y_{1,t} + \delta_{3,2}y_{2,t} + \sum_{k=1}^{K}\gamma_{3,k}d_{c,k,t} + \sum_{j=1}^{M}\gamma_{3,1,j}d_{1,j,t}$$
$$+ \sum_{j=1}^{N}\gamma_{3,2,j}d_{2,j,t} + \sum_{j=1}^{P}\gamma_{3,3,j}d_{3,j,t} + e_{3,t'}$$

where the instruments are the three lag returns. This system of equations is just identified.

Step 5: Perform likelihood ratio tests for contagion on the parameters $\gamma_{1,2,j}$ and $\gamma_{1,3,j}$ in the first equation in the system, $\gamma_{2,1,j}$ and $\gamma_{2,3,j}$ in the second equation in the system, and $\gamma_{3,1,j}$ and $\gamma_{3,2,j}$ in the third equation in the system.

4.4 The BKS Test

Step 1: Construct exceedances based on equation (17) for all asset returns.

Step 2: For asset returns i and j, classify the number of co-exceedances, ranging from 0, 1, 2.

Step 3: Construct an indicator variable that is $I = 0$ for no co-exceedances in asset returns i and j, $I = 1$ for exceedances in asset i but not asset j, $I = 2$ for exceedances in asset j but not asset i, and $I = 3$, for co-exceedances in assets i and k, where the indicator variable enters the likelihood function of equation (18).

Step 4: Estimate the multinomial logit model in equation (18), with the explanatory variables consisting of an intercept and the exceedances of asset k.

Step 5: Perform Wald tests on the parameter associated with the exceedances of asset return k.

Step 6: Repeat the tests for the other two combinations of asset returns.

5.   APPLICATIONS

To illustrate the application of the empirical methodologies of contagion, three distinct crisis episodes in equity markets over the last decade are investigated. These are the so-called Tequila crisis associated with the float of the Mexican peso in December 1994; the speculative attack on the Hong Kong stock market in October 1997 during the East Asian financial crisis, the Asian flu; and the more recent problems in Latin America associated with Argentina in 2001.

Both the Mexican (Tequila) and Hong Kong (Asian flu) examples correspond to the bivariate examples investigated in Forbes and Rigobon (2002), but are extended to a multivariate framework using additional contagion tests. These exercises illustrate the similarities and differences between the tests and the subsequent differences in the results that can be generated from the alternative tests, rather than provide definitive analysis of each of the crises. Here the aim is to provide an illustration of the implementation of the contagion methodologies outlined in the previous sections.

5.1   Background

Figure 1 illustrates the changes in volatility in equity markets over the three crises investigated in this chapter. The first column represents returns for Mexico, Argentina, and Chile during the Tequila crisis. The second column represents returns for Hong Kong, Korea, and Malaysia during the Asian flu. The final column represents returns for Argentina, Brazil, and Chile during the Argentine crisis. The reasons for the choice of sample periods and crisis subsamples are briefly described below.

5.1.1   The Tequila Crisis: 1994–95   On 20 December 1994 the Mexican exchange rate band was widened and the peso devalued sharply. The peg was abandoned and the Mexican peso was allowed to float on 22 December 1994. Mexican financial markets melted down in the days that followed

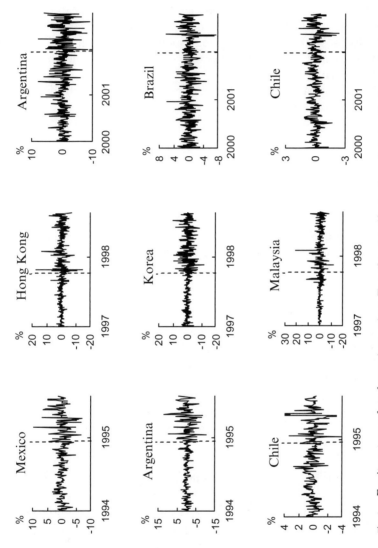

Fig. 1. Equity returns data for various crises: Tequila crisis (first column), Asian flu (second column), Argentine crisis (third column). The precrisis period in each figure is to left of the vertical dashed line, crisis period to the right.

the currency attack as equity markets experienced extreme volatility, domestic interest rates soared, and banks came under pressure; see Sachs, Tornell, and Velasco (1996) for a chronology of the crisis. The Mexican crisis affected other emerging markets, particularly other Latin American countries, in what has been referred to as the *Tequila crisis*. Here we consider transmission between the equity markets of Mexico, Argentina, and Chile.

The sample period chosen here comprises a precrisis period from 1 June 1994 to 18 December 1994, and a crisis period of 19 December 1994 to 2 March 1995. This is a total sample of 197 observations, 143 in the precrisis period and 54 in the crisis period. The crisis date is not dissimilar to that examined by Forbes and Rigobon (2002), who date the crisis as beginning on 19 December 1994, but ending on 31 December 1994, which is earlier than the empirical example considered here. The end of the crisis period in this chapter corresponds to the period of reforms in the Mexican banking system.

The noncrisis period assumed in this study is shorter than that of Forbes and Rigobon (2002), and this is because it is not clear in the data or the chronology of the crisis that the earlier period in 1994 is less volatile than the designated crisis period assumed in this chapter. For example, Mexican financial markets were quite volatile in the aftermath of the assassination of the PRI's presidential candidate Colosio on 23 March 1994, when Mexico lost about one-third of its foreign reserves in a few weeks, the currency hit the ceiling of its intervention band, and domestic interest rates rose sharply.

Covariances and correlations for the Tequila crisis are shown in table 1. There is a marked increase in both variances and covariances, and corresponding increases in the correlation coefficients. Table 2 provides a decomposition of the variances of the equity returns in the precrisis and crisis periods into various components, based on the DFGM model estimated with GMM.[4] In the precrisis period there is substantially diversifiable risk in Mexico and Chile, with the country factors contributing over 75 percent of total volatility. In the crisis period, both Mexico and Argentina experience substantial contagion effects, with evidence that the contagious links between these countries were reinforcing (66 percent of total volatility in Mexico is sourced as contagion from Argentina, and 75 percent of volatility in Argentina is sourced as contagion from Mexico).

5.1.2 The Asian Flu: 1997–98   Many East Asian currencies experienced rapid depreciation and high volatility during 1997, following the float of the Thai baht. In October 1997 the Hong Kong dollar experienced a speculative attack. This was successfully defended by its currency board. However, the turmoil translated into the equity market, which plunged dramatically over the period 20–23 October. This volatility was widely observed in other markets, including that of the United States, in the immediate aftermath of this speculative attack. Here we examine equity returns in Hong Kong, Korea, and Malaysia for the period from 1 January

Table 1. Variances and Covariances (Correlations above Diagonal) of Daily Percentage Equity Returns for Selected Sample Periods

	Precrisis Period			Crisis Period		
	(1)	(2)	(3)	(4)	(5)	(6)
Tequila crisis						
	Mexico	Argentina	Chile	Mexico	Argentina	Chile
Mexico	1.840	0.288	0.116	11.670	0.449	0.279
Argentina	0.549	1.969	0.387	6.223	16.443	0.755
Chile	0.118	0.408	0.363	1.150	3.695	1.457
Asian flu						
	Hong Kong	Korea	Malaysia	Hong Kong	Korea	Malaysia
Hong Kong	2.238	0.121	0.253	10.794	0.135	0.447
Korea	0.260	2.045	0.026	1.608	13.114	0.288
Malaysia	0.631	0.063	2.782	4.713	3.351	10.291
Argentine crisis						
	Argentina	Brazil	Chile	Argentina	Brazil	Chile
Argentina	3.758	0.590	0.189	10.374	0.435	0.351
Brazil	1.780	2.422	0.176	2.651	3.586	0.533
Chile	0.169	0.126	0.212	0.791	0.706	0.490

1997 to 19 October 1997 as the precrisis period, and 20 October 1997 to 31 August 1998 as the crisis period. There are 434 total observations, 208 in the precrisis period and 226 in the crisis period. The results can be directly compared with the bivariate example of Forbes and Rigobon (2002), who consider contagion between Hong Kong and Korea and Hong Kong and Malaysia. Again, the crisis period considered here is longer than that of Forbes and Rigobon. In this case it corresponds to the considerable turmoil and repeated attacks on the Hong Kong financial markets leading up to the Russian debt default on 17 August 1998.

As shown in table 1, the variances in the Asian equity markets increased by a factor of about 5 from the precrisis to the crisis period. There are corresponding increases in the covariances, with the largest increase in correlation between Korean and Malaysian returns (from 0.026 to 0.288). The decomposition of the Asian crisis in table 2 shows that in the precrisis period, returns in Korea and Malaysia were almost totally determined by country factors, suggesting opportunities for diversification. During the crisis period, contagion accounts for over 70 percent of total volatility for all three equity markets. The effect of Hong Kong provides the largest impact on Korea (at almost 75 percent of total volatility) and just under 50 percent on Malaysia. There is also a reinforcing linkage from Korea to Hong Kong, accounting for 60 percent of Hong Kong volatility.

Table 2. Variance Decompositions for the Tequila, Asian, and Argentine Crises Based on the DFGM Estimation (%)

Components	Precrisis Period			Crisis Period		
	(1)	(2)	(3)	(4)	(5)	(6)
Tequila crisis						
	Mexico	Argentina	Chile	Mexico	Argentina	Chile
World factor	12.882	63.424	24.773	2.909	13.842	14.396
Country factor	87.118	36.576	75.227	19.673	7.983	43.715
Origin of contagion						
Mexico	—	—	—	—	75.319	34.092
Argentina	—	—	—	66.407	—	7.797
Chile	—	—	—	11.011	2.856	—
Total	100.000	100.000	100.000	100.000	100.000	100.000
Variance	1.840	1.969	0.563	11.670	16.443	1.457
Asian flu						
	Hong Kong	Korea	Malaysia	Hong Kong	Korea	Malaysia
World factor	55.294	2.641	10.956	11.825	0.408	3.005
Country factor	44.706	97.359	89.044	9.560	15.036	24.426
Origin of contagion						
Hong Kong	—	—	—	—	74.450	49.915
Korea	—	—	—	60.514	—	22.653
Malaysia	—	—	—	18.101	10.106	—
Total	100.000	100.000	100.000	100.000	100.000	100.000
Variance	2.238	2.045	2.782	10.794	13.114	10.291
Argentine crisis						
	Argentina	Brazil	Chile	Argentina	Brazil	Chile
World factor	63.918	54.471	5.679	23.083	36.822	2.484
Country factor	36.082	45.529	94.321	13.030	30.777	41.249
Origin of contagion						
Argentina	—	—	—	—	11.959	52.612
Brazil	—	—	—	2.495	—	3.655
Chile	—	—	—	61.392	20.442	—
Total	100.000	100.000	100.000	100.000	100.000	100.000
Variance	3.758	2.422	0.212	10.374	3.586	0.490

5.1.3   The Argentine Crisis: 2001–02   Argentina experienced substantial turmoil in its financial markets in the second half of 2001, leading up to the float of the peso on 2 January 2002. Some background to the crisis is given in de la Torre, Levy Yeyati, and Schmukler (2003). We date the crisis here from 10 July 2001, when the Argentine government formally adopted a zero-deficit rule in order to retain access to international bond markets. In the intervening period between this announcement and the float of the

Table 3. Alternative Contagion Test Statistics during the Tequila Crisis, *p*-Values in Parentheses

Host Country	Recipient Country	DFGM	FR	FR-M	FG	BKS
Mexico	Argentina	21.892* (0.000)	−0.723 (0.765)	1.700 (0.192)	121.972* (0.000)	8.760* (0.003)
	Chile	2.524 (0.112)	0.022 (0.491)	0.074 (0.786)	38.139* (0.000)	0.005 (0.945)
	Both	37.858* (0.000)	—	2.653 (0.265)	78.259* (0.000)	13.033* (0.000)
Argentina	Mexico	67.257* (0.000)	−0.833 (0.798)	3.205* (0.073)	16.425* (0.000)	9.827* (0.002)
	Chile	4.375* (0.036)	−0.951 (0.577)	1.918 (0.166)	10.180* (0.001)	8.250* (0.004)
	Both	70.152* (0.000)	—	5.661* (0.059)	18.742* (0.000)	0.908 (0.341)
Chile	Mexico	9.974* (0.002)	0.239 (0.405)	0.071 (0.791)	—	0.005 (0.942)
	Argentina	2.871* (0.090)	0.531 (0.298)	36.150* (0.000)	—	8.765* (0.003)
	Both	14.257* (0.001)	—	40.883* (0.000)	—	12.515* (0.000)
Joint		101.825* (0.000)	—	65.378* (0.000)	101.897* (0.000)	—

Note: The FG test for this crisis does not have a local shock for Chile (they are all common shocks), so we cannot test for contagion from Chile. DFGM = Dungey et al. (2003) test; FR = Forbes and Rigobon (2002) test (M = multivariate); FG = Favero and Giavazzi (2002) test; BKS = Bae, Karolyi, and Stulz (2003) test.
*Indicates the presence of statistically significant contagion at the 10 percent level.

peso were protracted negotiations between Argentina, the U.S. Treasury, and the IMF. In the example here we consider contagion between Argentina, Chile, and Brazil over a crisis period of 9 July 2001 to 3 December 2001, compared with a precrisis period of 9 July 2000 to 8 July 2001. The total sample comprises 366 observations, with 261 in the precrisis period and 105 in the crisis period.

Table 1 for the Argentine crisis shows large increases in both variances and covariances between the precrisis and crisis periods. The biggest increases in correlation are between Argentina and Chile (0.189 to 0.351) and Brazil and Chile (0.176 to 0.533). Interestingly, the correlation between Brazilian and Argentinean returns falls marginally (0.590 to 0.435). Table 2 shows that in the precrisis period Argentina and Brazil exhibit similar variance decompositions, with the country factor contributing less than 50 percent in both cases. In contrast, 94 percent of volatility returns in Chile are associated with a country-specific factor. During the crisis period, Argentina and Brazil look different. Contagion contributes nearly two-thirds of Argentina's volatility compared with one-third of Brazil's. The most strik-

Table 4. Alternative Contagion Test Statistics during the Asian Flu, *p*-Values in Parentheses

Host Country	Recipient Country	DFGM	FR	FR-M	FG	BKS
Hong Kong	Korea	158.187*	−0.295	1.175	117.582*	2.210
		(0.000)	(0.616)	(0.278)	(0.000)	(0.137)
	Malaysia	1.574	−0.507	1.162	137.669*	6.015*
		(0.210)	(0.694)	(0.281)	(0.000)	(0.014)
	Both	182.063*	—	1.968	217.451*	10.019*
		(0.000)		(0.374)	(0.000)	(0.002)
Korea	Hong Kong	45.651*	−0.315	1.518	304.902*	2.146
		(0.000)	(0.624)	(0.218)	(0.000)	(0.143)
	Malaysia	12.085*	−0.257	1.031	356.649*	2.369
		(0.001)	(0.601)	(0.310)	(0.000)	(0.124)
	Both	439.764*	—	1.872	65.402*	8.517*
		(0.000)		(0.392)	(0.000)	(0.004)
Malaysia	Hong Kong	53.578*	−0.348	6.582*	146.704*	6.862*
		(0.000)	(0.636)	(0.010)	(0.000)	(0.009)
	Korea	0.773	−0.105	4.963*	73.385*	2.181
		(0.379)	(0.542)	(0.026)	(0.000)	(0.140)
	Both	70.005*	—	10.765*	202.745*	11.145*
		(0.000)		(0.005)	(0.000)	(0.001)
Joint		772.474*	—	14.357*	1085.287*	—
		(0.000)		(0.026)	(0.000)	

Note: See note to table 3.
*Indicates the presence of statistically significant contagion at the 10 percent level.

ing result is the apparent reinforcement of contagion effects between Argentina and Chile.

5.2 Results of Contagion Tests

Some preliminary information on the data characteristics of the crisis samples is provided in table 6. The table gives the number of observations in the precrisis and crisis periods for each test, but also gives the exceedances and co-exceedances based on the FG and BKS selection procedures, given in equations (15) and (17).

Three hypotheses are tested. Hypothesis 1 is the null of no contagion among all countries during the crisis period. Hypothesis 2 tests the null of no contagion from one country (the host country) to both other countries in the sample. Hypothesis 3 tests the null of no contagion between two individual countries within the group. The first two hypotheses are examined using the DFGM, multivariate FR, FG, and BKS tests. The third hypothesis can be examined using each of these tests and the FR test.

5.2.1 Contagion during the Tequila Crisis Table 3 provides the results of the contagion tests for the Tequila crisis. (A summary of the results is given in the first part of table 7.) Table 3 reports the results of the DFGM test, the bivariate FR test, the multivariate FR test, the FG test, and the BKS test. The left-hand column indicates the host country, from which contagion is sourced, and the second column indicates the country potentially in receipt of contagion. Each cell gives the value of the test statistic with the p-value in parentheses. An asterisk (*) denotes evidence of contagion at the 10 percent level, through a rejection of the null of no contagion.

The first result to note is that all tests find strong evidence against the first hypothesis of no contagion within the group (the test statistics are shown in the final row of table 3). For the second hypothesis of no contagion from the host country to the other countries there is broad agreement on significant contagion, as shown in the rows labelled "Both" in the table. The null of no contagion for hypothesis 2 is supported in the multivariate FR test for transmissions originating in Mexico and for the BKS test for contagion originating from Argentina. In the case of Chile there are no unique exceedances associated with Chile (see table 6), which is why there are no tests of contagion originating from Chile reported for the FG test.

The results for the tests on the third hypothesis, of no contagion between pairs of countries, provides mixed evidence. The FR test supports the null of no contagion, consistent with results reported in Forbes and Rigobon (2002). The multivariate version of the FR test finds some significant linkages, but fewer than other tests. The difference between the bivariate and multivariate FR tests reflects two things: one, the inclusion of additional variables; and two, the choice of the low-volatility period. The FG and DFGM tests are in agreement in rejecting the null of no contagion in all cases, with the exception being from Mexico to Chile, where the p-value for the DFGM test is 0.112. Inspection of table 6 shows that the number of exceedances used in the FG test for Argentina is one. Hence all the results reported for this test in table 3 hinge on the significance of that one observation.

The BKS test provides evidence for contagion from Argentina to the other countries individually, despite the earlier reported lack of contagion from Argentina to other countries jointly in testing hypothesis 2. The BKS test is conducted on the significance of an extreme shock from Argentina (exceedance) on corresponding contemporary extreme shocks in Mexico and Chile (co-exceedance). This explains why there can be significant contagion from one country to other countries individually, but insignificant tests of contagion to both countries simultaneously.

5.2.2   Contagion during the Asian Flu   Table 5 shows there is less agreement among the results of the contagion tests for the Asian crisis period. The final row of table 4 again shows that hypothesis 1, of no joint contagion, is rejected in each case. Under hypothesis 2, the DFGM, FG, and BKS tests reject the null of no contagion emanating from a host country to others in the sample using each country as the host in turn. The multivariate FR test rejects hypothesis 2 only in the case of contagion transmitted from Malaysia.

The FG tests reject the null of no contagion between each pair of countries in testing hypothesis 3. The DFGM tests agree, with the exceptions

Table 5. Alternative Contagion Test Statistics during the Argentine Crisis, *p*-Values in Parentheses

Host Country	Recipient Country	DFGM	FR	FR-M	FG	BKS
Argentina	Brazil	0.087	−1.426	16.874*	181.516*	16.129*
		(0.768)	(0.923)	(0.000)	(0.000)	(0.000)
	Chile	57.110*	0.221	0.279	699.079*	0.001
		(0.000)	(0.412)	(0.598)	(0.000)	(0.975)
	Both	161.182*	—	17.152*	562.294*	10.758*
		(0.000)		(0.000)	(0.000)	(0.001)
Brazil	Argentina	0.999	−0.944	0.080	356.493*	16.249*
		(0.318)	(0.827)	(0.778)	(0.000)	(0.000)
	Chile	2.933*	2.004*	22.989*	29.703*	4.758*
		(0.087)	(0.023)	(0.000)	(0.000)	(0.029)
	Both	16.525*		23.327*	191.042*	0.001
		(0.000)		(0.000)	(0.000)	(0.977)
Chile	Argentina	53.718*	0.376	1.822	19.338*	0.001
		(0.000)	(0.354)	(0.177)	(0.000)	(0.971)
	Brazil	1.138	1.599*	19.162*	15.739*	4.483*
		(0.286)	(0.055)	(0.000)	(0.001)	(0.034)
	Both	68.133*	—	29.514*	27.464*	9.125*
		(0.000)		(0.000)	(0.000)	(0.003)
Joint		225.491*	—	73.170*	1453.29*	
		(0.000)		(0.000)	(0.000)	

Note: See note to table 3.
*Indicates the presence of statistically significant contagion at the 10 percent level.

that no contagion is detected from Hong Kong to Malaysia, or Malaysia to Korea. These differences in the results possibly reflect that the FG assigns a separate parameter value to each exceedance, while in DFGM the contagion is all summarized by a single parameter. The same is true for BKS, where the test of contagion is based on a single parameter. Both the BKS and multivariate FR tests find only limited evidence of contagion between pairs of countries. The bivariate FR tests find no evidence to reject the null of no contagion. The only pair of countries in which all tests, other than the bivariate FR test, agree on rejecting the null of no contagion is from Malaysia to Hong Kong. (A summary of the test results for the Asian flu crisis is provided in the central panel of table 7.)

5.2.3 Contagion during the Argentine Crisis   Table 5 reports the evidence for contagion in the Argentine crisis, and is summarized in the final panel of table 7. As with the previous crises examined, hypothesis 1 of no contagion jointly in all countries is rejected by all tests. The tests also reject hypothesis 2 of no contagion from a host country to others in the sample, for each country as the host. The one exception to this is the BKS test, which finds no contagion from Brazil to both Argentina and Chile jointly. This

Table 6. The Number of Observations Involved in Testing the Significance of Contagion, by Crisis and Test

	Tests				
	DFGM	FR	FR-M	FG	BKS
Tequila effect					
Total observations	197	197	197	197	197
Precrisis observations	143	143	143	143	143
Crisis observations	54	54	54	54	54
Exceedances					
Mexico				6 (5)[a]	10
Argentina				5 (1)[a]	10
Chile				3 (0)[a]	10
Co-exceedances					
Mexico and Argentina				1	4
Mexico and Chile				—	2
Argentina and Chile				3	4
All				—	
Asian flu					
Total observations	434	434	434	434	434
Precrisis observations	208	208	208	208	208
Crisis observations	226	226	226	226	226
Exceedances					
Hong Kong				6 (5)[a]	22
Korea				7 (6)[a]	22
Malaysia				7 (7)[a]	22
Co-exceedances					
Hong Kong and Korea				1	4
Hong Kong and Malaysia				—	5
Korea and Malaysia				—	4
All				—	
Argentine crisis					
Total observations	366	366	366	366	366
Precrisis observations	261	261	261	261	261
Crisis observations	105	105	105	105	105
Exceedances					
Argentina				6 (4)[a]	18
Brazil				3 (1)[a]	18
Chile				5 (3)[a]	18
Co-exceedances					
Argentina and Brazil				1	6
Argentina and Chile				1	2
Brazil and Chile				—	4
All				1	

Note: Abbreviations are explained in table 3 note and in text.
[a]Unique exceedances are given in brackets. These are the observations that are used in the Faverro and Giavazzi test for contagion.

result reflects the low number of co-exceedances (two) between Argentina and Chile in the sample, as reported in table 6.

The tests of hypothesis 3, for no contagion between pairs of countries, produce mixed results. In one case, for contagion from Brazil to Chile, all five tests, including the bivariate FR test, agree on the presence of contagion. The evidence on contagion from Chile presents a mixed picture. On the one hand, all tests but the DFGM test agree on contagion from Chile to Brazil. On the other hand, both the DFGM and FG tests agree on contagion from Chile to Argentina. The results supporting contagion from Chile to Argentina are consistent with the variance decomposition presented in table 3, where just over 60 percent of volatility in Argentinean returns in the crisis period was due to contagion from Chile.

In the case of contagion from Argentina, the multivariate FR, FG, and BKS tests reject the null of no contagion to Brazil, and the DFGM and FG tests reject the null of contagion from Argentina to Chile. The latter result is consistent with the increase in the correlation in returns from the precrisis period to the crisis period for Argentina and Chile reported in table 1 (0.189 to 0.351). The evidence of contagion from Argentina to Brazil is at odds with the observed decrease in correlation between these returns from the noncrisis to the crisis period (0.590 to 0.435).

5.2.4 *Synthesis of Results*   Table 7 records the number of instances across tables 3 through 5 in which the null hypothesis of no contagion is rejected using each test in each crisis. Hypothesis 1 represents the joint test of no contagion, and the number of rejections is reported in the final column of table 7. The maximum potential number of rejections is three, and all methods in each sample reject the null of no contagion for the overall test.

Hypothesis 2 represents the test of no contagion from one host country to both other countries in the sample. The maximum potential number of rejections of the null of no contagion is four, the second-to-last column of table 7 shows that at least three tests agree on this in each case (and in each case the test that fails to reject the null of no contagion is the multivariate FR test).

Hypothesis 3 tests for no contagion between pairs of countries. Five tests are run in each case. Table 7 shows the speckled evidence of contagion presented by the tests. Only in the case of contagion from Brazil to Chile do all five tests agree. Most often the bivariate FR test fails to reject the null of no contagion.

Overall, the bivariate FR test appears to be a conservative test, with low power resulting in the test being biased toward a failure to reject the null of no contagion (this is consistent with the results of Billio and Pelizzon 2003). At the other extreme, the FG test tends to find too much evidence of contagion compared with the other results. This is partly the result of the test being a function of just a few outliers in the data, as shown in table 6. The FR multivariate version of the test does find more evidence of contagion than the bivariate version but not as much as the other multivariate tests. The DFGM test in general yields evidence of contagion that is con-

Table 7. Corroboration of Evidence across Tests: The Number of Tests That Reject the Null
Hypothesis of No Contagion in Each Case

Crisis	Host Country	Bivariate Links			Host to Others	Overall
		Mexico	Argentina	Chile		
Mexican	Mexico	—	3	1	3	
crisis	Argentina	4	—	3	3	3
	Chile	1	3	—	3	
		Hong Kong	Korea	Malaysia		
Asian	Hong Kong	—	2	2	3	
crisis	Korea	2	—	2	3	3
	Malaysia	4	2	—	4	
		Argentina	Brazil	Chile		
Argentine	Argentina	—	3	2	4	
crisis	Brazil	2	—	5	3	3
	Chile	2	4	—	4	
Possible high score		5	5	5	4	3

sistent with the change in the correlation structure and variance decomposition in the data presented in tables 1 and 2. Often the DFGM, FG, and BKS tests are in agreement, particularly in the host-to-others tests. In those cases where the BKS test fails to find contagion but the other tests do, the number of co-exceedances used in identifying contagion is low.

6. CONCLUSIONS

This chapter briefly reviews the relationships between four alternative tests for the presence of contagion in financial markets. The four tests considered are the latent factor model of Dungey et al. (2002, 2005), the correlation test popularized by Forbes and Rigobon (2002), the dummy-variables approach of Favero and Giavazzi (2002), and the probability-based test of Bae, Karolyi, and Stulz (2003). The main contribution of the chapter is to highlight the potential inconsistencies in tests of contagion arising from the way in which common shocks are modeled, how endogeneity bias is treated, and how crisis-period information is filtered to identify contagion. Each of the tests is applied to common data sets and periods. The tests are applied to daily equity market returns in three distinct crisis periods. The first is the so-called Tequila crisis of 1994–95, where contagion is tested for between Mexico, Argentina, and Chile. The second is the Hong Kong crisis of October 1997, testing for contagion between Hong Kong, Korea, and Malaysia. The final example is the Argentine crisis of 2001–02, where contagion is considered between Argentina, Brazil, and Chile.

The contribution of this chapter has been to examine how conclusions about the existence of contagion in a particular crisis and group of countries is affected by the methodology used. While there is agreement in the joint tests of contagion, there is little in more specific tests between particular countries: the joint tests reject the null hypothesis of no contagion, but the results are more mixed for pairs of countries, ranging from no contagion at all in the bivariate FR tests to rejection of no contagion between almost all pairs in the endogeneity-corrected FG test. The four tests differ in ways of modeling common shocks, controling for endogeneity, and filters to process crisis-period information. The next step in this research agenda is to discover how these features affect the finite sample properties and statistical performance of the tests by performing a range of Monte Carlo experiments.

APPENDIX: DATA DEFINITIONS

All data are from Thomson Financial Datastream.

Argentina: Buenos Aires Merval share price index [AGSHRPRCF]
Brazil: Brazil BOVESPA share price index [BRSHPRCF]
Chile: CL Share price index [CLI62 . . . F]
Hong Kong: Hang Seng index [HKSHRPRCF]
Korea: KOSPI share price index [KOSHRPRCF]
Malaysia: Kuala Lumpar SE composite index [MYSHRPRCF]
Mexico: IPC Mexico Bolsa share price index [MXSHRPRCF]

NOTES

1. The Fisher transformation is used in equation (6) to improve the asymptotic properties of the test (Forbes and Rigobon 2002). For further refinements of this transformation, see Kendall and Stuart (1969, p. 391). This transformation is valid for small values of the correlation coefficients, ρ_x and v_y, and relatively large samples. Problems may arise when very small samples are involved; see Dungey and Zhumabekova (2001), for example.

2. Potential methods for formalizing crisis date selection could be based on statistical procedures allowing for endogenous breaks or the determinant of the change in the covariance matrix (DCC) of Rigobon (2003).

3. The idea consists of simulating a high frequency model (say, hourly) and then sampling the simulated data to coincide with the observed data. A similar approach is used in estimating continuous time models from discrete data; see Gourieroux, Monfort, and Renault (1993).

4. As the model is just identified, the variances reported in table 1 are exactly decomposed into the components listed in table 2.

REFERENCES

Bae, K.-H., G. A. Karolyi, and R. M. Stulz, 2003, A New Approach to Measuring Financial Contagion, *Review of Financial Studies* 16, 717–763.

Baur, D., and N. Schulze, 2003, Coexceedances in Financial Markets: A Quantile Regression Analysis of Contagion, *University of Tuebingen Economics Discussion Paper* 253.

Berg, A., and C. Pattillo, 1999, Are Currency Crises Predictable? A Test, *International Monetary Fund Staff Papers* 46, 107–138.

Billio, M., and L. Pelizzon, 2003, Contagion and Interdependence in Stock Markets: Have They Been Misdiagnosed? *Journal of Economics and Business* 55, 405–426.

de la Torre, A., E. Levy Yeyati, and S. L. Schmukler, 2003, Living and Dying with Hard Pegs: The Rise and Fall of Argentina's Currency Board, *Economia: Journal of the Latin American and Caribbean Economic Association* 3, 43–99.

Dornbusch, R., Y. C. Park, and S. Claessens, 2000, Contagion: Understanding How It Spreads, *World Bank Research Observer* 15, 177–197.

Dungey, M., R. Fry, B. González-Hermosillo, and V. L. Martin, 2002, International Contagion Effects from the Russian Crisis and the LTCM Near-Collapse, *International Monetary Fund Working Paper* 02/74.

——, 2005, Empirical Modeling of Contagion: A Review of Methodologies. *Quantitative Finance,* forthcoming.

Dungey, M., and V. L. Martin, 2004, A Multifactor Model of Exchange Rates with Unanticipated Shocks: Measuring Contagion in the East Asian Currency Market, *Journal of Emerging Markets Finance,* 3, 305–330.

Dungey, M., and D. Zhumabekova, 2001, Testing for Contagion Using Correlations: Some Words of Caution, *Federal Reserve Bank of San Francisco, Pacific Basin Working Paper* PB01-09.

Edison, H. J., 2003, Do Indicators of Financial Crises Work? An Evaluation of an Early Warning System, *International Journal of Finance and Economics* 8, 11–53.

Eichengreen, B., A. K. Rose, and C. Wyplosz, 1995, Exchange Market Mayhem: The Antecedents and Aftermath of Speculative Attacks, *Economic Policy: A European Forum* 21, 249–296.

——, 1996, Contagious Currency Crisis, *National Bureau of Economic Research Working Paper* 5681.

Favero, C. A., and F. Giavazzi, 2002, Is the International Propagation of Financial Shocks Non-Linear? Evidence from the ERM, *Journal of International Economics* 57, 231–246.

Forbes, K. J., and R. Rigobon, 2002, No Contagion, Only Interdependence: Measuring Stock Market Comovements, *Journal of Finance* 57, 2223–2261.

Glick, R., and A. K. Rose, 1999, Contagion and Trade: Why Are Currency Crises Regional? *Journal of International Money and Finance* 18, 603–617.

Goldstein, M., G. L. Kaminsky, and C. M. Reinhart, 2000, *Assessing Financial Vulnerability: An Early Warning System for Emerging Markets* (Institute for International Economics, Washington, D.C.).

Gourieroux, C., A. Monfort, and E. Renault, 1993, Indirect Inference, *Journal of Applied Econometrics* 8, S85–S118.

Kaminsky, G. L., and C. M. Reinhart, 2003, The Center and the Periphery: The Globalization of Financial Turmoil, *National Bureau of Economic Research Working Paper* 9479.

Kaminsky, G. L., and S. L. Schmukler, 1999, What Triggers Market Jitters? A Chronicle of the Asian Crisis, *Journal of International Money and Finance* 18, 537–560.

Kendall, M. G., and A. Stuart, 1969, *Kendall's Advanced Theory of Statistics, Volume 1: Distribution Theory* (Charles Griffin and Co., London).

Knif, J., and S. Pynnonen, 1999, Local and Global Price Memory of International Stock Markets, *Journal of International Financial Markets, Institutions and Money* 9, 129–147.

Lowell, J., C. R. Neu, and D. Tong, 1998, Financial Crises and Contagion in Emerging Market Countries, *RAND Working Paper* MR-962.

Masson, P. R., 1999, Contagion: Macroeconomic Models with Multiple Equilibria, *Journal of International Money and Finance* 18, 587–602.

Pericoli, M., and M. Sbracia, 2003, A Primer on Financial Contagion, *Journal of Economic Surveys* 17, 571–608.

Rigobon, R., 2003, On the Measurement of the International Propagation of Shocks: Is the Transmission Stable? *Journal of International Economics* 61, 261–283.

Sachs, J. D., A. Tornell, and A. Velasco, 1996, Financial Crises in Emerging Markets: The Lessons from 1995, *Brookings Papers on Economic Activity* 1996 2, 147–215.

Taylor, M. P., 1987, Covered Interest Parity: A High-Frequency, High-Quality Data Study, *Economica* 54, 429–438.

Van Rijckeghem, C., and B. Weder, 2001, Sources of Contagion: Is It Finance or Trade? *Journal of International Economics* 54, 293–308.

4

Identifying Financial Crises

Jan P. A. M. Jacobs, Gerard H. Kuper, and Lestano

1. INTRODUCTION

Financial crises have a long history, as documented in Bordo and Eichengreen (2000) and Bordo et al. (2001). This includes the Mexican and Argentinean currency and debt crises of 1973–82 and 1978–81, respectively; the exchange rate crises following the abandonment of the European Exchange Rate Mechanism in 1992; the Tequila crisis resulting from the Mexican peso devaluation in 1994; the Asian flu of 1997 resulting from Thailand's devaluation; and the Russian cold arising from the collapse of the rouble in 1998. These episodes of international financial turmoil attracted worldwide attention, and their causes, impact, and policy implications have been studied extensively.

Both theoretical and empirical research has been put forward to understand the causes of financial crises. Some theoretical studies focus on fundamentals (Krugman 1979; Blanco and Garber 1986; Corsetti, Pesenti, and Roubini 1999a,b), while others move to nonfundamentals stories, such as self-fulfilling expectations (Obstfeld 1995, 1996; Morris and Shin 1998; Cole and Kehoe 2000) and financial panics (Radelet and Sachs 1998; Chang and Velasco 1998, 2001). Statistical and econometric models have been developed to test the relationship between crisis events and (non)fundamental factors including the development of early warning systems designed to prevent and manage crises, such as surveyed in Abiad (2003); and the models performance assessed by Berg, Borensztein, and Pattillo (2004). Other models look for evidence of the propagation of crises by tracking and testing shifts in correlations denoted in this literature as contagion.[1]

For all empirical studies, dating the occurrence of crises is crucial to distinguish between tranquil periods and crisis episodes. This chapter therefore first discusses how to measure and date three types of financial crises:

Jacobs: Department of Economics, University of Groningen, j.p.a.m.jacobs@eco.rug .nl; Kuper: University of Groningen, g.h.kuper@eco.rug.nl; Lestano: University of Groningen, lestano@eco.rug.nl. We would like to thank Mardi Dungey, Elmer Sterken, and Demosthenes N. Tambakis for helpful comments and suggestions.

currency crises, banking crises, and debt crises. The second major choice facing researchers is that of the control variables, or fundamentals, in examining financial crises. In the second part of this chapter we examine a wide selection of studies for choice of indicator and their significance in empirical applications.

2. DATING FINANCIAL CRISES

2.1 Currency Crises

This section considers the different methods used in the existing literature for identifying currency crises. These can be broadly classified as either event studies or studies based on some form of threshold criterion, often applied to an exchange market pressure index (EMPI). We briefly discuss various currency crisis–dating methods that transform EMPI into a binary crisis variable by means of exogenous thresholds. These dating schemes have in common that they are sensitive to different values of the threshold, to the time period considered, and to different exclusion window widths.[2] The last methods we distinguish use the EMPI, but identify crises without setting arbitrary thresholds.

Many studies on contagious currency crises use event-based definitions. Currency crises are identified qualitatively, by simply plotting the exchange rate series and picking up the high volatility; or by relying on the records of well-documented event chronologies from newspapers and journals, academic reviews, and reports of international organizations. Examples of events are abandonment of an exchange rate peg, devaluation, and suspension of convertibility. Granger, Huang, and Yang (2000) and Ito and Hashimoto (2002) use extreme jumps in exchange rates to determine events. Examples for news-based currency crisis dating are Kaminsky and Schmukler (1999), Glick and Rose (1999), Baig and Goldfajn (1999), Nagayasu (2001), and Dungey and Martin (2004). Bordo et al. (2001) identify a currency crisis by combining event studies with an index of speculative pressure exceeding a certain sample-dependent threshold.

Eichengreen, Rose, and Wyplosz (1995, 1996; hereinafter referred to as ERW) made an important early effort to develop a method to measure currency pressure and to date currency crises. Their definition of exchange rate pressure is inspired by the monetary model of Girton and Roper (1977): a speculative attack exists only in the form of extreme pressure in the foreign exchange market, which usually results in a devaluation (or revaluation), or a change in the exchange rate system (i.e., to float, fix, or widen the band of the exchange rate). However, speculative attacks on exchange rates can also be unsuccessful. When facing pressure on its currency, the country's authorities have the option to raise interest rates or to run down international reserves. Hence, speculative pressure is measured by an index (EMPI) that is a weighted average of normalized changes in the exchange rate, the ratio of gross international reserves to M1, and the nominal interest rates. All variables are relative to a reference country with a strong currency that serves as an anchor to other countries.

The EMPI is intuitively appealing. In the case of speculative pressure, the index captures changes in the domestic exchange rate if the attack is successful and changes in international reserves or nominal interest rates if the speculative attack does not lead to a devaluation. A period of speculative attack is identified when the index exceeds some upper bound. In their 1995 paper, ERW arbitrarily set a threshold of 2 standard deviations above the mean, while in ERW (1996) they set the threshold at 1.5 standard deviations above the mean. This threshold is based on news reports. If two or more potential crises occur closely together, the second and subsequent observations are excluded. So, an exclusion window is set to avoid counting the same crisis twice or more. ERW (1995) use a window width of twelve months, whereas in their 1996 paper they change the window to six months.

Frankel and Rose (1996) exclude unsuccessful speculative attacks from the exchange rate pressure concept. In their opinion international reserves are too rough a proxy to measure policy actions in defense of the currency. In addition, they argue that raising interest rates and exhausting international reserves is not standard practice to deal with speculative attacks in most developing countries. Therefore, they use only nominal exchange rates and define a currency crash as a nominal depreciation of the currency by at least 25 percent that is accompanied by an increase in the rate of depreciation of at least 10 percent. The latter cutoff point is used to avoid registering periods with high inflation, which are usually followed by high depreciation. Moreover, they use a three-year crisis window in order to avoid double-counting crashes. Esquivel and Larraín B. (1998), Bussiere and Mulder (2000), and Mulder, Perrelli, and Rocha (2002) follow the framework of Frankel and Rose (1996) by focusing on successful speculative attacks to date currency crises. Differences in the specification exist, however, in the choice of real versus nominal exchange rate depreciations and the magnitude and speed of the depreciation to qualify as a crisis.

Kaminsky, Lizondo, and Reinhart (1998), Kaminsky and Reinhart (1999, 2000), and Goldstein, Kaminsky, and Reinhart (2000) modify the EMPI by dropping the interest rate differentials, since in their sample—the 1970s and 1980s—interest rates were controlled by central banks. They also drop the reference country. In addition, foreign reserves are no longer scaled by money supply (M1), and the variables are not normalized. To avoid the problem that currency crises are associated with high inflation, the sample is split into periods with hyperinflation and low inflation with separate indices constructed for each subsample. The definition of a currency crisis is the same as in ERW, but the threshold to define a currency crisis is set to 3 standard deviations above the mean.

Many studies (Berg and Pattillo 1999; Caramazza, Ricci, and Salgado 2000; Weller 2001; Edison 2003; and Lestano, Jacobs, and Kuper 2003) follow Kaminsky, Lizondo, and Reinhart (1998), although considerable variation exists with respect to the inclusion of interest rate changes, the weights used, the threshold, and the treatment of high-inflation periods. Other studies use variants of the speculative pressure index approach. Kamin, Schindler, and Samuel (2001), for instance, construct the exchange rate pressure variable as a weighted average of two-month percentage changes in the real bilateral exchange rate against the dollar and in international reserves, with the weights being proportional to the inverse of the standard deviations of these series. Declines in these weighted averages in excess of 1.75 standard deviations signal a crisis month.

The exchange market pressure index of ERW has been criticized by Zhang (2001), who points out two problems. First, changes in international reserves and interest rates may cancel out if the speculative attack is successful. For example, a positive change in the exchange rate (in anticipation of a devaluation) may trigger a fall in the interest rate and an increase in international reserves. Second, movements in international reserves and the exchange rate can be volatile in some periods and relatively tranquil in other periods. Thus, an event that results in high volatility dominates the whole sample. To address both problems, Zhang suggests decomposing the exchange rate market pressure index of ERW into its components and using time-varying thresholds for each component. Interest rate variables are excluded, and the link to the reference country is dropped. Zhang arbitrarily sets the thresholds to 3 standard deviations above and below the mean.

The final group of currency crisis–dating methods does not rely on arbitrarily set thresholds to date currency crisis episodes. Some authors argue that potentially valuable information on the dynamics of EMPI is lost when the index is transformed into a binary variable. Therefore, Kwack (2000) and Vlaar (2000) simply use the EMPI itself as the dependent variable. Pozo and Amuedo-Dorantes (2003) and Haile and Pozo (2003) suggest exploiting the information in the tails of the distribution.[3] The reason for doing so is that the dating schemes discussed above are based on the arbitrary assumption that the index follows a well-behaved normal distribution. However, the normality condition need not necessarily hold due to fat tails in the data, skewness, or infinite second moments. In a study of the Asian crisis, Abiad (2003) proposes a Markov switching model with time-varying probabilities extending the work of Martinez-Peria (2002).[4] The model treats the states of tranquility or speculative pressure as a latent variable, and assumes that EMPI (or its components) is dependent on the latent variable. In addition, it is assumed that there is a certain probability of being in the same state or of moving from one state to the other. The strength or weakness of a country's fundamentals determines the transition probabilities. By estimating transition in a maximum likelihood framework, the crisis episodes are identified and characterized.

2.2 Banking Crises

The definition of banking crises is less precise than the definition of currency crises and hence more difficult to implement. Consequently, most of the existing methods that are widely used to date banking-problem episodes are event based. Recent studies on banking crises show important differences regarding crisis episodes. The most-cited studies for dating banking crises are Caprio and Klingebiel (1996); Lindgren, Garcia, and Saal (1996); Dermirgüç-Kunt and Detragiache (2000); Dziobek and Pazarbasioglu (1997); and Kaminsky and Reinhart (1999).

Caprio and Klingebiel (1996) start from a sample of sixty-nine countries for which information on bank crises is available from the mid-1970s to 1998. The banking crisis episodes are categorized into episodes that appeared to be systemic or borderline. Systemic periods are characterized by events in which the entire banking system has zero or negative net worth. Borderline episodes are defined as evidence of significant bank problems, such as bank runs, forced bank closures, mergers, or government takeovers. Their data are based on news and interviews with country economists. Their observations show that banking crises are more costly in emerging markets in which losses tend to be larger relative to income than in the industrial countries. Recently, Caprio and Klingebiel (2003) have corrected some discrepancies in their earlier list and updated it through 1998.

Lindgren, Garcia, and Saal (1996) draw a distinction between banking crises (systemic episodes—bank insolvency) and banking problems, defined as "significant extensive unsoundness short of crisis" (localized crises or nonsystemic episodes—bank illiquidity). *Banking crises* refer to evidence of bank runs or other substantial portfolio reallocations, collapsing financial firms, or massive government intervention. Their list of banking problems includes episodes from 1980 to mid-1996 and covers 181 International Monetary Fund (IMF) member countries, of which about three-quarters suffered from banking crises. They acknowledge the difficulty in assessing whether or not a bank is solvent. Bank loans, the primary asset of a banking system, are difficult to value and bank managers have an incentive to show loans as performing to accrue income. Lack of transparency in the provision of information and the existence of off-balance-sheet investments further complicate the analysis. Solvency only characterizes a bank at a point in time; a more forward-looking analysis would provide insight into the determinants of insolvency, including poor asset quality and earnings, management weakness, and insufficient oversight. Other traditional measures such as capital adequacy, asset quality, earnings, and liquidity offer some indication of solvency.

Dermirgüç-Kunt and Detragiache (1998) define a banking crisis as an episode of banking distress in which the ratio of nonperforming assets to total bank assets exceeds 10 percent and the costs of rescue operations exceed 2 percent of gross domestic product (GDP). Banking crises are also frequently identified by events such as bank failure, large-scale bank nationalization, deposit freezes, prolonged bank holidays, and bank shutdowns or mergers. They use a sample of sixty-five countries from 1980 to 1995.

Dziobek and Pazarbasioglu (1997) focus on systemic banking problems, defined as situations where distresses affect banks that hold at least 20 percent of total deposits of the banking system. Their total sample consists of twenty-four countries for the period 1991–95. The sample countries are divided into countries that recently completed their bank-restructuring efforts, or where the restructuring is still ongoing. Banking problem events are collected through questionnaires sent to country authorities, and IMF or World Bank staff specializing in banking-sector distress.

Finally, Kaminsky and Reinhart (1999) mark the start of banking crises by events that point at bank runs that lead to closure, merger, or takeover by the public sector of one or more financial institutions, or a large-scale government bail-out of one or more financial institutions that is followed by more bail-outs. A banking crisis ends when government assistance stops. Their sample includes twenty countries for the period 1970–95. Their banking-crisis identification relies heavily on existing studies of banking distress and on the financial news around the time of the crisis.

The first three studies specify both the beginning and the end of crises on an annual basis, but Kaminsky and Reinhart (1999) list crises at the monthly frequency. All of these studies register events for crisis dates, except Dermirgüç-Kunt and Detragiache (1998), who try to include quantitative measures. However, measurement problems exist. Central banks' quasi-fiscal operations for rescue purposes are difficult to quantify. In some respects, this is simply because central banks' accounting conventions differ from those of the government and the distinction between monetary and fiscal activities of the central bank is blurred. In addition, the main banking problems observed in recent years do not stem from the liabilities side of bank balance sheets. Since the introduction of deposit insurance, it is no longer possible to date a banking crisis on the basis of changes in bank deposits. The asset side of banks' balance sheets, indicators such as changes in prices in the real estate sector and nonperforming assets, are becoming more and more important. Unfortunately, both indicators are unavailable in a timely manner or are systematically distorted (Hawkins and Klau 2000).

Banking crises may be associated with currency crises through a number of channels of causation: a bank crisis may lead to a currency crisis or the other way around,[5] or common factors may cause both types of crisis. The last type of crisis is the so-called *twin crises* phenomenon. Twin crises were initially analyzed by Kaminsky and Reinhart (1999). They identify banking and currency crises in a restricted sample of twenty industrial and developing countries for the period 1970 until the mid-1990s and observe that there is no apparent link between currency and banking crises in the 1970s. However, the past two decades have witnessed that banking crises are closely associated with currency crises.

Kaminsky and Reinhart (1999) define twin crises as episodes in which the beginning of a banking crisis is followed by a balance-of-payments crisis within forty-eight months. Thereafter, the literature follows their definition but slightly adapts the time dimension. Glick and Hutchison (2001), for instance, identify the incidence of twin crises as instances in which a bank crisis is accompanied by a currency crisis in the previous, the current, or the following year. In contrast, Bordo et al. (2001) define twin crises as episodes in which currency crises and banking crises occur in the same or adjoining years.

2.3 Debt Crises

Since the onset of debt crises in the 1980s and 1990s, an extensive theoretical and empirical literature has dealt with the determinants of sovereign default and sovereign risk. Most of these studies have in common that they start from a definition of a debt crisis or a debt service difficulty or default. Typically, the incidence of a debt crisis is interpreted as a debt-rescheduling agreement or negotiation, arrears (amounts past due and unpaid) on principal repayments or interest payments, and an upper-tranche IMF agreement. Other studies use corporate default rates collected by commercial rating agencies, such as Standard and Poor's and Moody's Investors Service,[6] as a proxy for sovereign default events.

Some papers use combinations of debt crisis definitions; others simply make use of single events or measurement of either debt rescheduling or arrears. For instance, Berg and Sachs (1988), Lee (1991), Balkan (1992), Lanoie and Lemarbre (1996), and recently, Marchesi (2003) and Lestano, Jacobs, and Kuper (2003), have a common definition of a debt crisis using only the concept of debt rescheduling. All studies aim at selecting periods in which countries reschedule their external debt. Broadly speaking, *debt rescheduling* is defined as a mechanism whereby the debtors offer the creditors (commercial banks and governments of industrial countries) revised contracts that enable debtors not to default on their loans. The contract arrangements include an actual reduction of the principal and service of the debt and the postponement of payment.[7]

The approach of McFadden et al. (1985) and Hajivassiliou (1989, 1994) comprises all three elements in their debt default definition. They consider the presence of arrears on interest or principal as an additional expression of a debt-servicing problem. Overall, they define a country as experiencing a debt crisis in a given year if there is an event of debt rescheduling with commercial or official creditors, an upper-tranche IMF agreement is underway, or the amount of accumulated arrears on interest payments or principal repayments exceeds some minimum threshold. Detragiache and Spilimbergo (2001) adopt another approach and define a debt crisis if either or both of the following conditions occur: (a) arrears of principal or interest on external obligations toward commercial creditors (banks or bondholders) exceed 5 percent of total commercial debt outstanding and (b) a rescheduling or debt-restructuring agreement with commercial creditors exists as listed in the World Bank's *Global Development Finance.* Aylward and Thorne (1998) consider whether a country has external debt repayment problems and check whether a country was in arrears to the IMF or other creditors.

Recently, Manasse, Roubini, and Schimmelpfennig (2003) define a country to experience a debt crisis if Standard and Poor's classifies it as being in default or it receives a large nonconcessional IMF loan in excess of 100 percent of its quotum. Sy (2003) proposes to identify debt crises as sovereign bonds distress events. The sovereign bonds are classified as distressed securities if secondary market bond spreads are higher than a critical threshold. The threshold is set at 1,000 basis points or more above U.S. Treasuries.[8]

The interrelation between sovereign debt variables and currency and banking crises has also been studied. After assessing various currency crisis prediction models, Berg, Borensztein, and Pattillo (2004) emphasize that sovereign and domestic debt dynamics play a central role. They argue that debt and currency crises are related but distinct: most debt crises are associated with currency crises, but the reverse is not true. Reinhart (2002) explores the relationship between sovereign default and currency crises. Standard and Poor's sovereign credit ratings are used to define default. She finds that 84 percent of the defaults in the emerging-markets sample are linked with currency crises and almost half of the currency crises in the total sample are associated with defaults. She concludes that, in addition to their exchange rate disturbances, countries such as Mexico, South Korea, Thailand, and Turkey would most likely have experienced a sovereign default as well if they had not obtained vast international rescue packages.

Goldstein, Kaminsky, and Reinhart (2000) study the connections between currency and banking crises and changes in sovereign credit ratings issued by Moody's Investors Service. They find mixed evidence on the ability of the sovereign ratings to explain financial crises. There is evidence that the ratings have very low predictive power for currency crises, but this does not hold for banking crises. In contrast, Sy (2004) concludes that currency crises are not linked to the probability of sovereign default.

3. INDICATORS OF FINANCIAL CRISES

This section discusses potential indicators that have been employed in the empirical literature to describe the probability of financial crises. A comprehensive survey of various types of financial indicators can be found in Kaminsky, Lizondo, and Reinhart (1998) for currency crisis indicators before the start of the East Asian crisis; Bustelo (2000) and Burkart and Coudert (2002) on the East Asian crisis; and Abiad (2003) for recent studies. González-Hermosillo (1996), Dermirgüç-Kunt and Detragiache (1998), and Eichengreen and Arteta (2002) focus on banking crisis indicators, and Cline (1995) and Marchesi (2003) on debt crisis indicators. This section also includes a description of indicators that seem to work best and highlights some key findings on the significance of indicators in the literature.

The choice of financial indicators as predictors of financial crises is generally based on economic reasoning but is often limited by the availability of data. The studies summarized in tables 1–5 share the idea that it is possible to identify a number of domestic and external macroeconomic fundamental variables as the main determinants of financial crises. Some explanatory variables are exclusively for currency crises, banking crises, or debt crises;

Table 1. **Explanatory Variables for the External Sector (Current Account)**

Indicator	Interpretation	CC	BC	DC	References
Real exchange rate	A measure for the change in international competitiveness and a proxy for over(under)valuation. Overvalued real exchange rate is expected to produce higher probability of financial crisis.	+	+		Kaminsky, Lizondo, and Reinhart (1998); Berg and Pattillo (1999); Kamin, Schindler, and Samuel (2001); Edison (2003); Dermirgüç-Kunt and Detragiache (2000); Eichengreen and Arteta (2002)
Export growth	An indicator for a loss of competitiveness in international goods market. Declining export growth may be caused by an overvalued domestic currency and is hence a proxy for currency overvaluation. On the other hand, if export growth slows due to reasons unrelated to the exchange rate, this may cause devaluation pressure. In both cases, declining export growth can be a leading indicator for a sizeable devaluation.	−		−	Kaminsky, Lizondo, and Reinhart (1998); Berg and Pattillo (1999); Edison (2003); Marchesi (2003)
Import growth	Weak external sector is part of currency crisis. Enormous import growth could lead to worsening in the current account and has often been related with currency crises.	+			Kaminsky, Lizondo, and Reinhart (1998); Berg and Pattillo (1999); Edison (2003)

others are informative for more than one type of crisis. The first two columns in the tables list the indicator variable and give a brief economic interpretation of the mechanism by which they are anticipated to affect financial markets. The next three columns report the hypothesized sign of each indicator in each of the three types of crisis, currency crisis (CC), banking crisis (BC), and debt crisis (DC); a plus (minus) sign indicates that a high (low) value of the indicator reflects a high probability of a crisis. The final column lists the corresponding references that use each particular indicator.

The variables can be classified into several groups: the external sector (split by whether they pertain to either the current or capital account), the financial sector, the domestic real and public sectors, and finally, global influences.

Table 1. (continued)

Indicator	Interpretation	CC	BC	DC	References
Terms of trade	Increases in terms of trade strengthen a country's balance-of-payments position and hence lower the probability of crisis. Terms-of-trade deteriorations may precede currency crisis.	−	−	−	Kaminsky, Lizondo, and Reinhart (1998); Berg and Pattillo (1999); Kamin, Schindler, and Samuel (2001); Dermirgüç-Kunt and Detragiache (2000); Lanoie and Lemarbre (1996)
Ratio of the current account to GDP	A rise in this ratio is generally associated with large external capital inflows that are intermediated by the domestic financial system and could facilitate asset-price and credit booms. Increases in the current account surplus are expected to indicate a diminished probability to devalue and thus to lower the probability of a crisis.	−	−	−	Berg and Pattillo (1999); Kamin, Schindler, and Samuel (2001); Eichengreen and Arteta (2002); Lanoie and Lemarbre (1996); Marchesi (2003)

Note: CC, BC, and DC represent currency crisis, banking crisis, and debt crisis, respectively; GDP represents gross domestic product. Positive (negative) expected sign means that a high (low) value of the indicator causes a higher probability of a crisis.

In the first group, the external sector, there are seven variables, five of which are related to the current account and two to the capital account. These variables are certainly affected not only by domestic economic conditions and policies, but also by global conditions such as fluctuations in the bilateral dollar exchange rate, international capital flows, and commodity prices. The indicators in table 1 relate to changes in international competitiveness and changes in the current account of the balance of payments. Worsening of international competitiveness and a deterioration of the current account may lead to a higher probability of financial crises either directly or through overvalued exchange rates. Table 2 focuses on the capital account. With increasing globalization and financial integration, capital account problems make a country highly vulnerable to shocks. Manifestations of capital account problems could include declining foreign reserves and liabilities of the banking system, and foreign reserves mismatches.

The second group, the financial sector, contains sixteen indicators: nine financial indicators and seven domestic variables that are partly or fully driven by economic policy. Table 3 lists various financial variables that affect financial crises via different mechanisms. Many of these indicators

Table 2. Explanatory Variables for the External Sector (Capital Account)

Indicator	Interpretation	CC	BC	DC	References
Ratio of M2 to foreign exchange reserves	Captures extent to which the liabilities of the banking system are backed by foreign reserves. In the event of a currency crisis, individuals may rush to convert their domestic currency deposits into foreign currency, so this ratio captures the ability of the central bank to meet their demands.	+	+		Kaminsky, Lizondo, and Reinhart (1998); Berg and Pattillo (1999); Kamin, Schindler, and Samuel (2001); Edison (2003); Dermirgüç-Kunt and Detragiache (2000); Eichengreen and Arteta (2002)
Growth of foreign exchange reserves	A decline in foreign reserves is a reliable indicator that a currency is under devaluation pressure. A drop in reserves is not necessarily followed by devaluation; central bank may be successful in defending a peg, spending large amounts of reserves in the process. On the other hand, most currency collapses are preceded by a period of increased efforts to defend the exchange rate, which are marked by declining foreign reserves. Total value of foreign reserves is also used as indicator of a country's financial difficulty dealing with debt repayment.	−		−	Kaminsky, Lizondo, and Reinhart (1998); Berg and Pattillo (1999); Edison (2003); Marchesi (2003)

Note: CC, BC, and DC represent currency crisis, banking crisis, and debt crisis, respectively; Positive (negative) expected sign means that a high (low) value of the indicator causes a higher probability of a crisis.

indicate possible currency crises through excess liquidity. The causes of excess liquidity range from monetary policy to financial liberalization to weak banking systems. The domestic variables in table 4 include debt and deficit. High debt and deficits increase the vulnerability of the economy, especially in low-income countries and in countries with low national savings. In addition, low production growth, high inflation rates, and a burst in asset price bubbles often precede financial crises.

Finally, the global indicators in table 5 reflect major economic shifts in industrial countries and movements of oil prices. External events, such as

Table 3. Explanatory Variables for the Financial Sector

Indicator	Interpretations	CC	BC	DC	References
M1 and M2 growth	These indicators are measures of liquidity. High growth of these indicators might indicate excess liquidity, which may fuel speculative attacks on the currency, thus leading to a currency crisis.	+			Kamin, Schindler, and Samuel (2001)
M2 money multiplier	An indicator associated with financial liberalization. Large increases in the money multiplier can be explained by draconian reductions in reserve requirements.	+			Kaminsky, Lizondo, and Reinhart (1998); Berg and Pattillo (1999); Edison (2003)
Ratio of domestic credit to GDP	Very high growth of domestic credit may serve as a crude indicator of the fragility of the banking system. This ratio usually rises in the early phase of the banking crisis. It may be that as the crisis unfolds, the central bank is injecting money to the bank to improve its financial situation.	+	+		Kaminsky, Lizondo, and Reinhart (1998); Berg and Pattillo (1999); Edison (2003); Dermirgüç-Kunt and Detragiache (2000); Eichengreen and Arteta (2002)
Excess real M1 balance	Loose monetary policy can lead to currency crisis.	+			Kaminsky, Lizondo, and Reinhart (1998); Berg and Pattillo (1999); Edison (2003)
Domestic real interest rate	Real interest rate can be considered as proxy of financial liberalization, in which the liberalization process itself tends to lead to high real rates. High real interest rates signal a liquidity crunch, or have been increased to fend off a speculative attack.	+	+		Kaminsky (1998); Berg and Pattillo (1999); Edison (2003); Dermirgüç-Kunt and Detragiache (2000)
Lending and deposit rate spread	An increase of this indicator above some threshold level possibly reflects a deterioration in credit risk as banks are unwilling to lend or decline in loan quality.	+			Kaminsky, Lizondo, and Reinhart (1998); Berg and Pattillo (1999); Edison (2003)

continued

Table 3. continued

Indicator	Interpretations	CC	BC	DC	References
Commercial bank deposits	Domestic bank run and capital flight occur as crisis unfolds.	−			Kaminsky, Lizondo, and Reinhart (1998); Berg and Pattillo (1999); Edison (2003)
Ratio of bank reserves to bank assets	Adverse macroeconomic shocks are less likely to lead to crises in countries where the banking systems are liquid.		−		Dermirgüç-Kunt and Detragiache (2000)

Note: CC, BC, and DC represent currency crisis, banking crisis, and debt crisis, respectively; Positive (negative) expected sign means that a high (low) value of the indicator causes a higher probability of a crisis.

a sharp increase in U.S. interest rates and recessions in industrial countries, may contribute to a crisis. High world interest rates often induce capital outflows. For many East Asian countries, the depreciation of the Japanese yen against the U.S. dollar puts other regional currencies under pressure. A pronounced fall in the price of a commodity, such as oil, may have adverse effects on a country's trade balance and government revenue. Such factors can increase the likelihood of a currency crisis. Conversely, sharp increases in commodity prices may lead to a rise in imports and in the prices of nontraded goods. If the nominal exchange rate remains fixed, the real exchange rate can rise significantly, undermining the competitiveness of domestic industry.

It is important to note that some indicators are transformed to ensure that they are stationary and free from seasonal effects. Two types of transformations are applied: first differencing or percentage changes, and deviations from linear trends. In the case where the indicator has no visible seasonal pattern and is nontrending, its level form is maintained. Some unavailable indicators are proxied by closely related indicators—for example, industrial production substitutes for Organization for Economic Cooperation and Development (OECD) GDP. Scaling factors for different indicators are also used; for example, domestic credit, current account, and public debt are scaled by GDP.

Some indicators are multiple crisis indicators in the sense that the same indicator hints at more than one type of financial crisis. However, it is not certain whether such a multiple crisis indicator affects the probability of two or more types of financial crisis simultaneously, or whether it triggers one type of crisis that, in turn, rolls over to a second type of crisis, and a third. For instance, a drop in international competitiveness may result in a currency crisis, as a result of which a banking crisis evolves. Kaminsky and Reinhart (1999) point out the existence of a vicious cycle whereby banking sector problems lead to currency crises and these, in turn, have a negative

Table 4. Explanatory Variables for the Domestic Real and Public Sectors

Indicator	Interpretation	CC	BC	DC	References
Ratio of fiscal balance to GDP	Higher deficits are expected to raise the probability of crisis, since the deficits increase the vulnerability to shocks and investors' confidence.		+		Dermirgüç-Kunt and Detragiache (2000); Eichengreen and Arteta (2002)
Ratio of public debt to GDP	Higher indebtedness is expected to raise vulnerability to a reversal in capital inflows and hence to raise the probability of a crisis.	+	+	+	Kamin, Schindler, and Samuel (2001); Lanoie and Lemarbre (1996); Eichengreen and Arteta (2002)
Growth of industrial production	Recessions often precede financial crises.	−			Kaminsky, Lizondo, and Reinhart (1998); Berg and Pattillo (1999); Edison (2003)
Changes in stock prices	Burst of asset price bubbles often precede financial crises.	−			Kaminsky, Lizondo, and Reinhart (1998); Berg and Pattillo (1999); Edison (2003)
Inflation rate	The inflation rate is likely to be associated with high nominal interest rates and may proxy macroeconomic mismanagement, which adversely affects the economy and the banking system.		+	+	Dermirgüç-Kunt and Detragiache (2000); Lanoie and Lemarbre (1996); Marchesi (2003)
GDP per capita	High-income countries may be less likely to reschedule their debt than poorer countries since the costs of rescheduling would tend to be more onerous for more advanced economies. Deterioration of the domestic economic activity are expected to increase the likelihood of a banking crisis.		−	−	Dermirgüç-Kunt and Detragiache (2000); Eichengreen and Arteta (2002); Lanoie and Lemarbre (1996); Marchesi (2003)
National saving growth	High national savings may be expected to lower the probability of debt rescheduling.			−	Lanoie and Lemarbre (1996)

Note: CC, BC, and DC represent currency crisis, banking crisis, and debt crisis, respectively; Positive (negative) expected sign means that a high (low) value of the indicator causes a higher probability of a crisis.

Table 5. Explanatory Variables for the Global Economy

Indicator	Interpretation	CC	BC	DC	References
Growth of world oil prices	High oil prices are associated with recessions.	+			Edison (2003)
U.S. interest rate	International interest rate increases are often associated with capital outflows.	+	+		Edison (2003); Kamin, Schindler, and Samuel (2001); Eichengreen and Arteta (2002)
OECD GDP growth	Higher foreign output growth should strengthen exports and thus reduce the probability of a crisis.	−	−		Edison (2003); Kamin, Schindler, and Samuel (2001); Eichengreen and Arteta (2000)

Note: CC, BC, and DC represent currency crisis, banking crisis, and debt crisis, respectively; Positive (negative) expected sign means that a high (low) value of the indicator causes a higher probability of a crisis.

feedback on banks. Ultimately, they show that twin crises share some common determinants. Theoretical and empirical studies confirm that twin crises have been characterized by financial-sector liberalization (Glick and Hutchison 2001), easing of capital account restrictions (Goldfajn and Valdes 1997; Calvo and Mendoza 2000; Calvo and Reinhart 2000), financial fragility (Chang and Velasco 2000; Allen and Gale 2000), and market overreaction (Corsetti, Pesenti, and Roubini 1999b). Calvo and Reinhart (2000) and Burnside, Eichenbaum, and Rebelo (2003) observe that the effects of twin crises are more severe than pure banking and currency crises in terms of cost of bailout, loss of reserves, and real depreciation. In addition, the recovery of the domestic economy is more sluggish.

Table 6 summarizes nine empirical studies on financial crises: Kaminsky, Lizondo, and Reinhart (1998); Berg and Pattillo (1999); Kamin, Schindler, and Samuel (2001); Edison (2003); Dermirgüç-Kunt and Detragiache (2000); Eichengreen and Arteta (2002); Lanoie and Lemarbre (1996); Marchesi (2003); and Lestano, Jacobs, and Kuper (2003). These studies differ in the set of indicators, the transformations of the indicators, crisis definition and approach to assessing the outcomes. The first column of table 6 lists all indicators that are used in the empirical studies. The final four rows of the table describe the sample period, time span, and the number of countries covered.

The table allows the following conclusions. Berg and Pattillo (1999) and Edison (2003) augment the set of currency crisis indicators of Kaminsky, Lizondo, and Reinhart (1998) with global economy indicators, which are included to capture external shocks. All studies find that real exchange rates, export growth, and the ratio of M2 to international reserves are the most important indicators in explaining the probability of currency crises. Moreover, Kaminsky, Lizondo, and Reinhart (1998) and Berg and Pattillo (1999) observe that stock prices, industrial production, and international reserves are also statistically significant predictors of currency crisis occurrence. On the other hand, Kamin, Schindler, and Samuel (2001) find that the contributions of external balance and external shock indicators to the average probability of crisis are not high, but explain a significant share of the increases in the probability during the crisis years themselves. They interpret this as evidence that the domestic indicators are still the key determinants of vulnerability to crisis, but that external sectors often push vulnerable countries over the edge.

Dermirgüç-Kunt and Detragiache (2000) consider the role of macroeconomic variables, deposit insurance, and law enforcement in determining the likelihood of banking failure. They observe that the risk of a banking crisis becomes higher the lower output growth and the higher inflation, the domestic real interest rate, the ratio of M2 to international reserve, and domestic credit per GDP. They also find weak evidence that adverse terms of trade shocks increase the probability of a banking crisis. The size of the fiscal deficit and the rate of depreciation of the exchange rate do not seem to have an independent impact. An interesting finding is that a weak macroeconomic environment is not the sole indicator behind banking-sector fragility; structural characteristics of the banking sector and the economy also play a role. The authors conclude that the presence of an explicit deposit insurance scheme makes bank unsoundness more likely.

Using annual data on seventy-eight countries in the periods of 1975–97 to investigate the influence of domestic and external factors in bringing about banking problems, Eichengreen and Arteta (2002) find that domestic credit booms and government fiscal balance are strongly associated with banking crises. They also look at institutional explanations of banking crises and find that few of them yield robust results. More specifically, they find that domestic financial liberalization increases the probability of a banking crisis but that international financial liberalization (i.e., capital account liberalization), the presence of deposit insurance, and binary measures of institutional quality have unpredictable outcomes.

The recent study of Marchesi (2003) on the probability of debt crises concludes that none of the indicators listed in table 6 is significant. However, the study finds weak evidence that a debt rescheduling has a close relation with investments, the level of a country's indebtedness, and the existence of arrears in the payment of interest. Lanoie and Lemarbre (1996) do not support this result. They observe that the lower the rate of growth of GDP per capita and the larger external capital inflows, the higher the probability of debt rescheduling and debt crises. Marchesi also studies the relation between debt rescheduling and the adoption of IMF programs. The program consists of a set of policies in order to improve the economic condition of the debtor country, to enable the country to service its external debt better. The presence of an IMF program serves as a signaling device of a country's willingness and ability to undertake substantive economic reform, which is thus rewarded with debt relief. The author finds that participation in an IMF program lowers the expected probability of debt default.

Table 6. **Explanatory Variables: Empirical Results**

Indicator	KLR	BP	KSS	E	DKD	EA	LL	M	LJK		
	CC	CC	CC	CC	BC	BC	DC	DC	CC	BC	DC
External sector (current account)											
Real exchange rate	*	*	*	*	o	o			o	o	o
Export growth	*	*		*				o	o	o	o
Import growth	o	o		o					o	o	o
Terms of trade	o	o	*		o		o	o	o	o	o
Ratio of the current account to GDP		*	*			o	*				
External sector (capital account)											
Ratio of M2 to foreign exchange reserves	*	*	*	*	*	o			o	*	o
Growth of foreign exchange reserves	o	*		o				o		*	o
Financial sector											
M1 and M2 growth			*	o					*	*	*
M2 money multiplier	o	o		o							
Ratio of domestic credit to GDP	o	o		o	*	*				o	o
Excess real M1 balance	o	o		o							
Domestic real interest rate	o	o		o	*					*	
Lending and deposit rate spread	o		o		o						
Commercial bank deposits	o	o		o					*	*	*
Ratio of bank reserves to bank assets				o						o	
Domestic real and public sectors											
Ratio of fiscal balance to GDP		o			o	*			o	o	o
Ratio of public debt to GDP		o	*			o	o		o	o	o
Growth of industrial production	*			o					o	o	o
Changes in stock prices	*			o					o	o	o
Inflation rate					*			o	o	*	o

	1970–95	1970–96	1981–99	1970–99	1980–95	1975–97	1989–90	1983–96	1970–2001
GDP per capita					*	○	*	*	*
National saving growth								*	*
Global economy									
Growth of world oil prices			○	○		○		○	○
U.S. interest rate		*	○	○		○		○	○
OECD GDP growth		*	○	○				○	○
Observations	1970–95	1970–96	1981–99	1970–99	1980–95	1975–97	1989–90	1983–96	1970–2001
Frequency	monthly	monthly	monthly	monthly	annual	annual	annual	annual	monthly
Method	signal	probit	probit	signal	logit	probit	probit	probit	logit
Country coverage	20	23	26	28	65	78	93	87	6

Note: CC, BC, and DC represent currency crisis, banking crisis, and debt crisis, respectively; The marks ° and * denote insignificant and significant indicators, respectively. The papers included in this table are KLR: Kaminsky, Lizondo, and Reinhart (1998); BP: Berg and Pattillo (1999); KSS: Kamin, Schindler, and Samuel (2001); E: Edison (2003); DKD: Dermirgüç-Kunt and Detragiache (2000); EA: Eichengreen and Arteta (2002); LL: Lanoie and Lemarbre (1996); M: Marchesi (2003); LJK: Lestano, Jacobs, and Kuper (2003).

Lestano, Jacobs, and Kuper (2003) analyze the significance of all indicators listed in tables 1–5. Their empirical results suggest that rates of growth of money (M1 and M2), bank deposits, GDP per capita, and national savings correlate with all three types of financial crisis, whereas the ratio of M2 to foreign reserves and the growth of foreign reserves, the domestic real interest rate, and inflation play an additional role in banking crises and some varieties of currency crises. Moreover, based on an in-sample experiment using multivariate logit models, they prefer the currency dating method of Kaminsky, Lizondo, and Reinhart (1998) over other currency dating schemes.

It is difficult to assess these outcomes. The empirical papers deal with single crises only; they also differ in the types of analysis that have been used and employ different analytical methodologies. Some use signal extraction models, others use qualitative response models. Also, the time span, the frequency of the data, and the number of countries included in the analysis differ. Some papers use a short time span and cover a lot of countries—especially Lanoie and Lemarbre (1996)—while others cover a longer time span at the expense of a smaller country coverage. The studies also differ with respect to how they define a financial crisis. A general conclusion might be that the real exchange rate and the ratio of M2 to foreign exchange reserves are found to be significant in many empirical studies of currency crises, except in Lestano, Jacobs, and Kuper (2003). For banking crises, Dermirgüç-Kunt and Detragiache (1998) and Lestano, Jacobs, and Kuper found that the ratio of M2 to international reserves, domestic real interest rate, inflation rates, and GDP per capita play an important role. GDP per capita explains the probability of debt crises, except in Marchesi (2003).

To improve on the explanatory power of these models it might be useful to include measures of political stability (e.g., a corruption index) and of trade and equity market linkages to capture the idea of contagion. Another idea might be to link the various types of crises in one model. Finally, it may help to include not only the level of the indicators in the model, but also the changes therein. It can be argued that the way these factors develop over time has important consequences for the probability of a currency crisis to occur.

4. CONCLUSIONS

This chapter reviews the literature that focuses on the measurement and dating of financial crises. Three types of crises are distinguished: currency crises, banking crises, and debt crises. Event studies use a qualitative approach to identify currency crisis dates. Alternative currency-crisis dating schemes rely on the calculation of an exchange rate market pressure index. Most methods use a more or less arbitrary threshold to identify crises. These are the methods by Eichengreen, Rose, and Wyplosz (1995, 1996); Kaminsky, Lizondo, and Reinhart (1998); Frankel and Rose (1996); and Zhang (2001). Other methods for finding currency crisis dates are based on extreme values or Markov switching models and do not employ arbitrary thresholds.

The definition of banking crises is more difficult to implement. Different studies show different crisis episodes. Debt crisis studies have in common that they start from a definition of a debt crisis or a debt service difficulty or default. Differences arise from the fact that some papers use combinations of debt crisis definitions, whereas others simply make use of single events or measurement of either debt rescheduling or arrears.

In related work (Lestano, Jacobs, and Kuper 2003), we explore the dating outcomes for a common sample of countries and period and find that the different methodologies can reveal substantial differences in currency crisis chronologies.

In general, the explanatory power of indicators in models of financial crises is mixed. In many of the papers on currency crises, the real exchange rate and the ratio of M2 to foreign exchange reserves are found to be significant. For banking crises, the ratio of M2 to international reserves, the domestic real interest rate, inflation rates, and GDP per capita play an important role. GDP per capita explains the probability of debt crises.

NOTES

1. See Rigobon (2002) and Dungey et al. (this volume) for overviews.
2. See Lestano and Jacobs (2004) and Dungey et al. (this volume).
3. Compare also Koedijk, Schafgans, and Devries (1990).
4. See Jeanne and Masson (2000) and Cerra and Saxena (2002) for different Markov switching model specifications to date currency crises.
5. For instance, Eichengreen and Rose (2004) focus on the possible causal links from currency crises to banking crises, while Rossi (1999) studies the opposite causality effect, from banking to currency crises. See also Miller (1998) on the relationship between banking and currency crises.
6. See Moody's KMV (2000, 2003) and Standard and Poor's (1999, 2002) for details on the definition of default rates associated with the sovereign credit ratings, and Bhatia (2002) for an evaluation of sovereign credit rating methodologies.
7. Oka (2003) focuses on arrears to the IMF. Hajivassiliou (1987) and Li (1992) add the upper-tranche IMF agreement to their debt crisis definition. See IMF (2001) for details on the upper-tranche agreement.
8. Using extreme value theory and kernel density estimation suggested by Pozo and Amuedo-Dorantes (2003), Pescatori and Sy (2004) confirm that the 1,000-basis-points threshold corresponds to significant tail events.

REFERENCES

Abiad, A., 2003, Early Warning Systems: A Survey and a Regime-Switching Approach, *International Monetary Fund Working Paper* 03/32.

Allen, F., and D. Gale, 2000, Optimal Currency Crises, *Carnegie-Rochester Conference Series on Public Policy* 53, 177–230.

Aylward, L., and R. Thorne, 1998, Countries' Repayment Performance vis-à-vis the IMF: An Empirical Analysis, *International Monetary Fund Staff Papers* 45, 595–618.

Baig, T., and I. Goldfajn, 1999, Financial Market Contagion in the Asian Crisis, *International Monetary Fund Staff Papers* 46, 167–195.

Balkan, E. M., 1992, Political Instability, Country Risk and Probability of Default, *Applied Economics* 24, 999–1008.

Berg, A., E. Borensztein, and C. Pattillo, 2004, Assessing Early Warning Systems: How Have They Worked in Practice? *International Monetary Fund Working Paper* 04/52.

Berg, A., and C. Pattillo, 1999, Predicting Currency Crises: The Indicators Approach and an Alternative, *Journal of International Money and Finance* 18, 561–586.

Berg, A., and J. Sachs, 1988, The Debt Crisis: Structural Explanations of Country Performance, *Journal of Development Economics* 29, 271–306.

Bhatia, A. V., 2002, Sovereign Credit Ratings Methodology: An Evaluation, *International Monetary Fund Working Paper* 02/170.

Blanco, H., and P. M. Garber, 1986, Recurrent Devaluation and Speculative Attacks on the Mexican Peso, *Journal of Political Economy* 94, 148–166.

Bordo, M. D., and B. Eichengreen, 2000, Is the Crisis Problem Growing More Severe? *Presented at the Sveriges Riksbank conference "Asset Prices and Monetary Policy" June 16–17, 2000.*

Bordo, M. D., B. Eichengreen, D. Klingebiel, M. S. Martinez-Peria, and A. K. Rose, 2001, Is the Crisis Problem Growing More Severe? *Economic Policy* 16, 51–82.

Burkart, O., and V. Coudert, 2002, Leading Indicators of Currency Crises for Emerging Countries, *Emerging Markets Review* 3, 107–133.

Burnside, C., M. Eichenbaum, and S. Rebelo, 2003, On the Fiscal Implications of Twin Crises, in M. P. Dooley and J. A. Frankel, eds., *Managing Currency Crises in Emerging Markets* (pp. 218–222). Chicago: University of Chicago Press.

Bussiere, M., and C. Mulder, 2000, Political Instability and Economic Vulnerability, *International Journal of Finance and Economics* 5, 309–330.

Bustelo, P., 2000, Novelties of Financial Crises in the 1990s and the Search for New Indicators, *Emerging Markets Review* 1, 229–251.

Calvo, G. A., and E. G. Mendoza, 2000, Capital-Markets Crises and Economic Collapse in Emerging Markets: An Informational-Frictions Approach, *American Economic Review* 90, 59–64.

Calvo, G. A., and C. M. Reinhart, 2000, When Capital Inflows Come to a Sudden Stop: Consequences and Policy Options, in P. Kenen and A. Swoboda, eds., *Reforming the International Monetary and Financial System* (International Monetary Fund, Washington, DC).

Caprio, G., Jr., and D. Klingebiel, 1996, Bank Insolvencies: Cross-Country Experience, *World Bank Policy Research Working Paper* 1620.

———, 2003, Episodes of Systematic and Borderline Financial Crisis, *World Bank manuscript.*

Caramazza, F., L. Ricci, and R. Salgado, 2000, Trade and Financial Contagion in Currency Crises, *International Monetary Fund Working Paper* 00/55.

Cerra, V., and S. C. Saxena, 2002, Contagion, Monsoons, and Domestic Turmoil in Indonesia's Currency Crisis, *Review of International Economics* 10, 36–44.

Chang, R., and A. Velasco, 1998a, The Asian Liquidity Crisis, *National Bureau of Economic Research Working Paper* 6796.

———, 2000, Financial Fragility and the Exchange Rate Regime, *Journal of Economic Theory* 92, 1–34.

———, 2001, A Model of Financial Crises in Emerging Markets, *Quarterly Journal of Economics* 116(2), 489–517.

Cline, W. R., 1995, *International Debt Reexamined* (Institute for International Economics, Washington, DC).

Cole, H. L., and T. J. Kehoe, 2000, Self-Fulfilling Debt Crises, *Review of Economic Studies* 67, 91–116.

Corsetti, G., P. Pesenti, and N. Roubini, 1999a, Paper Tigers? A Model of the Asian Crisis, *European Economic Review* 43, 1211–1236.

———, 1999b, What Caused the Asian Currency and Financial Crisis? *Japan and the World Economy* 11, 305–373.

Dermirgüç-Kunt, A., and E. Detragiache, 1998, The Determinants of Banking Crises in Developing and Developed Countries, *International Monetary Fund Staff Papers* 45, 81–109.

———, 2000, Monitoring Banking Sector Fragility: A Multivariate Logit Approach, *World Bank Economic Review* 14, 287–307.

Detragiache, E., and A. Spilimbergo, 2001, Crises and Liquidity: Evidence and Interpretation, *International Monetary Fund Working Paper* 01/2.

Dungey, M., and V. L. Martin, 2004, A Multifactor Model of Exchange Rates with Unanticipated Shocks: Measuring Contagion in the East Asian Currency Market, *Journal of Emerging Markets Finance* 3, 305–330.

Dziobek, C., and C. Pazarbasioglu, 1997, Lessons from Systemic Bank Restructuring: A Survey of 24 Countries, *International Monetary Fund Working Paper* 97/161.

Edison, H. J., 2003, Do Indicators of Financial Crises Work? An Evaluation of an Early Warning System, *International Journal of Finance and Economics* 8, 11–53.

Eichengreen, B., and C. Arteta, 2002, Banking Crises in Emerging Markets: Presumptions and Evidence, in M. I. Bleger and M. Skreb, eds., *Financial Policies in Emerging Markets* (pp. 47–94). Cambridge: MIT Press.

Eichengreen, B., and A. K. Rose, 2004, Staying Afloat When the Wind Shifts: External Factors and Emerging-Market Banking Crises, in G. A. Calvo, M. Obstfeld, and R. Dornbusch, eds., *Money, Capital Mobility, and Trade: Essays in Honor of Robert A. Mundell* (MIT Press, Cambridge).

Eichengreen, B., A. K. Rose, and C. Wyplosz, 1995, Exchange Market Mayhem: The Antecedents and Aftermath of Speculative Attacks, *Economic Policy: A European Forum* 21, 249–296.

———, 1996, Contagious Currency Crises: First Tests, *Scandinavian Journal of Economics* 98, 463–484.

Esquivel, G., and F. Larraín, 1998, Explaining Currency Crises, *Harvard Institute for International Development, Development Discussion Paper* 666.

Frankel, J. A., and A. K. Rose, 1996, Currency Crashes in Emerging Markets: An Empirical Treatment, *Journal of International Economics* 41, 351–366.

Girton, L., and D. Roper, 1977, A Monetary Model of Exchange Market Pressure Applied to Postwar Canadian Experience, *American Economic Review* 67, 537–548.

Glick, R., and M. M. Hutchinson, 2001, Banking and Currency Crises: How Common Are Twins? in R. Glick, R. Moreno, and M. M. Spiegel, eds., *Financial Crises in Emerging Markets* (Cambridge University Press, Cambridge).

Glick, R., and A. K. Rose, 1999, Contagion and Trade: Why Are Currency Crises Regional? *Journal of International Money and Finance* 18, 603–617.

Goldfajn, I., and R. O. Valdes, 1997, Capital Flows and the Twin Crises: The Role of Liquidity, *International Monetary Fund Working Paper* 97/87.

Goldstein, M., G. L. Kaminsky, and C. M. Reinhart, 2000. *Assessing Financial Vulnerability: An Early Warning System for Emerging Markets* (Institute for International Economics, Washington, DC).

González-Hermosillo, B., 1996, Banking Sector Fragility and Systemic Sources of Fragility, *International Monetary Fund Working Paper* 96/12.

Granger, C. W. J., B.-N. Huang, and C.-W. Yang, 2000, A Bivariate Causality between Stock Prices and Exchange Rates: Evidence from Recent Asian Flu, *Quarterly Review of Economics and Finance* 40, 337–54.

Haile, F. D., and S. Pozo, 2003, Exchange Rate Regimes and Currency Crises: An Evaluation Using Extreme Value Theory, *unpublished manuscript.*

Hajivassiliou, V. A., 1987, The External Debt Repayments Problems of LDCs: An Econometric-Model Based on Panel Data, *Journal of Econometrics* 36, 205–230.

———, 1989, Do the Secondary Markets Believe in Life after Debt? in I. Hvain and I. Diwan, eds., *Dealing with the Debt Crisis* (pp. 276–291). Washington, DC: World Bank.

———, 1994, A Simulation Estimation Analysis of the External Debt Crises of Developing Countries, *Journal of Applied Econometrics* 9, 109–131.

Hawkins, J., and M. Klau, 2000, Measuring Potential Vulnerabilities in Emerging Market Economies, *Bank for International Settlements Working Paper* 91.

International Monetary Fund, 2001, *Financial Organization and Operations of the IMF* (International Monetary Fund, Washington, DC).

Ito, T., and Y. Hashimoto, 2002, High Frequency Contagion of Currency Crises in Asia, *National Bureau of Economic Research Working Paper* 9376.

Jeanne, O., and P. Masson, 2000, Currency Crises, Sunspots and Markov-Switching Regimes, *Journal of International Economics* 50, 327–350.

Kamin, S. B., J. W. Schindler, and S. L. Samuel, 2001, The Contribution of Domestic and External Factors to Emerging Market Devaluation Crises: An Early Warning Systems Approach, *Board of Governors of the Federal Reserve System, International Finance Discussion Paper* 711.

Kaminsky, G. L., S. Lizondo, and C. M. Reinhart, 1998, Leading Indicators of Currency Crises, *International Monetary Fund Staff Paper* 45, 1–48.

Kaminsky, G. L., and C. M. Reinhart, 1999, The Twin Crises: The Causes of Banking and Balance-of-Payments Problems, *American Economic Review* 89, 473–500.

———, 2000, On Crises, Contagion, and Confusion, *Journal of International Economics* 51, 145–168.

Kaminsky, G. L., and S. L. Schmukler, 1999, What Triggers Market Jitters? A Chronicle of the Asian Crisis, *Journal of International Money and Finance* 18, 537–560.

Koedijk, K. G., M. M. A. Schafgans, and C. G. Devries, 1990, The Tail Index of Exchange-Rate Returns, *Journal of International Economics* 29, 93–108.

Krugman, P., 1979, Model of Balance-of-Payments Crises, *Journal of Money Credit and Banking* 11, 311–325.

Kwack, S. Y., 2000, An Empirical Analysis of the Factors Determining the Financial Crisis in Asia, *Journal of Asian Economics* 11, 195–206.

Lanoie, P., and S. Lemarbre, 1996, Three Approaches to Predict the Timing and Quantity of LDC Debt Rescheduling, *Applied Economics* 28, 241–246.

Lee, S. H., 1991, Ability and Willingness to Service Debt as Explanation for Commercial and Official Rescheduling Cases, *Journal of Banking and Finance* 15, 5–27.

Lestano, and J. P. A. M. Jacobs, 2004, A Comparison of Currency crisis dating methods: East Asia, 1970–2002, Department of Economics, University of Groningen, The Netherlands, *CCSO Working Paper* 2004/12

Lestano, J. P. A. M. Jacobs, and G. Kuper, 2003, Indicators of Financial Crises Do Work! An Early-Warning System for Six Asian Countries, Department of Economics, University of Groningen, *CCSO Working Paper* 2003/13.

Li, C. A., 1992, Debt Arrears in Latin-America: Do Political Variables Matter? *Journal of Development Studies* 28, 668–688.

Lindgren, C.-J., G. G. H. Garcia, and M. I. Saal, 1996, *Bank Soundness and Macroeconomic Policy* (International Monetary Fund, Washington, DC).

Manasse, P., N. Roubini, and A. Schimmelpfennig, 2003, Predicting Sovereign Debt Crises, *International Monetary Fund Working Paper* 03/221.

Marchesi, S., 2003, Adoption of an IMF Programme and Debt Rescheduling: An Empirical Analysis, *Journal of Development Economics* 70, 403–423.

Martinez-Peria, M. S., 2002, A Regime-Switching Approach to the Study of Speculative Attacks: A Focus on EMS Crises, *Empirical Economics* 27, 299–334.

McFadden, D., R. Eckaus, G. Feder, V. Hajivassiliou, and S. O'Connell, 1985, Is There Life after Debt? An Econometric Analysis of the Creditworthiness of Developing Countries, in G. W. Smith and J. T. Cuddington, eds., *International Debt and the Developing Countries* (World Bank Group, Washington, DC).

Miller, V., 1998, The Double Drain with a Cross-Border Twist: More on the Relationship between Banking and Currency Crises, *American Economic Review* 88, 439–443.

Moody's KMV, 2000, Historical Default Rates of Corporate Bond Issuers, 1920–1999, *Moody's Investors Service, Global Credit Research, Special Comment.*

———, 2003, Sovereign Bond Defaults, Rating Transitions, and Recoveries (1985–2002), *Moody's Investors Service, Global Credit Research, Special Comment.*

Morris, S., and H. S. Shin, 1998, Unique Equilibrium in a Model of Self-Fulfilling Currency Attacks, *American Economic Review* 88, 587–597.

Mulder, C. B., R. Perrelli, and M. Rocha, 2002, The Role of Corporate, Legal and Macroeconomic Balance Sheet Indicators in Crisis Detection and Prevention, *International Monetary Fund Working Paper* 02/59.

Nagayasu, J., 2001, Currency Crisis and Contagion: Evidence from Exchange Rates and Sectoral Stock Indices of the Philippines and Thailand, *Journal of Asian Economics* 12, 529–546.

Obstfeld, M., 1995, The Logic of Currency Crises, in B. Eichengreen, J. Frieden, and J. von Hagen, eds., *Monetary and Fiscal Policy in an Integrated Europe* (Springer, Heidelberg, Germany).

———, 1996, Models of Currency Crises with Self-Fulfilling Features, *European Economic Review* 40, 1037–1047.

Oka, C., 2003, Anticipating Arrears to the IMF: Early Warning Systems, *International Monetary Fund Working Paper* 03/18.

Pescatori, A., and A. N. R. Sy, 2004, Debt Crises and the Development of International Capital Markets, *International Monetary Fund Working Paper* 04/44.

Pozo, S., and C. Amuedo-Dorantes, 2003, Statistical Distributions and the Identification of Currency Crises, *Journal of International Money and Finance* 22, 591–609.

Radelet, S., and J. D. Sachs, 1998, The East Asian Financial Crisis: Diagnosis, Remedies, Prospects, *Brookings Papers on Economic Activity*, 2, 1–90.

Reinhart, C. M., 2002, Default, Currency Crises, and Sovereign Credit Ratings, *World Bank Economic Review* 16, 151–170.

Rigobon, R., 2002, *International Financial Contagion: Theory and Evidence in Evolution* (Research Foundation of The Association for Investment Management and Research, Charlottesville, VA).

Rossi, M., 1999, Financial Fragility and Economic Performance in Developing Economies: Do Capital Controls, Prudential Regulation and Supervision Matter? *International Monetary Fund Working Paper* 99/66.

Standard and Poor's, 1999, Sovereign Defaults: Hiatus in 2000? *Standard & Poor's Credit Week, December 22.*

———, 2002, Rating Performance 2002, Default, Transition, Recovery, and Spreads, *Research from Standard and Poor's Risk Solutions.*

Sy, A. N. R., 2004, Rating the Rating Agencies: Anticipating Currency Crises or Debt Crises, *Journal of Banking and Finance* 28, 2845–2867.

Vlaar, P. J. G., 2000, Currency Crisis Models for Emerging Markets, *De Nederlandsche Bank Staff Report* 45.

Weller, C. E., 2001, Financial Crises after Financial Liberalisation: Exceptional Circumstances or Structural Weakness? *Journal of Development Studies* 38, 98–127.

Zhang, Z., 2001, Speculative Attacks in the Asian Crisis, *International Monetary Fund Working Paper* 01/189.

5

High-Frequency Contagion between Exchange Rates and Stock Prices during the Asian Currency Crisis

Takatoshi Ito and Yuko Hashimoto

1. INTRODUCTION

Frequent currency crises among emerging-market economies have become one of the most important global financial problems in the 1990s and 2000s. The most prominent crises include Mexico in 1994; Thailand, Korea, and Indonesia in 1997; Russia in 1998; Brazil in 1999; and Argentina in 2001–02. Among them, the Asian crisis differs from other crises in its speed, depth, and breadth of contagion, and it has been the focus of many studies as described in, for example, Corsetti, Pesenti, and Roubini (1998), Flood and Marion (1999), Radelet and Sachs (2000), Ito (2000), and Ito and Hashimoto (2002), to name a few. The simultaneous occurrence of a currency crisis and financial-sector (banking-sector) crisis triggered a sharp drop in stock prices in the region, so that a feature of this crisis is the simultaneous fall of currency and stock prices across countries. Of course, the simultaneous fall of stock prices and currencies—that is, contagion across different asset prices—is by no means limited to this crisis period or even to crisis-hit countries; worldwide stock market declines were apparent during the Depression and Black Monday 1987. Even during stable periods, movements in the prices of different assets—currencies and equities—are likely to influence each other directly in the major markets.[1] However, the comovement of asset prices has generally been found to strengthen during unstable periods in the 1980s and 1990s; see, for example, Rigobon (2003), who investigates Latin American bond markets from 1994 to 2001, and the approaches described in Dungey et al. (this volume). The contemporaneous interactions between stock prices and exchange rates in a crisis-hit country emerge on the presumption of strong interconnections between asset prices.

Ito: Department of Economics, University of Tokyo, tito@e-u.tokyo.ac.jp; Hashimoto: Faculty of Economics, Toyo University, yhashi@toyonet.toyo.ac.jp.

There are good reasons to anticipate linkages between currency and equity markets. In the case of a currency market shock, such as a sharp depreciation or speculative attack, the domestic monetary authority may raise interest rates in an attempt to reduce capital outflows (or increase capital inflows) to avoid further depreciation. Higher interest rates, however, may exert downward pressure on stock prices. Even if the country survives speculative pressure on the exchange rate, it may still suffer the negative shock through a decline in stock prices, as evidenced by Hong Kong in October 1997 and the summer of 1998. In August 1998, the Hong Kong Monetary Authority purchased stocks to defend financial markets from the so-called double-play—a simultaneous attack on the currency and equity markets. The result was that Hong Kong did not suffer from the Asian currency crisis in terms of exchange rate depreciation, but experienced stock price declines. Thus, contagion from the crisis can be said to have had a great impact, even in Hong Kong.

Stock price declines sometimes work as a leading indicator of crises; see, for example, Goldstein, Kaminsky, and Reinhart (2000). The slowdown of an economy affects stock prices, prompting international investors to withdraw their capital and putting downward pressure on the currency. In the case of Thailand, the stock price had peaked in the mid-1990s and already declined by half on the eve of crisis. This substantial three-year decline in stock prices led the weakened economy into another recession and finally plunged it into currency crisis. However, in other cases, stock prices only reacted to the currency crisis, such as in Indonesia, where sharp depreciations triggered the insolvency of corporations and banks that had currency mismatches on their balance sheets. Stock prices fell once the currency depreciated sharply. Thus, by examining stock price reactions and exchange rate behaviors jointly, we gain a more detailed insight into contagion during the crisis.

There are at least five channels of spillovers among foreign exchange rates and stock prices. The first channel is the spillover effect from the exchange rate shock to stock prices, as outlined above. The second channel runs from stock price shocks to the exchange rate, based on the perspective that the stock price reflects economic fundamentals. The third channel originates from a third factor (other than shocks in foreign exchange market/stock market)—for example, shocks due to monetary policy. The fourth channel is contagion among the currencies, which was the topic of Ito and Hashimoto (2002) and empirical literature including Frankel and Rose (1996), Glick and Rose (1999), and Bekaert, Harvey, and Ng (2005). The final transmission channel is cross-border contagion among different stock markets, which has an active empirical literature represented by such papers as King, Sentana, and Wadhwani (1994) and Bae, Karolyi, and Stulz (2003). The theoretical literature on contagious links spans each of these channels, and is overviewed in Dornbusch, Park, and Claessens (2000) and represented more recently by Allen and Gale (2000) and Kodres and Pritsker (2002).

This chapter examines the contagion between daily exchange rates and stock prices during the Asian crisis. Ito and Hashimoto (2002) proposed a method to identify the direction of causality among currencies in crisis. This chapter extends that methodology to examine the interaction between exchange rate depreciations and stock price declines, and is able to provide detail on causality between the shocks which cannot be provided in a framework focused on correlations between these markets. In this chapter, we identify the interconnections between stock and foreign exchange markets and characterize the contemporaneous responses of each market during the crisis period.

Two branches of the empirical literature are closely related to this chapter. The first one addresses the interaction between the foreign exchange market and the stock market. Forbes and Rigobon (2002) analyze contagion using vector autoregression (VAR), taking into account the omitted variables and heteroskedasticity to claim evidence of limited stock market contagion during the Asian crisis. Pavlova and Rigobon (2004) show that exchange rates serve as a transmission channel for stock price movements. There are relatively few other papers that examine the transmissions between the asset markets in this crisis, an exception being Granger, Huang, and Yang (2000).[2] The second stream of related literature is estimation methodology. Many of the previous studies use VAR methodology, which considers only the presence of correlation in the financial markets; see, for example, Bekaert and Hodrick (1992), Forbes and Rigobon (2002) and Debelle and Ellis (this volume). Our methodology has several advantages over the VAR method. First, the dependent variable in our model is constructed to capture only large responses, eliminating noise. The focus on larger responses is consistent with the literature, which argues that contagion is a nonlinear process, so that extreme observations should be modeled separately—see, for example, Bekaert, Harvey, and Ng (2005). Second, the origin of shocks and the direction of causality are determined by comparing daily changes of the exchange rates (or stock prices) before running regressions. Third, by our employing these steps, the number of explanatory variables is fewer than in comparable VAR studies, so that the estimation is more efficient.[3]

Other macro-based empirical analyses of contagion are not implementable using high-frequency data. The explanatory variables are only available on a much lower frequency. For example, Kaminsky and Reinhart (2000) investigate the spillover effects of stock price returns using logit estimation and find that U.S., Japanese, and German markets play an important role in the spillover relationships in the case of the Brazilian, Thai, and Russian crises at a monthly frequency.

This chapter investigates the interaction between the exchange rates and stock market prices in Asian financial markets using daily observations in the aftermath of the 1997 crisis. Based on the concept of an "origin" country and an "affected" country in the spillover relationship, developed in Ito and Hashimoto (2002), we identify contagion causality within the day. The steps we follow are first to estimate the threshold value distinguishing currency depreciation and stock price declines due to contagion from those due to noise. The model then identifies the channels of contagion between three alternatives: the effect of the hard-hit origin country, the trend in the market, and effects from other countries. The model predicts that the exchange rates and stock prices are correlated internationally even at a high-frequency (daily) level, providing support to theoretical inferences in favor of financial contagion between the foreign exchange and stock markets—as, for example, in Pavlova and Rigobon (2004).

There are four major transmissions to be considered here: contagion between currency markets, contagion between stock markets, contagion from currencies to stocks, and contagion from stocks to currencies. The major findings in these respects are as follows. Between exchange rates we find that the Indonesian and Korean, but not the Thai, dollar exchange rates affected other currencies in the region. This may be contrary to casual observation that the currency crisis spread from Thailand to other countries in the second half of 1997. Contagion among stock markets was not significant for most pairs of countries, consistent with the findings in Forbes and Rigobon (2002). In the currency markets we find that shocks from the Indonesian, Korean, and Thai exchange rates had large impacts on the stock prices of other countries, including Hong Kong, so that the currency crisis can be said to have had effect even in Hong Kong. Shocks from other currencies did not significantly affect the stock prices of the sample countries. Contagion from stock market shocks to currencies was generally insignificant, with two important exceptions. These were that the Thai baht was quite sensitive to shocks in stock prices of other countries, and that the Hong Kong stock price shocks were found to have substantial effects on other Asian exchange rates in the midst of the crisis.

The rest of the chapter is organized as follows. In section 2, movements of the exchange rates and stock prices of the region during the crisis period are reviewed. In section 3, we present the estimation methodology used in this chapter. Section 4 shows the results of estimations based on the Tobit equations that include contagion terms. Section 5 presents conclusions.

2. DATA AND EMPIRICAL EVIDENCE ON CURRENCIES AND STOCK PRICES

This chapter considers daily data for the period 4 January 1994 to 7 July 1999 on nominal bilateral exchange rates against the U.S. dollar and stock price indices[4] for eight Asian countries: Hong Kong, Indonesia, Korea, Malaysia, the Philippines, Singapore, Taiwan, and Thailand. The data source is Datastream. The exchange rate data are shown in figure 1 for the subperiod of 30 June 1997 to 7 July 1999, normalized to 100 at the beginning of the subsample. This is a period of considerable turmoil in the Asian economies, following the series of speculative attacks and floats or devaluations from July 1997. Most Asian currencies had recovered stability in line with economic recovery in mid-1998.

Figure 2 shows the stock price indices for the same subsample of 30 June 1997 to 7 July 1999. The picture is less clear cut than for currencies. During

30 June 1997 = 100

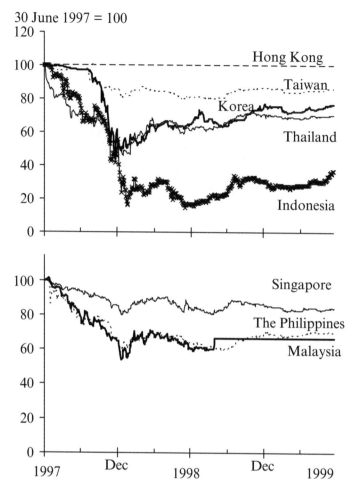

Fig. 1.   Asian exchange rates against the U.S. dollar (30 June 1997 = 100).

the precrisis period some stock prices were relatively stable and others rose. The exception is Thailand, which exhibited a downward trend in the precrisis period, particularly post–October 1996. Thailand is arguably the origin of stock price declines in other markets evident later in the sample. In April and July 1997 declines in stock prices appear to have spilled into the Philippines, followed by Indonesia in August 1997. From September 1997, more rapid declines are evident in Malaysia, Indonesia, and South Korea. The magnitude of stock price declines eases post–December 1997, and like currencies, stock prices recovered in mid-1998 along with the economic recovery.

Figures 1 and 2 suggest that the exchange rate devaluations of Thailand, the Philippines, and Indonesia seem to be preceded by the stock price declines in 1997.[5] Stock prices were falling in Thailand as early as late 1996 and

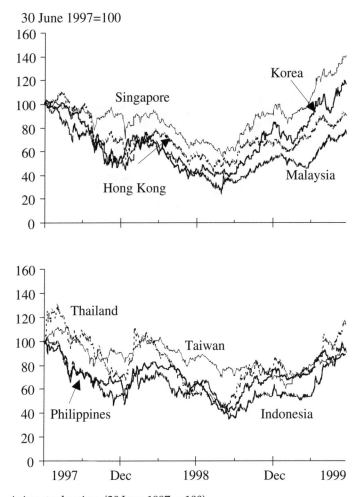

Fig. 2.   Asian stock prices (30 June 1997 = 100).

in the first half of 1997, prior to the float of the Thai baht on 2 July 1997. In the same fashion, the Philippines experienced a large fall in stock prices in April and July 1997, before the large devaluation of the peso in September 1997. Falling Indonesian stock prices in early August preceded the float of the rupiah and its slump to a historic low in November. This prima facie evidence for the direction of linkages between the equity and currency markets in the Asian crisis has also been noted by McKibbin and Martin (1998).

However, there has been relatively little work on transmissions between equity and currency markets during periods of financial crisis. Most studies of financial crises concentrate on a single index. A popular approach has been to identify contagion as a significant change in correlation coefficient between assets; see Forbes and Rigobon (2002). However, in practice this has been limited in most studies to bivariate comparisons, although Dungey et al. (this volume) illustrate a multivariate extension of this approach. A further undesirable element of the correlation approach is that it fails to identify either the cause of the transmission or the crisis spillover channel. This chapter uses the definition first developed by Ito and Hashimoto (2002).[6] A traditional channel of contagion in the literature refers to a depreciation of a currency to depreciations of other currencies. We observe, however, that a large decline could occur in the stock prices that could spread to the exchange rate of that country or stock prices of other countries. We first identify the origin of the depreciation (or stock price decline) and then statistically analyze the causes and the propagation of the crisis. To place this in context we investigate the interaction between exchange rate behaviors and stock price movements during both crisis and noncrisis periods.

Since the high-frequency dynamics of exchange rates and stock prices include an element of noise behavior, it is difficult to identify whether a large depreciation (stock price decline) arises from a shock or is merely noise. Here we use an identifying assumption to distinguish contagion from noise based on a threshold. Basically, we assume that all movements of less than a certain size are noise. This may miss potentially contagious linkages from smaller shocks, but is consistent with the literature on contagion concerned with the transmission of extreme observations. Once we have identified the appropriate sample observations by extracting potentially contagious events from noise, we estimate the possible relationship between equity price and currency movements to analyze their characteristics.

3. POTENTIAL CHANNELS OF TRANSMISSION

There are several channels and factors that may transmit a shock in exchange rates to stock prices, and vice versa. The first channel is the spillover effect from the exchange rate shock to stock prices. There are two competing effects through this channel. If the exchange rate depreciation is orderly and moderate, the depreciation boosts trade competitiveness for the depreciating country at least temporarily, in the presence of nominal domestic price rigidities, and is expected to have a positive effect on the stock prices. This is the case of the Indonesian and Korean stock prices at the early stage of Asian currency crisis, when the exchange rates of these two countries were relatively stable and stock prices were rising. On the other hand, a sharp and rapid depreciation will induce a fall in stock prices, due to the change in sentiment (confidence) of market participants and an increased probability of corporate failure for those with foreign currency–denominated liabilities. In addition, the central bank may raise interest rates to defend the currency, and the higher interest rate will cause a decline in stock prices.[7] Although the signs of spillover effects from the exchange rate to stock prices cannot be theoretically determined, a sharp depreciation (as opposed to a moderate, orderly depreciation) tends to cause stock prices to decline.

The second channel is the one from stock prices to the exchange rate. From the perspective that the stock price reflects economic fundamentals, news of weak fundamentals weakens confidence and is associated with slower economic growth, smaller profit opportunities, and currency depreciation.

The third channel is contagion among currencies. This was the topic of Ito and Hashimoto (2002), and other papers on the contagion of currency crises. It refers to the spread of crises through countries in reaction to news that is not necessarily fundamentals based.

The final transmission channel is cross-border contagion among different stock markets. Market interdependencies, such as macroeconomic similarities and trade linkages, result in a fall in a single country's stock price contagiously spilling over to other countries. Regardless of an individual country's macroeconomic fundamentals and other financial markets, a negative shock in one country spreads to another through real and financial linkages. There is a large literature on the comovements of stock prices among industrialized countries (e.g., King, Sentana, and Wadhwani 1994). As an example of this type of channel, consider a country that has declining stock prices and is likely to experience an economic slowdown, and hence reduces its imports. In the medium run, this will negatively affect its trade partners' exports. Although this import-export linkage may take several months to work through, the impact of stock market declines, especially large ones, across countries linked in this manner is immediate. Investors tend to downgrade their assessment of countries with trade linkages to the affected country. Indeed, a change in sentiment toward, or risk assessment of, an entire region serves as a transmission channel of stock price declines.

4.   THE MODEL

Denote the return in the exchange rate (or stock price) for country i as $r_{i,t}$ as follows:

$$r_{i,t} = \ln(S_{i,t}) - \ln(S_{i,t}) \tag{1}$$

where $S_{i,t}$ is the value of the bilateral exchange rate (or stock price). In a number of instances a rapid fall in $r_{i,t}$ is followed by an immediate, and almost offsetting, rise in $r_{i,t+1}$. To reduce the impact of quickly reversed changes in the returns for either currency or equity returns, we construct a weighted cumulative change that takes on information from previous periods. These weighted indices are denoted $wsp_{i,t}$ for equity markets and $wfx_{i,t}$ for the currency markets, and are constructed as

$$wsp_{i,t} = 0.5r_{i,t} + 0.25r_{i,t-1} + 0.125r_{i,t-2} + 0.0625r_{i,t-3} + 0.0625r_{i,t-4} \tag{2}$$
$$wfx_{i,t} = 0.5r_{i,t} + 0.25r_{i,t-1} + 0.125r_{i,t-2} + 0.0625r_{i,t-3} + 0.0625r_{i,t-4}.$$

Hence the weighted returns take into account activity from the previous trading week of five days, with greater weight on more recent observations. In this way we concentrate on sustained drops in returns; see Ito and Hashimoto (2002).

Our framework supposes that crises spread from the hard-hit countries to the others. To identify the hardest-hit countries in each market, or the origin country for the shocks, we use the distributions of $wsp_{i,t}$ and $wfx_{i,t}$. At each point t the largest fall in these weighted indices is identified as the hardest-hit country at that point in time. In addition, we impose that to be an origin country for the shocks, the largest value of the weighted indices must exceed the arbitrary threshold of a 2 percent decline in returns. That is, the origin shocks are chosen according to the criteria

at time t origin country for equities $= j$ if $\{wsp_{j,t} > 2\%\}$ and $\{wsp_{j,t} > wsp_{i,t} \, \forall i \neq j\}$

at time t origin country for currencies $= j$ if $\{wfx_{j,t} > 2\%\}$ and $\{wfx_{j,t} > wfx_{i,t} \, \forall i \neq j\}$.

Applying this method to the stock and currency market returns of the eight Asian markets produces the list of origin countries for exchange rate depreciations and stock price falls shown in tables 1 and 2. The hardest hits were experienced in Thailand in July 1997, Indonesia in August–September 1997 and again after January 1998, and Korea from October 1997 to January 1998. Comparing tables 1 and 2 provides evidence that many of the large falls in stock prices were preceded by the currency crisis. The frequency of large declines (origin countries) for equity markets soared after the Thai currency crisis.

4.1 Friction Model

A common problem in financial market returns data is differentiating signals from noise. One way of dealing with this is to use the tails of the distribution of the returns as the more interesting data, as, for example, in Bae, Karolyi, and Stulz (2003) for equities.

In this chapter, we employ a practical approach to account for the noise in the exchange rate and stock price behavior. Consider the case where the exchange rate (or stock price) return observed for country i, y_i^*, is represented by the process

$$y_i^* = x_i' b_i + e_i, \tag{3}$$

where x_i represents a vector of explanatory variables, with loadings b, and an error given by e_i. Thresholds are then applied to divide the series y_i^* into one of three categories: (a) rises in the exchange rate, (b) change due purely to noise, and (c) potentially contagious falls in returns. To identify each of these categories, two threshold values are defined, a_1 and a_2, where $a_1 \leq 0 \leq a_2$. Equation (4), below, illustrates the three cases. When $y_{i,t}^* > a_2$ the return is classified as positive. When $y_{i,t}^*$ lies between the two thresholds, the movements are classified as noise, and when the decline in $y_{i,t}^*$ is greater than the lower threshold this is identified as a potentially contagious fall in returns. Using the series $y_{i,t}$ as the indicator variable, this is expressed as

Table 1. Daily Origin of Exchange Rate Shocks, July 1997–March 1999

Month	Day	Origin Country	Devaluation (%)
1997			
July	2	Thailand	−3.40
	3	Thailand	−2.22
	4	Thailand	−2.06
	14	The Philippines	−5.30
	21	Indonesia	−2.83
	23	Thailand	−2.06
August	15	Indonesia	−2.99
	18	Indonesia	−3.23
	27	Indonesia	−2.93
	28	Indonesia	−3.19
September	2	Indonesia	−2.39
	3	Thailand	−2.81
	4	Thailand	−3.74
	18	The Philippines	−2.06
	29	Indonesia	−2.38
	30	Indonesia	−2.33
October	1	Indonesia	−3.19
	3	Indonesia	−4.32
	6	Indonesia	−2.56
	20	Taiwan	−2.45
November	20	Korea	−5.52
	25	Korea	−2.24
	28	Korea	−2.92
December	1	Korea	−2.21
	2	Korea	−2.82
	3	Thailand	−3.66
	8	Korea	−5.39
	9	Korea	−6.88
	10	Korea	−6.73
	11	Korea	−8.02
	12	Indonesia	−10.97
	15	Indonesia	−6.72
	16	Thailand	−3.66
	22	Korea	−10.12
	23	Korea	−10.12
	24	Indonesia	−4.32
	25	Indonesia	−2.34
	31	Korea	−3.96
1998			
January	2	Indonesia	−14.38
	5	Indonesia	−13.08
	6	Indonesia	−11.93
	7	Indonesia	−7.57
	8	Indonesia	−18.31
	12	Thailand	−2.39
	16	Indonesia	−4.01

Table 1. (continued)

Month	Day	Origin Country	Devaluation (%)
1998 (cont'd)			
January	19	Indonesia	−7.87
	20	Indonesia	−4.72
	21	Indonesia	−11.10
	22	Indonesia	−12.87
	23	Indonesia	−12.77
	26	Indonesia	−3.85
February	12	Malaysia	−3.04
	13	Indonesia	−9.30
	16	Indonesia	−3.99
	17	Korea	−2.17
	23	Indonesia	−2.62
March	4	Indonesia	−3.31
	5	Indonesia	−6.84
	6	Indonesia	−4.24
	9	Indonesia	−2.40
April	16	Indonesia	−2.23
	21	The Philippines	−2.49
May	6	Indonesia	−6.12
	7	Indonesia	−4.99
	13	Indonesia	−10.37
	14	Indonesia	−3.24
	19	Indonesia	−12.50
	28	Indonesia	−5.17
June	10	Indonesia	−5.08
	11	Indonesia	−4.66
	12	Indonesia	−4.02
	15	Indonesia	−4.48
	16	Indonesia	−4.32
	17	Indonesia	−6.82
	29	Malaysia	−2.01
August	6	Korea	−3.21
	11	Indonesia	−2.27
September	8	Indonesia	−3.44
	9	Indonesia	−2.22
October	27	Indonesia	−2.08
November	2	Indonesia	−2.74
	3	Indonesia	−4.26
	4	Indonesia	−3.98
December	15	Indonesia	−2.29
1999			
January	13	Indonesia	−3.84
	14	Indonesia	−2.08
March	11	Indonesia	−2.17

Table 2. Origin of Daily Stock Market Shocks, January 1994–May 1999

Month	Day	Origin Country	Devaluation (%)
1994			
January	11	Malaysia	−3.382
	12	Malaysia	−5.068
	13	Malaysia	−4.250
	14	Taiwan	−2.391
	18	Thailand	−2.152
	20	Thailand	−2.176
	25	Malaysia	−2.639
February	7	Thailand	−3.864
	14	Taiwan	−2.215
	16	Hong Kong	−2.223
	25	Hong Kong	−2.338
	28	Taiwan	−2.470
March	1	The Philippines	−2.750
	2	The Philippines	−2.424
	4	The Philippines	−2.392
	9	The Philippines	−2.609
	18	Hong Kong	−2.742
	21	Hong Kong	−3.979
	22	Indonesia	−2.025
April	21	Hong Kong	−2.104
May	4	Hong Kong	−2.459
October	6	Taiwan	−2.850
	11	Taiwan	−4.272
November	1	Taiwan	−3.175
	22	Hong Kong	−2.386
	23	Thailand	−3.433
December	9	Hong Kong	−2.348
1995			
January	3	Hong Kong	−2.213
	12	Thailand	−2.116
	13	The Philippines	−3.186
	23	Thailand	−2.886
February	27	The Philippines	−2.078
April	17	Taiwan	−2.311
July	19	Taiwan	−2.527
	20	Taiwan	−2.620
August	9	Taiwan	−2.260
	11	Taiwan	−2.739
November	20	The Philippines	−2.039
December	14	Korea	−2.117
	18	Korea	−2.323
1996			
January	5	Taiwan	−3.430
	29	Taiwan	−2.700
March	11	Hong Kong	−3.737
	13	Hong Kong	−2.174

Table 2. (continued)

Month	Day	Origin Country	Devaluation (%)
1996 (cont'd)			
May	20	Taiwan	−2.391
July	29	Indonesia	−2.305
October	4	Thailand	−2.053
	8	Thailand	−4.189
	28	The Philippines	−2.633
1997			
January	7	Korea	−2.242
February	4	Thailand	−3.427
	14	Thailand	−2.147
March	4	Thailand	−2.279
	7	Thailand	−4.563
	24	Taiwan	−2.406
April	8	The Philippines	−2.244
	29	The Philippines	−2.622
	30	The Philippines	−2.489
May	15	Thailand	−2.540
	16	Thailand	−2.464
	19	The Philippines	−2.083
June	9	Thailand	−2.023
	19	Thailand	−2.313
	20	Thailand	−3.085
July	9	The Philippines	−2.562
	10	The Philippines	−2.744
August	5	Malaysia	−2.551
	7	Indonesia	−2.163
	15	Indonesia	−2.756
	18	Indonesia	−2.738
	19	Hong Kong	−2.185
	20	Thailand	−2.088
	22	Indonesia	−2.182
	25	Indonesia	−3.810
	26	Thailand	−3.987
	27	Thailand	−2.331
	28	The Philippines	−5.402
	29	Hong Kong	−4.746
September	1	Hong Kong	−4.310
	2	Taiwan	−2.457
	3	Malaysia	−3.418
	4	Malaysia	−2.915
	12	Indonesia	−2.114
	18	Malaysia	−2.165
	22	Malaysia	−2.321
	23	Korea	−2.004

continued

Table 2. (continued)

Month	Day	Origin Country	Devaluation (%)
1997 (cont'd)			
October	3	Indonesia	−2.259
	8	Korea	−2.037
	15	Hong Kong	−2.468
	16	Korea	−2.556
	17	Taiwan	−2.108
	20	Taiwan	−4.357
	21	Hong Kong	−3.435
	22	Hong Kong	−4.658
	23	Hong Kong	−7.569
	24	Malaysia	−2.593
	27	Korea	−4.463
	28	Hong Kong	−8.475
	29	Thailand	−3.535
	30	Korea	−3.169
	31	Korea	−3.107
November	7	Korea	−2.308
	11	Indonesia	−2.291
	12	Hong Kong	−2.433
	17	Korea	−2.234
	18	Malaysia	−3.900
	19	Malaysia	−3.440
	20	Malaysia	−7.229
	21	Indonesia	−2.266
	24	Korea	−4.854
	25	Korea	−3.588
	26	Malaysia	−2.882
	28	Korea	−3.629
December	1	Korea	−3.825
	2	Korea	−3.914
	9	Korea	−2.996
	10	Hong Kong	−2.143
	11	Hong Kong	−3.864
	12	Korea	−5.242
	15	Indonesia	−6.215
	16	Malaysia	−2.677
	23	Korea	−4.231
	24	Korea	−4.260
	25	Korea	−2.291
1998			
January	5	Malaysia	−2.864
	6	Malaysia	−3.444
	7	Hong Kong	−3.818
	8	The Philippines	−3.960
	9	The Philippines	−6.210
	12	Hong Kong	−6.163
	22	The Philippines	−3.084

Table 2. (continued)

Month	Day	Origin Country	Devaluation (%)
1998 (cont'd)			
February	5	Thailand	−2.195
	11	Indonesia	−3.406
	12	Indonesia	−6.178
	13	Indonesia	−2.595
	16	Korea	−3.767
	17	Korea	−2.488
March	5	Korea	−2.656
	6	Korea	−2.545
	9	Korea	−2.859
	30	Korea	−2.207
April	1	Korea	−2.001
	2	Korea	−2.488
	3	Korea	−3.502
	16	Malaysia	−2.068
	23	Korea	−2.432
	29	Indonesia	−2.350
May	1	Indonesia	−2.123
	4	Korea	−3.199
	5	Indonesia	−2.002
	6	Indonesia	−3.264
	11	Korea	−2.100
	12	Korea	−2.518
	13	Indonesia	−3.240
	14	Thailand	−2.181
	18	Indonesia	−2.379
	20	Thailand	−2.587
	25	Korea	−3.730
	26	Korea	−4.838
	27	Hong Kong	−2.803
	28	Hong Kong	−2.065
	29	Thailand	−2.010
June	1	Taiwan	−2.659
	2	Thailand	−2.996
	8	Singapore	−2.042
	10	Hong Kong	−3.175
	11	The Philippines	−2.516
	12	Korea	−4.309
	15	Korea	−4.552
	16	Korea	−3.775
July	10	Malaysia	−2.967
	13	Malaysia	−2.377
	22	Malaysia	−2.065
	23	Korea	−2.386
	29	Malaysia	−2.839

continued

Table 2. (continued)

Month	Day	Origin Country	Devaluation (%)
1998 (*cont'd*)			
August	3	Hong Kong	−2.303
	4	The Philippines	−2.131
	5	Indonesia	−3.063
	6	Indonesia	−2.422
	7	Hong Kong	−2.804
	10	Malaysia	−2.473
	11	Malaysia	−3.917
	12	The Philippines	−3.850
	13	Malaysia	−2.721
	17	Malaysia	−2.448
	18	Korea	−2.081
	21	Malaysia	−2.426
	24	Indonesia	−3.312
	25	Indonesia	−2.018
	27	Malaysia	−2.005
	28	The Philippines	−3.749
	31	Hong Kong	−3.704
September	1	Hong Kong	−3.353
	10	The Philippines	−3.173
	11	The Philippines	−2.242
	15	Indonesia	−4.884
	17	Indonesia	−2.278
	18	Indonesia	−3.559
	21	Indonesia	−4.754
	22	The Philippines	−2.221
October	2	Taiwan	−2.645
	5	Hong Kong	−2.071
	27	Korea	−2.304
November	9	The Philippines	−2.299
	10	The Philippines	−3.259
	11	Thailand	−3.624
	13	Thailand	−2.695
	25	Indonesia	−2.961
December	3	Thailand	−2.821
	4	Thailand	−2.183
	17	Korea	−2.656
1999			
January	5	Taiwan	−2.130
	26	Thailand	−2.368
February	8	Malaysia	−3.783
	9	Korea	−2.451
	10	Thailand	−2.069
	19	Korea	−2.022
May	7	Hong Kong	−2.009
	13	Korea	−2.730
	17	Korea	−2.324
	26	Thailand	−2.586

$$y_{i,t} \begin{cases} > 0 & y_{i,t}^* > a_2 \\ = 0 & a_2 \geq y_{i,t}^* \geq a_1 \\ < 0 & y_{i,t}^* < a_1 \end{cases} \tag{4}$$

We simplify estimating the threshold values for equation (4), by assuming symmetry between those values, so that $a_1 = -a_2$. Then, the log-likelihood function will be

$$\ln L = \sum_{i \in (y^* < a_1)} \ln \left\{ \Phi \left[\frac{y^* + a_1 - x'b}{\sigma} \right] \frac{1}{\sigma} \right\}$$

$$+ \sum_{i \in (a_1 \leq y^* \leq a_2)} \ln \left\{ \Phi \left[\frac{y^* + a_2 - x'b}{\sigma} \right] \frac{1}{\sigma} - \Phi \left[\frac{y^* + a_1 - x'b}{\sigma} \right] \frac{1}{\sigma} \right\}$$

$$+ \sum_{i \in (a_2 < y^*)} \ln \left\{ \Phi \left[\frac{y^* + a_2 - x'b}{\sigma} \right] \frac{1}{\sigma} \right\}.$$

The independent x_i variables used in explaining the high-frequency behavior of returns of one country in equation (3) may be attributed to a number of potential candidates. In the application here, we consider the three types of explanatory variables: first, the difference between the domestic stock prices and other Asian stock prices, denoted SPKAIRI; second, the difference between the home exchange rate and other Asian exchange rates, denoted FXKAIRI; and finally, the origin country for the shocks to exchange rates and stock prices, denoted FXORIGIN and SPORIGIN, respectively. So, in equation (3), $x_i = $ [FXKAIRI$_i$, SPKAIRI$_i$, FXORIGIN, SPORIGIN]'. Details of construction of these indicators are given in the following section.

FXKAIRI$_i$ and SPKAIRI$_i$ account for the difference between the financial market of home country, i, and other Asian countries' financial markets. In the midst of crisis, a country with overvalued stock prices and exchange rates is more likely to be a candidate of speculative attack regardless of the macroeconomic performance of the country. Investors often pull their capital out of countries in the same region after one country is hit by a crisis. The investors' perception of overvaluation depends on several factors, but a relatively smaller rate of depreciation (stock price fall) may be one of the signals that investors use to assess a country as overvalued. The final variables, FXORIGIN$_j$ and SPORIGIN$_j$, are dummy variables that consider the impact of the origin country j; FXORIGIN and SPORIGIN represent vectors of origin shocks across all the countries in the sample.

5. ESTIMATION

In this section, the impact of a large negative return in currencies (equities) in one country on other countries is examined. The model incorporates the idea of contagion—when the five-day weighted average of currency depreciation (stock price fall) breaks the threshold barrier for noise movements, it may be due to the contagion. In the estimation, we examine whether the differences between the domestic stock returns and other Asian stock returns (domestic exchange rate changes and other Asian exchange rate changes) and that of the origin country were statistically more likely to be associated with the possibility of contagion. The dependent variable used in the estimation was estimated using the friction model of the previous section and is thus available for all countries, whether contagion exists or not.

In examining the effects of contagion we are particularly interested in examining the cross-border effects of (infrequent) large changes in the exchange rates or stock prices on those of other countries. The impact of relative changes in the exchange rates (or stock prices) on today's exchange rate change (or stock return) is used to control for small (everyday) changes.

The daily changes of the stock prices and exchange rates in one country may follow a two-stage process. The first stage is an autoregressive response to the previous day's movements in exchange rates and stock prices relative to other countries, and the second is a nonlinear response to large shocks. With regard to the autoregressive response, if the currency of one country depreciates with other currencies in the region, trade competitiveness and corporate profitability do not change, so that the current day's exchange rate will be little affected. On the other hand, if depreciation (stock price declines) occurs in only one country, that country experiences an idiosyncratic shock that has trade competitiveness implications. The market may take some time to digest the information, and investors will likely respond to change the exchange rate or the stock prices on the following day. Therefore, whether the exchange rate changes (or stock price changes) are regionwide or idiosyncratic has different implications for today's exchange rate (or the stock price). We will model this inference by choosing the relative exchange rate change as the independent variable, while the currency (or the stock price) of one country is the dependent variable.

In the second stage, large depreciations (or sharp declines in the stock prices) have nonlinear effects on the exchange rates and stock prices of other countries as well as the country of origin. Both the nonlinearity and identification of origin countries are captured by defining explanatory variables based on declines in the relevant asset price beyond a threshold value. These large shocks have cross-border implications, as the shocks of the different origin countries may have different effects. Hence, the large changes in the exchange rates (or the stock prices) of different countries are included as separate independent variables.

The regression model we employ in this section is a Tobit model. The general formulation of the model is given as follows:

$$y_i^* = x_i' b_i + e_i$$

$$y_{i,t} \begin{cases} = y_{i,t}^* & \text{if} \quad y_{i,t}^* > a_1 \\ = 0 & \text{if} \quad y_{i,t}^* \leq a_1 \end{cases}$$

where a_1 is the threshold value. The variable y represents the collection of all y_i. The probability that $y = 0$ is calculated as

$$\text{Prob}(y = 0)$$
$$= \text{Prob}(y^* \le 0)$$
$$= \text{Prob}(x'b + e \le 0)$$
$$= \text{Prob}(e \le -x'b)$$
$$= \Phi(-x'b/\sigma).$$

Then, the likelihood that $y = y^*$ can be rewritten as

$$f(y = y^* | y^* > a_1)$$
$$= \text{Prob}(y^* > a_1)$$
$$= f(y = y^*)$$
$$= \Phi\left[\left(\frac{y - x'b}{\sigma}\right)\right]\frac{1}{\sigma}.$$

The log likelihood for this Tobit regression model is

$$\ln L = \sum_{i \in (y_i = 0)} \ln\left\{\Phi\left[\frac{-x'b}{\sigma}\right]\right\} + \sum_{i \in (y_i = y_i^*)} \left(\ln\left\{\Phi\left[\frac{-x'b}{\sigma}\right]\right\} - \ln \sigma\right),$$

where $x = $ [FXKAIRI,SPKAIRI,FXORIGIN,SPORIGIN]. The variables FXKAIRI and SPKAIRI are used to control for small changes between the home and other Asian countries' currency and equity returns. More precisely, they are defined as a difference between the weighted cumulative change index of equation (2) for the home country and the averaged weighted cumulative change index of other Asian countries. That is,

$$\text{FXKAIRI}_{i,t} = wfx_{i,t} - \frac{1}{7}\sum_{j=1, j\neq i}^{7} wfx_{j,t}$$

$$\text{SPKAIRI}_{i,t} = wsp_{i,t} - \frac{1}{7}\sum_{j=1, j\neq i}^{7} wsp_{j,t}.$$

FXORIGIN and SPORIGIN are dummy variables representing the presence of an origin shock in a particular country and market. While FXKAIRI, SPKAIRI, and SPORIGIN are 8×1 vectors, FXORIGIN is a 6×1 vector because the (five-day averaged) exchange rates of Hong Kong and Singapore did not show depreciations over 2 percent, and therefore these two countries were excluded from "origin."

Examining the estimated coefficients, the following insights are obtained. The stock price movements are autocorrelated (SPKAIRI has a positive coefficient)—that is, loss of confidence in the stock market tends to be carried over to the next day in the same country. A depreciation of a country on one day may result in stock price declines on the following day because the depreciation is regarded as loss of confidence and triggers the monetary tightening in the country. That is, the depreciation affects adversely the stock market of the country on the following day (FXKAIRI has a negative coefficient). The stock price movement is also adversely affected by several factors, such as the large declines in the value of currency or the stock prices of other countries of the previous day. That is, a shock in the origin country has a significant impact on stock price movements (FXORIGIN and SPORIGIN have positive coefficients).

The decline in stock prices due to loss of confidence in the country tends to have a negative impact on the exchange rate of that country the following day. That is, the stock price decline results in depreciation (SPKAIRO has a negative coefficient). The exchange rate tends to show an autoregressive nature. That is, a depreciation in one country results in a depreciation in that same country the following day (FXKAIRI has a positive coefficient). The exchange rate movements suffer contagious effects from stock markets and foreign exchange markets of other countries. In particular, the exchange rates are adversely affected by large declines in the value of the currency or the stock prices in an origin country on the previous day (FXORIGIN and SPORIGIN have positive coefficients).

6. RESULTS

Table 3 shows the estimated threshold, a_1, for both exchange rates and stock prices. The results support the contention that changes in the exchange rate or stock price exceeding 1 percent in either direction can be regarded as substantially different from noise over the sample period. In the Tobit estimation below, we set the threshold at 1 percent, in contrast to the 2 percent threshold used in tables 1 and 2.

Table 3. Estimated Threshold for the Exchange Rate and Stock Prices for Three Sample Periods: 1997–99, 1997–98, and 1998–99

	Exchange Rates			Stock Prices		
	1997–99	1997–98	1998–99	1997–99	1997–98	1998–99
Hong Kong	0.010***	0.010***	0.009***	0.010***	0.010***	0.008***
	(0.001)	(0.001)	(0.001)	(0.001)	(0.001)	(0.001)
Indonesia	0.010***	0.011***	0.010***	0.010***	0.011***	0.010***
	(0.001)	(0.001)	(0.001)	(0.001)	(0.001)	(0.001)
Korea	0.011***	0.012***	0.010***	0.011***	0.012***	0.010***
	(0.001)	(0.001)	(0.001)	(0.001)	(0.001)	(0.001)
Malaysia	0.009***	0.010***	0.008***	0.009***	0.010***	0.008***
	(0.001)	(0.001)	(0.002)	(0.001)	(0.001)	(0.002)
The Philippines	0.008***	0.007***	0.008***	0.008***	0.008***	0.008***
	(0.001)	(0.001)	(0.001)	(0.001)	(0.001)	(0.001)
Singapore	0.007***	0.007***	0.007***	0.007***	0.007***	0.007***
	(0.000)	(0.001)	(0.001)	(0.000)	(0.001)	(0.001)
Taiwan	0.007***	0.007***	0.007***	0.006***	0.006***	0.007***
	(0.000)	(0.000)	(0.001)	(0.000)	(0.000)	(0.001)
Thailand	0.008***	0.009***	0.008***	0.008***	0.008***	0.008***
	(0.001)	(0.001)	(0.001)	(0.001)	(0.001)	(0.001)

Note: Standard errors in parentheses.
***Significant at the 1 percent level.

The Tobit estimates are reported in tables 4 to 9. We run regressions for three sample periods: the entire sample (1 July 1997–7 July 1999), the first-half sample (1 July 1997–18 June 1998), and the second-half sample (19 June 1998–7 July 1999).

The dependent variable takes the value 1 if the fluctuations of exchange rates (stock prices) exceed 1 percent and 0 otherwise. In the case of stock price changes there are sufficient changes exceeding 1 percent to estimate the Tobit model for each country in each sample period. However, in the case where the dependent variable is a change in exchange rates, there is an insufficient number of changes exceeding the threshold value in the second-half sample for any country but Indonesia, consistent with table 1. Hence the exchange rate Tobit model is estimated for all countries for the total and first-half samples, but only for Indonesia in the second-half sample.

6.1   Results for Exchange Rates

The estimates of the parameters on the exchange rate are shown in tables 4 through 6. Table 4 reports results for the entire sample period, table 5 reports the first-half sample results, and table 6 reports the second-half sample results. The effect of the performance of the local stock market relative to regional stock markets (the variable SP_i) has a significant coefficient in two countries of the five considered during the first-half period, and is significant for Indonesia in the second-half sample. In Malaysia (third column of table 4), the decline in relative stock prices led to further depreciation of the exchange rate. In Indonesia the fall in local relative stock prices (SP_i) contributed to falls in the exchange rate even after mid-1998 (table 6).

The effect of the relative exchange rates in the region (the FX_i coefficient) is significant in all countries for the total period and first-half period, but insignificant in Indonesia in the second half of the sample. The coefficient estimates are all positive, indicating that the decline in exchange rate accelerated its depreciation.

The effects of the origin of the shocks in stock prices (the SPORIG variables) are relatively minor. The exceptions are the generally significant effect of stock price shocks originating from Hong Kong and the effects of almost all stock price shocks on the Thai exchange rate (the final column of table 4). Given the devaluation of the Thai baht, the downturn in the stock markets in the region weakened the exchange rate of Thailand. With this exception, the contagious impact of the origin countries of stock price shocks on exchange rates was found to be relatively small.

In contrast to the stock price origin, the impact of the origin of the exchange rate shock is remarkable. The effect of the FXORIG variables for shocks originating in Indonesia and Korea appears to be significant in most countries.

In summary, the Asian exchange rates during the crisis were found to be particularly vulnerable to Hong Kong stock price shocks, and shocks originating with Indonesian and Korean exchange rates. In the case of the Thai

Table 4. Estimated Coefficients from Tobit Estimation with Exchange Rates as the Dependent Variable 1997–99

	Indonesia	Korea	Malaysia	The Philippines	Thailand
SPKAIRI	0.045	−0.078	−0.276***	0.071	0.150**
	(0.205)	(0.201)	(0.113)	(0.190)	(0.075)
FXKAIRI	0.585***	0.837***	0.565***	0.785***	0.675***
	(0.130)	(0.256)	(0.202)	(0.247)	(0.169)
SPORIGIN—Hong Kong	0.028***	0.019**	0.011**	0.0074	0.007**
	(0.011)	(0.010)	(0.005)	(0.009)	(0.004)
SPORIGIN—Indonesia	0.019*	0.013*	0.003	0.006	0.010***
	(0.013)	(0.009)	(0.005)	(0.008)	(0.004)
SPORIGIN—Korea	−0.003	0.013*	0.004	0.008	0.008***
	(0.009)	(0.009)	(0.004)	(0.006)	(0.003)
SPORIGIN—Malaysia	−0.004	0.011	0.003	0.012*	0.008**
	(0.013)	(0.011)	(0.005)	(0.007)	(0.004)
SPORIGIN—The Philippines	−0.021	0.008	−0.001	0.013	0.010**
	(0.019)	(0.015)	(0.008)	(0.011)	(0.005)
SPORIGIN—Singapore	−0.223	−0.147	−0.065	0.036**	−0.073
	(1091.47)	(2983.27)	(123)	(0.018)	(13138.4)
SPORIGIN—Taiwan	0.008	−0.155	0.008	−0.122	0.019
	(0.023)	(922)	(0.009)	(1210)	(0.006)***
SPORIGIN—Thailand	−0.003	−0.149	0.012**	−0.132	0.010**
	(0.015)	(246)	(0.006)	(1970)	(0.006)
FXORIGIN—Indonesia	0.033***	0.020***	0.017***	0.023***	0.012***
	(0.010)	(0.007)	(0.003)	(0.006)	(0.003)

132

FXORIGIN—Korea	0.058***	0.025**	0.012**	0.023***	0.014***
	(0.013)	(0.0013)	(0.006)	(0.009)	(0.004)
FXORIGIN—Malaysia	0.075***	-0.153	-0.088	-0.112	-0.065
	(0.031)	(834)	(348)	(641)	(189)
FXORIGIN—The Philippines	-0.204	-0.141	-0.1012?	-0.009	-0.068
	(0.005)	(717)	(0.000)	(0.020)	(877)
FXORIGIN—Taiwan	-0.219	0.016	0.015	0.025	0.002
	(0.078)	(2000)	(0.017)	(1590)	(0.014)
FXORIGIN—Thailand	-0.237	-0.138	-0.000	0.012	0.009*
	(305)	(417)	(0.009)	(0.012)	(0.006)
Sigma	0.040***	0.029***	0.014***	0.022***	0.012***
	(0.003)	(0.004)	(0.002)	(0.003)	(0.001)

Note: Standard errors in parentheses.
***Significant at the 1 percent level.
**Significant at the 5 percent level.
*Significant at the 10 percent level.

Table 5. Estimated Coefficients from Tobit Estimation with Exchange Rates as the Dependent Variable 1997–98

	Indonesia	Korea	Malaysia	The Philippines	Thailand
SPKAIRI	0.351	−0.002	−0.348***	0.108	0.138**
	(0.274)	(0.218)	(0.135)	(0.210)	(0.075)
FXKAIRI	0.585***	0.878***	0.412**	0.698***	0.518***
	(0.145)	(0.255)	(0.181)	(0.240)	(0.151)
SPORIGIN—Hong Kong	0.031***	0.015*	0.008*	0.004	0.005*
	(0.001)	(0.011)	(0.005)	(0.009)	(0.004)
SPORIGIN—Indonesia	0.025*	0.010	−0.001	0.004	0.008**
	(0.014)	(0.010)	(0.005)	(0.008)	(0.004)
SPORIGIN—Korea	−0.006	0.008	0.000	0.004	0.006**
	(0.010)	(0.010)	(0.004)	(0.007)	(0.003)
SPORIGIN—Malaysia	−0.005	0.005	−0.001	0.009	0.006*
	(0.001)	(0.012)	(0.006)	(0.008)	(0.004)
SPORIGIN—The Philippines	−0.005	0.006	−0.004	0.015	0.010**
	(0.015)	(0.017)	(0.008)	(0.013)	(0.005)
SPORIGIN—Singapore	−0.236	−0.145	−0.077	−0.136	−0.071
	(828)	(1577.26)	(1168.77)	(89172.8)	(14703.0)
SPORIGIN—Taiwan	0.013	−0.153	0.006	−0.114	0.020**
	(0.028)	(499)	(0.009)	(248)	(0.007)
SPORIGIN—Thailand	0.009	−0.159	0.010*	−0.122	0.009*
	(0.019)	(373)	(0.006)	(291)	(0.006)
FXORIGIN—Indonesia	0.027**	0.017**	0.013***	0.019***	0.008***
	(0.012)	(0.008)	(0.003)	(0.006)	(0.003)

FXORIGIN—Korea	0.050***	0.018*	0.007	0.017**	0.010***
	(0.013)	(0.013)	(0.005)	(0.009)	(0.004)
FXORIGIN—Malaysia	0.073**	-0.154	-0.080	-0.115	-0.064
	(0.033)	(659)	(163)	(471)	(128)
FXORIGIN—The Philippines	-0.220	-0.142	-0.083	-0.010	-0.007
	(462)	(586)	(4670)	(0.020)	(483)
FXORIGIN—Taiwan	-0.247	0.014	0.011	0.014	-0.005
	(785)	(1030)	(0.016)	(654)	(0.013)
FXORIGIN—Thailand	-0.261	-0.139	-0.005	0.077	0.008*
	(288)	(3.01)	(0.009)	(0.018)	(0.006)
Sigma	0.042***	0.028***	0.013***	0.021***	0.011***
	(0.003)	(0.004)	(0.002)	(0.003)	(0.001)

Note: Standard errors in parentheses.
***Significant at the 1 percent level.
**Significant at the 5 percent level.
*Significant at the 10 percent level.

Table 6. **Estimated Coefficients from Tobit Estimation with Exchange Rates as the Dependent Variable 1998–99**

	Indonesia
SPKAIRI	−0.494**
	(0.222)
FXKAIRI	0.264
	(0.216)
SPORIGIN—Hong Kong	−0.132
	(9830)
SPORIGIN—Indonesia	−0.013
	(0.014)
SPORIGIN—Korea	−0.132
	(868)
SPORIGIN—Malaysia	n.a.
SPORIGIN—The Philippines	n.a.
SPORIGIN—Singapore	n.a.
SPORIGIN—Taiwan	n.a.
SPORIGIN—Thailand	−0.102
	(276)
FXORIGIN—Indonesia	0.021**
	(0.001)
Sigma	0.012*
	(0.004)

Note: Standard errors in parentheses; n.a. indicates an insufficient number of observations.
**Significant at the 5 percent level.
*Significant at the 1 percent level.

baht, exchange rate shocks originating in almost all stock markets were significant.

6.2 Results for Stock Prices

The estimation results for stock prices are shown in tables 7 through 9. Table 7 reports results of the entire sample period, table 8 reports the first-half results, and table 9 reports the latter-half sample results.

The effect of the relative stock market prices (SP$_i$) is significant at standard levels of significance in six of the eight countries examined during the first-half period, and for all but Malaysia in the second-half sample. The parameter sign is as expected, indicating that decreasing stock prices led to a further decline. The relative exchange rate effect (FX$_i$) coefficient is significant in five of the eight countries in all sample periods.

The impact of the origin of the stock price shock (SPORIG) on stock prices differs across the sample periods. During the first-half period, shocks sourced from Hong Kong, Korea, Malaysia, and the Philippines are the most prominently statistically significant. In the second-half sample, Indonesia, Singapore, and Taiwan are the most likely to be sources of statistically significant stock price shocks. These results are consistent with the fact that the Hong Kong stock market was targeted in a speculative attack in October 1997 and the Korean stock price index declined sharply in late 1997, while stock prices in Indonesia remained unstable even after 1998 due to its economic and political instability.

The effects on the stock prices of the origin of exchange rate shocks (FXORIG) identify Indonesia, Korea, and Thailand as the three main originators of shocks that have statistically significant effects on others. The effect of the exchange rate origin on stock prices is dramatically reduced for the latter-half sample period, reflecting the return of stability to the foreign exchange markets in the region.

In summary, our estimation results clearly show the evidence of contagion between an exchange rate and a stock price of the same country or of different countries during the crisis period. It also shows that the contagious impact on exchange rates was mainly due to the Hong Kong stock price fall and the Indonesian and Korean depreciations. In contrast, stock prices are found to be more influenced by both exchange rate and stock price shocks from other countries.

6.3 Stylizing the Results

Tables 10 and 11 summarize the estimation results. The panels provide the parameter signs and significance levels of the results, with boldface entries representing significant coefficients of the expected sign. Focus initially on the first-half, or crisis, sample, for the crisis period of July 1997 to June 1998 shown in table 10. Counting the number of bold entries in the lower half of that table, it is evident that shocks originating with exchange rates affect both other countries' exchange rates and other countries' stock prices. Indonesian- and Korean-sourced exchange rate shocks were particularly influential on Asian currency and stock markets.

In contrast, counting the bold entries in the upper half of table 10, it is apparent that the contagious effect of stock price–originated shocks on other countries' stock prices seems relatively minor, compared with the stock price effect on exchange rates. As discussed in the previous two subsections, the contagious links between stock and currency markets are asymmetric. We find contagion among exchange rates and from stock prices to exchange rates, but relatively minor evidence of contagion among stock prices.

It is obvious from the final column of table 10 that the Thai exchange rate was affected by the stock price movements not only from domestic stock prices, but also by other Asian stock price behaviors. One might conjecture a process of the collapse of exchange rates in Thailand as the gradual deterioration of fundamentals led to a stock price fall that finally triggered the currency crisis of July 1997. In addition, the battered stock markets in Asia accelerated the continuing fall of exchange rates after August 1997.

By examining the stock price reactions, we have gained new insights into contagion during this crisis. The results show that the Hong Kong stock price was affected by the Indonesian, Korean, and Thai currency

Table 7. Estimated Coefficients from Tobit Estimation with Stock Returns as the Dependent Variable 1997–99

	Hong Kong	Indonesia	Korea	Malaysia	The Philippines	Singapore	Taiwan	Thailand
SPKAIRI	0.356***	0.402***	0.346***	0.123***	0.237***	0.298***	−0.070	0.056
	(0.086)	(0.072)	(0.060)	(0.052)	(0.066)	(0.081)	(0.060)	(0.048)
FXKAIRI	−1.210***	0.148***	0.171**	−0.006	−0.118	−0.821***	−0.530***	0.068
	(0.179)	(0.045)	(0.087)	(0.122)	(0.097)	(0.153)	(0.138)	(0.101)
SPORIGIN	−0.005	0.007**	−0.003	0.006**	0.005**	0.002	−0.002	0.004*
Hong Kong	(0.004)	(0.004)	(0.004)	(0.003)	(0.003)	(0.003)	(0.003)	(0.003)
SPORIGIN	−0.001	0.001	−0.000	−0.001	0.002	−0.005*	−0.009***	0.002
Indonesia	(0.003)	(0.004)	(0.003)	(0.003)	(0.003)	(0.003)	(0.003)	(0.003)
SPORIGIN	−0.006**	−0.004	−0.002	0.000	−0.006***	−0.004**	−0.011***	0.002
Korea	(0.003)	(0.003)	(0.003)	(0.003)	(0.002)	(0.002)	(0.003)	(0.002)
SPORIGIN	−0.010**	−0.000	0.002	0.007**	0.001	−0.009***	−0.008***	−0.004
Malaysia	(0.004)	(0.004)	(0.003)	(0.003)	(0.003)	(0.004)	(0.003)	(0.003)
SPORIGIN	0.006	−0.001	0.003	0.005*	0.003	0.006**	−0.004	0.002
The Philippines	(0.005)	(0.005)	(0.004)	(0.004)	(0.004)	(0.003)	(0.004)	(0.004)
SPORIGIN	−0.005	−0.098	0.004	−0.093	0.004	0.002	−0.004	−0.078
Singapore	(0.011)	(333)	(0.011)	(404)	(0.009)	(0.009)	(0.008)	(205)
SPORIGIN	0.001	−0.004	0.000	0.006	−0.003	−0.003	0.010**	−0.002
Taiwan	(0.008)	(0.008)	(0.007)	(0.006)	(0.006)	(0.006)	(0.005)	(0.006)
SPORIGIN	−0.013**	−0.014**	−0.011**	−0.009**	−0.007**	−0.009**	−0.009**	0.001
Thailand	(0.006)	(0.006)	(0.005)	(0.005)	(0.004)	(0.004)	(0.004)	(0.003)
FXORIGIN	−0.021***	−0.014***	−0.002	−0.004*	0.001	−0.011***	−0.012***	−0.005**

	(1)	(2)	(3)	(4)	(5)	(6)	(7)
Indonesia	(0.004)	(0.002)	(0.002)	(0.002)	(0.003)	(0.003)	(0.002)
FXORIGIN	−0.018***	−0.001	0.001	−0.009**	−0.020***	−0.012***	−0.002
Korea	(0.006)	(0.005)	(0.004)	(0.005)	(0.006)	(0.005)	(0.004)
FXORIGIN	−0.010	−0.005	0.001	−0.000	0.002	−0.069	−0.003
Malaysia	(0.012)	(0.011)	(0.011)	(0.010)	(0.009)	(210)	(0.010)
FXORIGIN	−0.102	−0.003	−0.013	−0.077	−0.005	n.a.	−0.000
The Philippines	(323)	(204)	(0.011)	(131)	(0.010)	n.a.	(0.009)
FXORIGIN	0.010	−0.092	−0.000	0.005	0.004		0.013
Taiwan	(0.017)	(465)	(0.015)	(0.013)	(0.013)		(0.014)
FXORIGIN	−0.028***	−0.114	−0.019***	−0.012**	−0.087	−0.010**	−0.010*
Thailand	(0.009)	(2129.7)	(0.008)	(0.006)	(332)	(0.006)	(0.006)
Sigma	0.015***	0.015***	0.014***	0.012***	0.011***	0.010***	0.012***
	(0.001)	(0.001)	(0.001)	(0.001)	(0.001)	(0.001)	(0.001)

Note: Standard errors in parentheses; n.a. indicates an insufficient number of observations.
***Significant at the 1 percent level.
**Significant at the 5 percent level.
*Significant at the 10 percent level.

Table 8. Estimated Coefficients from Tobit Estimation with Stock Returns as the Dependent Variable 1997–98

	Hong Kong	Indonesia	Korea	Malaysia	The Philippines	Singapore	Taiwan	Thailand
SPKAIRI	0.459***	0.570***	0.289***	0.385***	0.273***	0.356**	0.063	0.011
	(0.121)	(0.106)	(0.084)	(0.085)	(0.094)	(0.123)	(0.093)	(0.062)
FXKAIRI	−0.984***	0.108**	0.237***	0.013	−0.094	−0.789***	−0.556***	0.091
	(0.200)	(0.050)	(0.102)	(0.120)	(0.103)	(0.178)	(0.166)	(0.112)
SPORIGIN	−0.006	0.009**	−0.001	0.006**	0.008***	0.004	−0.001	0.003
	(0.006)	(0.004)	(0.005)	(0.003)	(0.003)	(0.003)	(0.003)	(0.003)
Hong Kong SPORIGIN	0.000	−0.003	0.001	0.002	0.003	−0.003	−0.010**	0.005*
	(0.000)	(0.005)	(0.005)	(0.003)	(0.003)	(0.004)	(0.003)	(0.003)
Indonesia SPORIGIN	0.000	−0.001	0.001	0.003	0.003	−0.003	−0.009***	0.002
	(0.000)	(0.004)	(0.004)	(0.003)	(0.003)	(0.003)	(0.004)	(0.003)
Korea SPORIGIN	−0.004	−0.002	0.001	0.001	−0.005**	−0.009**	−0.009**	−0.004
	(0.004)	(0.005)	(0.004)	(0.002)	(0.003)	(0.004)	(0.004)	(0.003)
Malaysia SPORIGIN	−0.007	0.005	0.002	0.002	0.001	0.012***	−0.004	−0.000
	(0.005)	(0.006)	(0.004)	(0.004)	(0.003)	(0.004)	(0.004)	(0.004)
The Philippines SPORIGIN	0.010*	0.005	0.005	0.009**	0.008*		−0.004	−0.000
	(0.006)	(0.006)	(0.006)	(0.004)	(0.005)		(0.005)	(0.005)
Singapore SPORIGIN	−0.003	−0.105	−0.093	−0.086	−0.079	−0.083	−0.073	−0.082
	(0.017)	(1008.13)	(414)	(467)	(335)	(210)	(621)	(244)
Taiwan SPORIGIN	−0.001	−0.002	0.006	0.012*	−0.005	−0.007	0.016***	0.005
	(0.011)	(0.011)	(0.009)	(0.007)	(0.008)	(0.009)	(0.007)	(0.008)
Thailand SPORIGIN	−0.006	−0.009	−0.006	−0.000	−0.002	−0.007*	−0.005	0.004
	(0.008)	(0.007)	(0.006)	(0.005)	(0.005)	(0.005)	(0.005)	(0.005)
FXORIGIN	−0.020***	−0.012**	−0.003	−0.003*	0.000	−0.011***	−0.013***	−0.004**

	(1)	(2)	(3)	(4)	(5)	(6)	(7)	(8)
Indonesia	(0.005)	(0.004)	(0.003)	(0.002)	(0.002)	(0.003)	(0.003)	(0.003)
FXORIGIN	-0.018*** (0.007)	-0.006 (0.006)	-0.005 (0.006)	-0.001 (0.004)	-0.010** (0.005)	-0.021*** (0.006)	-0.013*** (0.006)	-0.003 (0.004)
Korea	-0.009 (0.014)	-0.014 (0.014)	-0.007 (0.013)	-0.003 (0.010)	0.000 (0.010)	0.001 (0.010)	-0.077 (334)	-0.005 (0.010)
FXORIGIN	0.111 (320)	-0.102 (208)	-0.003 (0.012)	-0.012 (0.010)	-0.079 (142)	-0.005 (0.010)	-0.088 (34198.8)	0.000 (0.009)
Malaysia	0.014 (0.020)	-0.094 (425)	-0.005 (0.018)	-0.007 (0.014)	0.008 (0.015)	0.008 (0.015)	n.a.	0.006 (0.015)
FXORIGIN	-0.030*** (0.011)	-0.114 (1354.66)	-0.098 (171)	-0.020*** (0.007)	-0.013** (0.006)	-0.096 (459)	-0.011** (0.006)	-0.011** (0.007)
The Philippines								
FXORIGIN								
Taiwan								
FXORIGIN								
Thailand								
Sigma	0.017*** (0.001)	0.016*** (0.001)	0.015*** (0.001)	0.012*** (0.001)	0.012*** (0.001)	0.012*** (0.001)	0.011*** (0.001)	0.013*** (0.001)

Note: Standard errors in parentheses; n.a. indicates an insufficient number of observations.

***Significant at the 1 percent level.

**Significant at the 5 percent level.

*Significant at the 10 percent level.

Table 9. Estimated Coefficients from Tobit Estimation with the Stock Returns as Dependent Variable 1998–99

	Hong Kong	Indonesia	Korea	Malaysia	The Philippines	Singapore	Taiwan	Thailand
SPKAIRI	0.115*	0.198**	0.344***	−0.034	0.168**	0.193**	−0.124**	0.113*
	(0.081)	(0.085)	(0.067)	(0.073)	(0.080)	(0.088)	(0.073)	(0.066)
FXKAIRI	−2.492***	0.261***	−0.132	−0.537**	−0.061	−0.873***	−0.993***	0.054
	(0.465)	(0.102)	(0.207)	(0.322)	(0.271)	(0.286)	(0.359)	(0.283)
SPORIGIN Hong Kong	0.003	0.001	−0.060	0.004	−0.004	0.001	−0.002	0.005
	(0.005)	(0.007)	(339)	(0.008)	(0.005)	(0.004)	(0.005)	(0.004)
SPORIGIN Indonesia	−0.000	0.010**	−0.002	−0.017**	0.002	−0.006	−0.005	−0.007*
	(0.004)	(0.005)	(0.004)	(0.009)	(0.004)	(0.005)	(0.004)	(0.005)
SPORIGIN Korea	−0.063	−0.81	−0.007*	−0.119	−0.010**	−0.008*	n.a.	−0.002
	(56.1)	(90.7)	(0.004)	(14456.7)	(0.006)	(0.005)		(0.004)
SPORIGIN Malaysia	−0.073	0.007	0.005	0.005	0.003	−0.007*	−0.003	−0.003
	(11754.4)	(0.006)	(0.004)	(0.007)	(0.005)	(0.005)	(0.004)	(0.005)
SPORIGIN The Philippines	0.001	−0.014*	0.002	−0.006	−0.004	−0.005	−0.002	0.005
	(0.004)	(0.009)	(0.005)	(0.008)	(0.006)	(0.005)	(0.004)	(0.005)
SPORIGIN Singapore	−0.002	−0.088	0.012*	n.a.	0.019	0.021***	0.001	−0.066
	(0.009)	(7314.64)	(0.009)		(0.010)	(0.009)	(0.008)	(2762.63)
SPORIGIN Taiwan	0.009*	−0.003	n.a.	−0.006	0.001	0.003	−0.002	n.a.
	(0.007)	(0.010)		(0.012)	(0.008)	(0.007)	(0.007)	
SPORIGIN Thailand	−0.059	−0.082	n.a.	−0.107	−0.014**	−0.007*	−0.066	−0.003
	(259)	(112)		(922)	(0.006)	(0.005)	(16009.7)	(0.004)
FXORIGIN	−0.024***	−0.017***	−0.003	−0.098	0.001	−0.014***	−0.011***	−0.011**

	(0.006)	(0.007)	(0.004)	(71.3)	(0.004)	(0.005)	(0.004)	(0.005)
Indonesia								
FXORIGIN	n.a.	n.a.	n.a.	n.a.	n.a.	n.a.	n.a.	n.a.
Korea								
FXORIGIN	n.a.	n.a.	n.a.	n.a.	n.a.	n.a.	n.a.	n.a.
Malaysia								
FXORIGIN	n.a.	n.a.	n.a.	n.a.	n.a.	n.a.	n.a.	n.a.
The Philippines								
FXORIGIN	n.a.	n.a.	n.a.	n.a.	n.a.	n.a.	n.a.	n.a.
Taiwan								
FXORIGIN	n.a.	n.a.	n.a.	n.a.	n.a.	n.a.	n.a.	n.a.
Thailand								
Sigma	0.008***	0.013***	0.009***	0.015***	0.010***	0.008***	0.008***	0.009***
	(0.001)	(0.001)	(0.001)	(0.002)	(0.001)	(0.001)	(0.001)	(0.001)

Note: Standard errors in parentheses; n.a. indicates an insufficient number of observations.
***Significant at the 1 percent level.
**Significant at the 5 percent level.
*Significant at the 10 percent level.

Table 10. Contagion Effects for Sample Period July 1997 to June 1998

From	To	Stock Price								Exchange Rate				
		Hong Kong	Indonesia	Korea	Malaysia	The Philippines	Singapore	Taiwan	Thailand	Indonesia	Korea	Malaysia	The Philippines	Thailand
Stock price origin	Hong Kong	−	+**	−	+**	+***	+	−	+	+***	+*	+*	+	+*
	Indonesia	+	−	+	+	+	−	−**	+**	+**	+	−	+	+**
	Korea	−	−	+	+	−**	−	−***	+	−	+	+	+	+***
	Malaysia	−	−	+	−	+	−**	−**	−	−	+	−	+	+*
	The Philippines	+*	+	+	+*	+	+***	n.a.	+	+**	+	−	+	+**
	Singapore	−	−	−	−	−	−	+**	+	+	−	−	−	−
	Taiwan	−	−	+	+*	−	−	+**	+	+	−	−	−	+***
	Thailand	−	−	−	−	−	−*	+	−	−	−	+*	−	+*
Exchange rate origin	Indonesia	−***	−***	−	−	+	−***	−***	+	+**	+**	+***	+***	+***
	Korea	−***	−	−	−	−**	−***	−***	−**	+***	+*	+	+**	+***
	Malaysia	−	−	−	−	+	+	−	−	+**	−	−	−	−
	The Philippines	−	−	−	−	−	−	+	+	−	−	−	−	−
	Taiwan	+	−	+	+	+	+	n.a.	+	−	+	+	+	−
	Thailand	−***	−	−	−***	−**	−	−**	−**	−	−	−	+	+*

Note: Standard errors in parentheses; n.a. indicates an insufficient number of observations.
***Significant at the 1 percent level.
**Significant at the 5 percent level.
*Significant at the 10 percent level.

depreciations during the crisis. Although Hong Kong was said to have avoided contagion during the crisis in terms of the exchange rate regime, it is apparent from these findings that Hong Kong also suffered contagion from the crisis in terms of transmissions from currencies to stock prices.

Surprisingly, neither stock prices nor exchange rates of other Asian countries had a contagious effect on the Korean exchange rate.[8] Only Hong Kong stock prices significantly affected the Korean exchange rate in the results. Although a more careful examination of Korean financial markets is required, the results support the common perception that the Korean crisis in 1997 was the simultaneous occurrence of twin (currency and banking) crises and was not a fundamentals-based crisis.

Table 11 is the same summary table for the period of July 1998 to June 1999. This is a period of recovery from the bottom of currency crisis for most countries. Only Indonesia was still in turmoil. There was no contagion to any exchange rate but the Indonesian rupiah from itself. There were some adverse contagious effects from the Indonesian rupiah to stock prices of other countries (except Korea, Malaysia, and the Philippines). There were some contagion effects from stock price declines in one country to stock price declines of other countries (such as Korea to Singapore and the Philippines), but no widespread pattern was detected.

7. CONCLUDING REMARKS

In this chapter we analyze the comovement of the exchange rates and stock prices among eight Asian countries during the Asian currency crisis of 1997–99 with a view to identifying contagious transmissions between them. New insights into contagion in the crisis are gained by examining the stock price reactions and exchange rate movements in a common framework. In this chapter we use a friction model and a Tobit model to analyze the impact of a negative shock in one asset price on others. In estimation, we take into account the difference between mildly affected countries and severely affected countries, large declines in the exchange rates (or stock prices) relative to others in the region, and the asset price trend in each country.

Our major findings are as follows. First, the Indonesian, Korean, and Thai exchange rates had large impacts on the stock prices of other countries, while other currencies did not affect stock prices elsewhere. Second, the Hong Kong stock market was significantly affected by the depreciation of the Indonesian, Korean, and Thai currencies. Therefore, contagion during the Asian crisis can be said to have a great impact even in Hong Kong. Third, the Indonesian and Korean, but not Thai, exchange rates had impacts on other currencies in the region. This may be contrary to casual observation that the currency crisis spread from Thailand to other countries in the second half of 1997. Fourth, contagion among stock markets was not significant for most pairs of countries. Fifth, the Hong Kong stock price was found to have substantial effects on Asian exchange rates in the midst of

Table 11. Contagion Effects for Sample Period July 1998 to June 1999

		Stock Price								Exchange Rate
From	To	Hong Kong	Indonesia	Korea	Malaysia	The Philippines	Singapore	Taiwan	Thailand	Indonesia
Stock price origin	Hong Kong	+	+	−	+	−	+	−	+	−
	Indonesia	−	+**	−	−**	+	−	−	−*	−
	Korea	−	−		−	−**	−*	n.a.	−	−
	Malaysia	−	+	+*	+	+	−	−	+	n.a.
	The Philippines	+	−*	+	−	−	−	−	+	n.a.
	Singapore	−	−	+	n.a.	+**	+***	+	−	n.a.
	Taiwan	+	−	n.a.	−	+	+	−	n.a.	n.a.
	Thailand	−	−	n.a.	−	−**	−*	−	−	−
Exchange rate origin	Indonesia	−***	−***	−	−	+	−***	−***	−**	+**
	Korea	n.a.	n.a.	n.a.	n.a.	n.a.	n.a.	n.a.	n.a.	n.a.
	Malaysia	n.a.	n.a.	n.a.	n.a.	n.a.	n.a.	n.a.	n.a.	n.a.
	The Philippines	n.a.	n.a.	n.a.	n.a.	n.a.	n.a.	n.a.	n.a.	n.a.
	Taiwan	n.a.	n.a.	n.a.	n.a.	n.a.	n.a.	n.a.	n.a.	n.a.
	Thailand	n.a.	n.a.	n.a.	n.a.	n.a.	n.a.	n.a.	n.a.	n.a.

Note: Standard errors in parentheses; n.a. indicates an insufficient number of observations.
***Significant at the 1 percent level.
**Significant at the 5 percent level.
*Significant at the 10 percent level.

crisis. Sixth, Thai exchange rates were quite sensitive to shocks in stock prices of other countries. Seventh, in general the spillovers from stock price shocks to exchange rates were not significant, with two important exceptions: significant effects from most regional stock markets to the Thai baht, and shocks from the Hong Kong stock market affected most currencies in the region.

Our results show evidence of contagion between an exchange rate and a stock price for selected pairs of countries during the crisis period. The contagious impact on exchange rates was mainly due to the Hong Kong stock price fall and Indonesian and Korean depreciations. In contrast to the impact on exchange rates, stock prices are found to be influenced by a wider variety of both exchange rates and stock prices of other countries.

NOTES

1. See, for example, Hung and Cheung (1995), Malliaropulos (1998), Ng (2000), and Forbes and Rigobon (2002).

2. A number of other papers consider transmissions between equity and currency markets in other periods (Bekaert and Hodrick 1992) or transmissions across other asset classes (Hartmann, Straetmans, and de Vries 2004) in integrated models, while a larger literature models transmissions for individual asset classes in the Asian crisis period, including Debelle and Lewis (this volume).

3. Khalid and Kawai (2003), for example, analyze the crisis contagion among nine Asian countries based on a VAR framework and conclude that there was no spillover effect between stock markets and foreign exchange markets during the 1997 crisis. The difficulty with their VAR estimation is the use of too many (twenty-seven) explanatory variables in the model—three variables (daily stock prices, exchange rates, and interest rates) for nine countries. The inclusion of the autoregressive terms in the model also weakens the ability of the model to detect the underlying relationship.

4. Hang Seng Price Index (Hong Kong), Jakarta SE Composite Price Index (Indonesia), Korea SE Composite Price Index (Korea), Kuala Lumpur Composite Price Index (Malaysia), Philippines SE Composite Price Index (the Philippines), Singapore DBS 50 Price Index (Singapore), Taiwan Weighted Index (Taiwan), Bangkok Book Club (Thailand).

5. The decline in stock prices in Asia in mid-October 1997 was a spillover from a sharp drop of Hong Kong stock prices.

6. Ito and Hashimoto (2002) first provide the methodology to demonstrate a clear cause-and-effect relationship in exchange-rate-depreciation (stock price declines) spillover relationships. They also found a positive relationship between trade link indices and the contagion coefficients, implying that the bilateral trade linkage is an important crisis transmission channel in the exchange rate markets; see also Glick and Rose (1999).

7. In October 1997, the Hong Kong dollar was targeted by speculative attacks and the Currency Board system raised interest rates, resulting in a decline in stock prices. In order to avoid the financial market turmoil due to the stock price fall, several measures were taken in the speculative attack in August 1998, including buying up stocks with public funds to shore up the stock market. Countries with fixed ex-

change rate regimes—for example, People's Republic of China and Malaysia (from September 1998)—experienced a rise in interest rates under devaluation pressure.

8. We think that the Korean exchange rate depreciations, most notably from the end of November to the end of December, occurred more independently than being affected by other currencies in the short run. It shows up as "origins" rather than "being affected" in the high-frequency data. Of course, conventional wisdom is that the Korean currency crisis is a result of contagion from Thailand and Indonesia, but this may be only true with a long time lag of several weeks; and that is very difficult to capture in an econometric analysis, because most of the effects would become endogenous in time aggregation of more than a week. We have a precise definition of what contagion in high frequency means, and according to our definition, the Korean exchange rate is not affected by contagion.

REFERENCES

Allen, F., and D. Gale, 2000, Financial Contagion, *Journal of Political Economy* 108, 1–33.

Bae, K.-H., G. A. Karolyi, and R. M. Stulz, 2003, A New Approach to Measuring Financial Contagion, *Review of Financial Studies* 16, 717–763.

Bekaert, G., C. R. Harvey, and A. Ng, 2005, Market Integration and Contagion, *Journal of Business* 78, part 2, forthcoming.

Bekaert, G., and R. J. Hodrick, 1992, Characterizing Predictable Components in Excess Returns on Equity and Foreign-Exchange Markets, *Journal of Finance* 47, 467–509.

Corsetti, G., P. Pesenti, and N. Roubini, 1998, What Caused the Asian Currency and Financial Crisis? Part I: A Macroeconomic Overview, *National Bureau of Economic Research Working Paper* 6833.

Dornbusch, R., Y. C. Park, and S. Claessens, 2000, Contagion: Understanding How It Spreads, *World Bank Research Observer* 15, 177–197.

Flood, R., and N. Marion, 1999, Perspectives on the Recent Currency Crisis Literature, *International Journal of Finance and Economics* 4, 1–26.

Forbes, K. J., and R. Rigobon, 2002, No Contagion, Only Interdependence: Measuring Stock Market Comovements, *Journal of Finance* 57, 2223–2261.

Frankel, J. A., and A. K. Rose, 1996, Currency Crashes in Emerging Markets: An Empirical Treatment, *Journal of International Economics* 41, 351–366.

Glick, R., and A. K. Rose, 1999, Contagion and Trade: Why Are Currency Crises Regional? *Journal of International Money and Finance* 18, 603–617.

Goldstein, M., G. L. Kaminsky, and C. M. Reinhart, 2000, *Assessing Financial Vulnerability: An Early Warning System for Emerging Markets* (Institute for International Economics, Washington, DC).

Granger, C. W. J., B.-N. Huang, and C.-W. Yang, 2000, A Bivariate Causality between Stock Prices and Exchange Rates: Evidence from Recent Asian Flu, *Quarterly Review of Economics and Finance* 40, 337–354.

Hartmann, P., S. Straetmans, and C. G. de Vries, 2004, Asset Market Linkages in Crisis Periods, *Review of Economics and Statistics* 86, 313–326.

Hung, B. W.-S., and Y.-L. Cheung, 1995, Interdependence of Asian Emerging Equity Markets, *Journal of Business Finance and Accounting* 22, 281–288.

Ito, T., 2000, Capital Flows in Asia, in S. Edwards, ed., *Capital flows and the emerging economies: Theory, evidence, and controversies, National Bureau of Economic Research Conference Report series* (University of Chicago Press, Chicago).

Ito, T., and Y. Hashimoto, 2002, High-Frequency Contagion of Currency Crises in Asia, *National Bureau of Economic Research Working Paper* 9376.

Kaminsky, G. L., and C. M. Reinhart, 2000, On Crises, Contagion, and Confusion, *Journal of International Economics* 51, 145–168.

Khalid, A. M., and M. Kawai, 2003, Was Financial Market Contagion the Source of Economic Crisis in Asia? Evidence Using a Multivariate VAR Model, *Journal of Asian Economics* 14, 131–156.

King, M., E. Sentana, and S. Wadhwani, 1994, Volatility and Links between National Stock Markets, *Econometrica* 62, 901–933.

Kodres, L. E., and M. Pritsker, 2002, A Rational Expectations Model of Financial Contagion, *Journal of Finance* 57, 769–799.

Malliaropulos, D., 1998, International Stock Return Differentials and Real Exchange Rate Changes, *Journal of International Money and Finance* 17, 493–511.

McKibbin, W. J., and W. Martin, 1998, The East Asian Crisis: Investigating Causes and Policy Responses, *Australian National University, Working Papers in Trade and Development* 93/6.

Ng, A., 2000, Volatility Spillover Effects from Japan and the U.S. to the Pacific Basin, *Journal of International Money and Finance* 19, 207–233.

Pavlova, A., and R. Rigobon, 2004, Asset Prices and Exchange Rates, *MIT Sloan Working Paper no.* 4322-03.

Radelet, S., and J. Sachs, 2000, The Onset of the East Asian Financial Crisis, in P. Krugman, ed., *Currency Crises, National Bureau of Economic Research Conference Report Series* (University of Chicago Press, Chicago).

Rigobon, R., 2003, On the Measurement of the International Propagation of Shocks: Is the Transmission Stable? *Journal of International Economics* 61, 261–283.

6

The Response of Financial Markets in Australia and New Zealand to News about the Asian Crisis

Eleanor Debelle and Luci Ellis

1. INTRODUCTION

As financial markets become more integrated, shocks can be transmitted more quickly between them. In times of market turmoil, this implies that the effects of negative shocks might be felt in markets far removed from the originating market. What is more, it appears that in some instances markets that are expected to be affected by market turmoil elsewhere unexpectedly escape. An understanding of why this might occur is vital in developing views on appropriate policy responses to financial crises. Here we present a case study of such an incident. During the 1997–98 East Asian financial crisis, the economies of Australia and New Zealand were widely expected to feel its effects, due to geographical proximity and trading links in the region; see, for example, the summary of contemporary forecasts in Summers (2001). However, in the case of Australia this did not occur to the extent expected by market commentators. To illustrate the transmission, and nontransmission, of this particular crisis, we investigate the spillover of financial market volatility, specifically the impact of news from Asia (Korea, Thailand, and Indonesia, as well as Malaysia and the Philippines) during the 1997–98 financial crisis, on financial markets in Australia and New Zealand. We examine the initial impact of key events and announcements in the Asian crisis period and the spillover of these effects, as measured by both financial prices and proxies of their volatility.

Ellis: Reserve Bank of Australia, EllisL@rba.gov.au, corresponding author. We are indebted to colleagues at the Reserve Bank of Australia, to participants at seminars at the BIS and the London School of Economics, and to Mardi Dungey for invaluable comments and suggestions. We are also grateful to Adam Cagliarini for technical advice, and Clare Padua for assistance with the data. Any errors are ours alone. The opinions expressed in this chapter are those of the authors and should not be attributed to the Reserve Bank of Australia.

We find that news—both positive and negative—that came out of Asia during the crisis clearly had repercussions for the Antipodean markets. But these effects must be put in perspective: Developments in the U.S. market generally had a much greater influence on Australasian price movements and volatility than cross-market shocks originating in the Asian crisis economies. This result is in line with previous work on the importance of overseas returns in Australian markets (Kortian and O'Regan 1996). We also find evidence indicating that stock markets reacted to developments in Asia with a lag, after the United States reacted, rather than reacting directly to the news itself, related perhaps to the argument that large financial markets act as centers, directing shocks to the periphery of other markets (Kaminsky and Reinhart 2003).

Our results indicate that the volatility in Australian and New Zealand financial markets was generally as great or greater in late 1998—which we term the "world crisis" period—than in the 1997–98 period, when the main news events of the Asian financial crisis occurred. We also find that the apparent spillover of financial market shocks from Asia to Australia and New Zealand was small and—for some asset classes—*smaller* in the Asian crisis period than previously. This implies that the shocks originating in Asia were less important for Australian and New Zealand markets than were the global "common" shocks affecting all of these markets simultaneously.

Australia and New Zealand provide an interesting case study in part because the countries reacted differently to the crisis. The evidence suggests that the *volatility* seen in Australian and New Zealand markets was not affected by the different stances of monetary policy, or by the differing natures of the monetary policy regimes in the two countries. The effects of developments in Asia on volatility in Australian and New Zealand financial markets were remarkably similar, despite the distinctly different methods used to conduct monetary policy over that period. These results may reflect the short-run measure of volatility that we adopt in this chapter, however. The *levels* of the financial market variables in Australia and New Zealand display differing profiles: there were large divergences in stock and bond prices over the period. On the other hand, the exchange rates of the two currencies against the U.S. dollar moved together, reflecting that these currencies are generally traded as a bloc.

This chapter draws on the literature on contagion (see Dornbusch, Park, and Claessens 2000 and Pericoli and Sbracia 2003 for a survey). Calvo and Mendoza (1999) show that contagion of financial market volatility might increase as world markets become more integrated. In certain circumstances, the costs of gathering and analyzing information about unfamiliar foreign markets may outweigh the perceived benefits. This can result in investors' choosing to act on the basis of rumors unrelated to market fundamentals, instead of on complete information. In addition, fund managers may face incentives that encourage herd behavior in portfolio allocation decisions. Both of these effects can result in contagion of financial volatility from markets in one country to those in other countries.

Masson (1999) has defined *contagion* as the portion of financial market volatility that cannot be explained by normal factors such as domestic fundamentals and global common shocks. However, much of the contagion literature focuses on the propagation of exchange rate crises and does not deal explicitly with the transmission of volatility outside crisis periods (Dungey and Martin 2001 and Ito and Hashimoto, in this volume, are exceptions). This chapter bears greater resemblance to the literature on "meteor showers and heat waves," which studies geographic (time zone) patterns in the volatility of particular securities (Engle, Ito, and Lin 1990; Fleming and Lopez 1999). We seek to identify the effect of "meteors"—as measured by news events or volatility in one market—on returns and volatility in other markets.

Previous work on the effects of macroeconomic news on Australian financial market prices and volatility has focused on announcements made at prescheduled times, such as Australian CPI releases (Campbell and Lewis 1998; Kim 1996). In these cases, the content of an announcement may be a surprise, but its timing is not. Therefore, it is possible for market participants to plan their contingent trading strategies in advance. If the timing of an announcement is not known in advance, however, traders have less opportunity to plan for its effects. Previous empirical work for other countries has suggested that unscheduled announcements tend to have more persistent effects on financial returns than do scheduled announcements (Almeida, Goodhart, and Payne 1998), although the difference can be measured in hours. In general, studies of this kind examine the impact of economic announcements on "own" financial markets. The present chapter, however, focuses on the effects of unscheduled (though potentially anticipated) announcements relating to one group of countries on the financial markets of other countries.

The chapter proceeds as follows. In section 2, we discuss the reasons that financial markets in Australia and New Zealand might have been affected by the financial crisis in Asia. We also discuss our measure of news events and the financial market data to be analyzed. Section 3 contains the empirical evidence on the response of financial markets in Australia and New Zealand to these news events, in terms of both volatility and price movements. In section 4, we examine whether the spillover of financial market returns is greater in times of crisis than in more normal times, using results from vector autoregressions (VARs). Section 5 contains concluding remarks.

2. MOTIVATION AND DATA

2.1 The Impact of News on Financial Markets

A large literature exists on the impact of macroeconomic news on financial market prices sampled at high frequencies (Campbell and Lewis 1998; Fleming and Remolona 1997; Almeida, Goodhart, and Payne 1998; Kim and Sheen 2000; and Kim 1999 are some recent examples).

One distinction between most of this event-study literature and the present essay is that the former generally examines the effects of news events on financial markets in the country in which the news originated. We focus on the effects of news on third-country markets. In addition, most of the previous literature examines the effect of official macroeconomic data releases, which generally have prescheduled release dates and times.

Asian time zones largely overlap the Australian and New Zealand domestic trading zones. We would, therefore, expect that in most cases the reaction of Australian and New Zealand markets would begin on the same day that the Asian news events occurred. There may be some instances, however, in which the news events in Asia occurred after the market closes in Australia and New Zealand, and so the reaction will have occurred on the following day.

2.2   Identifying the Timing of News Events

The first step in assessing how news about the Asian financial crisis affected other countries' financial markets is to identify the events that constitute news. We use a combination of two preexisting chronologies, one from the Bank for International Settlements (BIS; 1998, table VII.6, p. 131), and the other from the International Monetary Fund (IMF; 1998, box 2.12, p. 49), as well as the Reserve Bank of Australia's (RBA's) daily market reports. A table listing the events from these sources is shown in the appendix. It should be noted that in some cases the dates cited in the IMF chronology differ from those in other IMF papers (e.g., Lane et al. 1999). Where possible, we have verified the dates using news-wire stories and other sources. The IMF and BIS chronologies ended in June and March 1998, respectively; we extended the chronology in this chapter to end-August 1998 using the RBA's daily market reports.

We distinguish between events that are considered "good" or "bad" news. We classify events relating to agreements between international agencies and crisis countries, announcements of rollovers of debt, and certain reforms as good news; all other news events listed in the appendix are considered to be bad news. The classification of events as positive or negative is shown in the right-most column in the table in the appendix. Our listing is similar to the classification used by Kaminsky and Schmukler (1999), based on the chronology compiled by Nouriel Roubini (1999), and to that of Baig and Goldfajn (1998), compiled from news-wire stories.[1]

Kaminsky and Schmukler (1999) report that the days on which some of the most volatile movements in Asian financial markets occurred were not necessarily associated with specific news events relating to the crisis. There are a number of possible explanations for this. First, markets might react to cumulations of news, so that a seemingly small or unimportant news event can engender a greater response if it follows a series of news events (the "straw that broke the camel's back" effect). Second, there may be some herding behavior by traders, so that sudden changes in financial prices can occur even in the absence of significant news. Third, the news events considered may be less relevant to asset markets than the trading strategies used by market participants. To maximize returns from these trading strategies, it may be necessary to take advantage of particular market conditions, such as thin volume, which may not occur on news-event days.

2.3 The Financial Market Data, Episodes, and Volatility

The data used to measure financial market returns and volatility for Australia and New Zealand in this study are the broad indices of stock prices—the All Ordinaries Index (AOI) for Australia and the New Zealand Stock Exchange's NZSE40 for New Zealand; bilateral exchange rates for the Australian and New Zealand dollars against the U.S. dollar; and the prices on futures contracts for Australian and New Zealand ten-year bonds, which trade on the Sydney Futures Exchange (SFE) and the New Zealand Futures and Options Exchange (NZFOE).[2] We use daily market-close data for stock prices and bond futures prices, and 4 P.M. (Australian Eastern Standard Time) readings for the bilateral exchange rates; we calculate volatility as the absolute value of daily percentage changes in prices (returns), or squared percentage changes.

We examine financial market behavior in Australia and New Zealand from the beginning of 1994 to the end of August 1999. The sample is divided into four subperiods or episodes: precrisis, from 1 January 1994 to 30 April 1997; Asian crisis, from 1 May 1997 to 31 August 1998; world crisis, from 1 September 1998 to 31 December 1998; and postcrisis, the first eight months of 1999.[3] The Asian crisis period spans sixteen calendar months, starting at the beginning of the month in which the first major news event occurred (see the appendix). We defined the end of the Asian crisis as being the onset of financial crises outside the Asian region; accordingly, we separately identify a world crisis period, which we take as ending at the end of 1998 when most markets had calmed down considerably. The postcrisis period is therefore limited to the first eight months of 1999.

We were constrained from beginning the precrisis period any earlier than January 1994 by the availability of the composite Asian financial indices described and used in section 4. We also wanted to avoid selecting a sample for the precrisis period that was too short, as the exact beginning of the Asian crisis is not necessarily clear. As early as July 1996, there was notable pressure on the Thai baht, following the collapse of the Bangkok Bank of Commerce. There was also pressure in January 1997, following the release of poor export and fiscal data (IMF 1998). Therefore, we chose to start the sample long before there was any indication of trouble in the region.[4]

The 1994 start date also captures the onset of the global bond bear market in February 1994, a period characterized by falling bond prices and more volatile financial markets in general. It was followed by a substantial recovery in financial markets, which continued through to the beginning of the Asian crisis period. Capturing both market phases seemed a balanced approach.

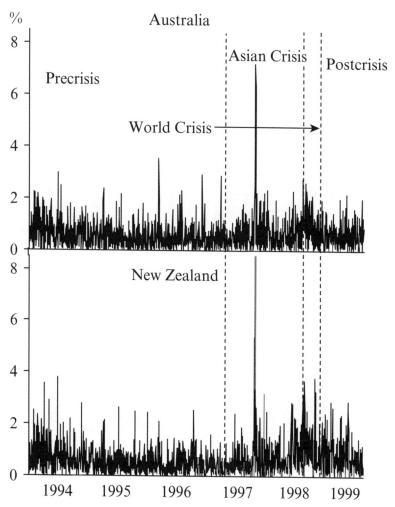

Fig. 1. Stock market volatility

2.3.1 *Stock Market Volatility*   Figure 1 plots the absolute daily percentage change in Australian and New Zealand stocks during the four periods described above. The standard pattern of financial market volatility is apparent: in both countries, stock market volatility fluctuates over time and tends to cluster. Volatility of Australian stocks appears, on average, to be slightly lower than for New Zealand, although overall, the patterns of fluctuations look very similar. This is evident throughout most of the sample, but most clearly during late October 1997—where the large spikes represent the large stock market sell-off at that time—and subsequently, in the world crisis period.[5] There does not appear to be much difference in volatility between the precrisis, Asian crisis, and postcrisis periods (with the ex-

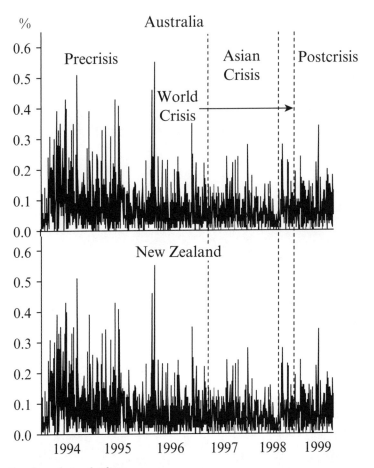

Fig. 2. Bond market volatility

ception of the large spike in October 1997), whereas the world crisis period clearly exhibits a higher level of volatility for both countries.

2.3.2 Bond Market Volatility   It is clear that volatility in bond market returns—the absolute percentage change in the price on the futures contract—is much smaller than stock price volatility (see figure 2). This partly reflects the pricing conventions on the Sydney Futures Exchange. However, there appears to be more evidence of volatility clustering in the bond market, with the 1994 period characterized by very volatile returns, followed by a period of relative calm in the second half of 1995. Again, these patterns are evident in both Australia and New Zealand, although, unlike the case for stock price volatility, bond price volatility is much higher for Australia and appears to be more persistent. Overall, however, volatility in the Australian and New Zealand bond markets seems highly correlated, with volatility in the precrisis period much higher for both countries than

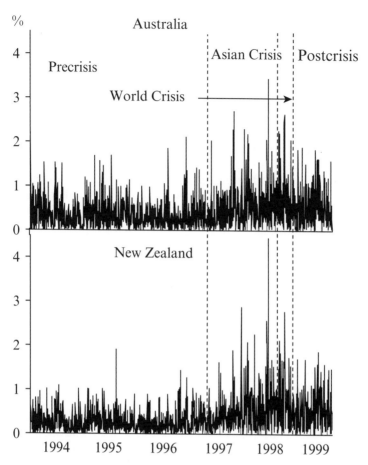

Fig. 3. Foreign exchange market volatility

in the other periods. This is consistent with the global sell-off in bond markets throughout 1994 and early 1995.

2.3.3 Foreign Exchange Market Volatility   Volatility of both the AUD/USD and the NZD/USD exchange rates increased markedly during the Asian crisis, building toward the end of the period, and remained high into the world crisis period (figure 3). This result suggests that the Asian and world crises had their largest impacts on the exchange rates of the two countries. The increased daily volatility during the later part of the Asian crisis period and in the world crisis period was associated with large depreciations in the AUD/USD and NZD/USD exchange rates. By contrast, the bond and stock markets rallied during most of this period. In part, this may reflect a "flight to quality" by investors.

Although the volatility in the exchange rates of these currencies against the U.S. dollar varied considerably in the crisis periods, the volatility in the

AUD/NZD cross-rate was relatively stable. The relatively constant volatility of the AUD/NZD cross-rate reflects that these two currencies are generally traded as a bloc.

3.   THE RESPONSE TO NEWS

In this section, we use some simple summary statistics and econometric techniques to measure the impact of news on financial market volatility and returns during the Asian crisis. Within the Asian crisis period, we distinguish between "news" days and "no-news" days, defined as days on which a news event did not occur, and which neither immediately preceded nor immediately followed a news day. Days on which a news event did not occur, but which were adjacent to at least one news day, are identified separately as "prenews" and "postnews" days.

3.1   Summary Statistics

The top third of table 1 summarizes volatility in the Australian and New Zealand stock markets—as measured by the average absolute percentage change in Australian and New Zealand stocks—for all news-event days (prenews, news, and postnews days) and no-news days during the Asian crisis period. The table also shows the corresponding measures for the world crisis, precrisis, and postcrisis periods, as well as the Asian crisis period taken as a whole.

Table 1.   Daily Financial Market Volatility

	Average Absolute Daily Percentage Returns							
	News Days during Asian Crisis							
	Pre-news	News	Post-news	No news	Precrisis	Asian Crisis	World Crisis	Postcrisis
Stock prices								
Australia	0.77	0.91	1.00	0.59	0.55	0.70	0.77	0.62
New Zealand	1.01	0.97	1.24	0.63	0.55	0.79	1.03	0.74
Bond prices								
Australia	0.06	0.06	0.06	0.06	0.08	0.06	0.07	0.07
New Zealand	0.05	0.05	0.07	0.05	0.06	0.05	0.06	0.05
Exchange rates								
Australia	0.59	0.67	0.66	0.46	0.33	0.52	0.62	0.52
New Zealand	0.56	0.63	0.62	0.44	0.26	0.51	0.65	0.52

Note: There are 868 precrisis days, 348 Asian crisis days, 88 world crisis days, and 173 postcrisis days. During the crisis period, there are 65 news days, 196 no-news days, 65 pre-news days, and 64 post-news days. There are 42 days that fall into more than one category.

Several facts stand out. First, during the Asian crisis, all news-event days were noticeably more volatile for both Australian and New Zealand stock indices than were days when news events did not occur. Second, volatility in both stock indices in the precrisis period was significantly lower (in a statistical sense, using a one-tailed test with a significance level of 5 percent) than during the Asian crisis, but similar to no-news days during the crisis. It was also lower than in both subsequent periods (world crisis and postcrisis). Third, volatility in the world crisis period was similar to that in the Asian crisis for Australian stocks; but for New Zealand stocks, the world crisis period exhibited significantly higher volatility.

The variation in bond market volatility was much smaller than for the other financial markets considered. For both Australia and New Zealand, there was seldom more than a 0.01 percentage-point difference between the mean absolute movements in the bond futures prices across the subperiods (table 1). Mean difference tests (shown in Ellis and Lewis 2001) do not indicate any significant news effects during the Asian crisis period for Australia or New Zealand. Pre-news days, news days, and post-news days did not engender any greater volatility in Australian and New Zealand bond markets, on average, than days when news events did not occur. Reflecting the severe sell-off in bond markets in 1994, mean volatility in the precrisis periods was significantly greater than for the Asian and postcrisis periods for both the Australian and New Zealand markets, but not greater than in the world crisis period. Although these are statistically significant differences, they are very small from an economic perspective.

The effect of the Asian crisis on Australian and New Zealand financial markets is particularly evident for exchange rates. There was an apparent news effect: the mean absolute returns on all news-event days were significantly greater than for no-news days for both exchange rates. In the Asian crisis, world crisis, and postcrisis periods, both exchange rates were significantly more volatile, on average, than in the precrisis period. This suggests that these differences reflected a generalized increase in volatility stemming from heightened uncertainty triggered by the crises, rather than transmissions specifically to Australia and New Zealand. Moreover, the world crisis period exhibited greater volatility than the Asian crisis period in both countries, although not significantly so for Australia.

3.2 Econometric Evidence

In this section, we seek to quantify the effect of news on financial markets. Based on our chronology, we constructed a news-event dummy series that took the value +1 for good news, −1 for bad news, and zero otherwise. We then estimated VARs of the daily returns on Australian and New Zealand assets and on a benchmark U.S. financial asset (S&P500 stock price index for the VAR explaining stock returns, and the futures contract on the thirty-year benchmark Treasury bond for the bond price VAR), for the precrisis, world crisis, and postcrisis periods. For the Asian crisis period, we augmented the

VAR with the current and lagged values of the news-event dummy series. This is similar to the methodology used by Baig and Goldfajn (1999).

Since bilateral exchange rates are relative prices—in this case, to the U.S. dollar—it is not possible to use this exact approach for the exchange rates. Instead, we estimated VARs of the AUD/USD and NZD/USD with the Commodity Research Bureau (CRB) Commodity Price Index, which is intended to proxy for the effects of global shocks on commodity-exporting countries. For each of the VAR systems, we used two lags of the endogenous variables, which was the preferred number of lags according to the Schwartz information criterion. We included the current-dated and first lag of the news variable for the Asian crisis period.

The results from these models should be taken as indicative rather than decisive, not least because linear VARs are hardly the best available model of financial asset returns. In particular, the residuals from most of these models are non-normal; specifically, they have marked ARCH properties. However, when we estimated single-equation models incorporating the same variables and lag structure to these VARs, allowing for GARCH residuals, the qualitative results on the importance of the news events in Asian and U.S. developments were unchanged.

The VAR results for the stock market are shown in table 2. The estimated coefficients on the news dummy series are positive but insignificant for Australian and New Zealand stocks. The coefficients on the lagged S&P500, however, are large and highly significant for both countries in all periods. This suggests that the news dummies do not appear to have much independent effect on Australian and New Zealand stock markets, once overnight events in U.S. markets are controlled for; these markets are dominated by overnight developments in the United States.[6] However, there is some evidence that Australian and New Zealand market participants react to events in Asia *indirectly* via the United States. The contemporaneous news dummies are just significant in the equation for the S&P500, and they are of the expected sign. This might explain why the post news days exhibited greater average volatility in both countries' stock markets than did news days (table 1). It also suggests possible inefficient information processing. If Asian news had systematically moved the S&P500, which then systematically moved Australian and New Zealand stock markets, it begs the question why the Australian and New Zealand markets did not react on the day of the news event. One answer may be that timing issues prevented these markets from reacting contemporaneously—for example, if the event occurred after the Antipodean markets closed.

The results for bonds indicate an even smaller response to the news events, once the overnight movements in the U.S. Treasury market are controlled for (table 3).[7] The estimated coefficients are broadly similar across the four subperiods, with the inclusion of the news-event dummies making little difference to the estimation results for the Asian crisis. Again, overnight movements in the U.S. long bond mattered more for Australian and New Zealand bond returns than did the Asian crisis news events.

Table 2. VAR Estimates for Daily Stock Returns

	Precrisis			Asian Crisis			World Crisis			Postcrisis		
	AOI	NZSE40	SP	AOI	NZSE40	SP	AOI	NZSE40	SP	AOI	NZSE40	SP
Constant	−0.02	−0.03	0.06**	−0.02	−0.08	0.05	0.04	0.04	0.38**	−0.03	−0.01	−0.03
	(−0.72)	(−1.31)	(2.21)	(−0.48)	(−1.52)	(0.67)	(0.45)	(0.28)	(2.15)	(−0.63)	(−0.23)	(−0.25)
AOI_{-1}	0.07	0.17***	0.01	0.00	0.33***	−0.08	−0.17	0.07	−0.21	−0.12	0.13	0.03
	(1.59)	(3.76)	(0.30)	(0.08)	(4.29)	(−0.83)	(−1.45)	(0.45)	(−0.97)	(−1.35)	(1.18)	(0.20)
AOI_{-2}	−0.06	0.00	−0.03	0.07	0.14*	0.02	−0.05	−0.02	−0.16	−0.05	0.20***	0.04
	(−1.64)	(0.06)	(−0.74)	(1.21)	(1.80)	(0.24)	(−0.49)	(−0.13)	(−0.85)	(−0.69)	(1.97)	(0.30)
$NZSE40_{-1}$	−0.04	0.02	0.04	−0.06	−0.08	0.05	−0.04	−0.04	0.12	−0.03	0.12	−0.20
	(−0.95)	(0.45)	(1.07)	(−1.16)	(−1.26)	(0.62)	(−0.48)	(−0.35)	(0.74)	(−0.46)	(1.41)	(−1.61)
$NZSE40_{-2}$	0.03	0.04	0.01	−0.01	−0.02	0.08	−0.08	0.14	−0.02	0.07	−0.16**	0.03
	(0.83)	(0.88)	(0.32)	(−0.20)	(−0.27)	(1.11)	(−1.01)	(1.36)	(−0.16)	(1.19)	(−1.97)	(0.28)
$S\&P_{-1}$	0.57***	0.43***	0.09**	0.45***	0.45***	0.09	0.38***	0.46***	−0.09	0.38***	0.35***	−0.02
	(15.27)	(10.66)	(2.27)	(10.63)	(8.54)	(1.45)	(6.61)	(5.88)	(−0.83)	(8.27)	(5.77)	(−0.23)
$S\&P_{-2}$	−0.14***	−0.11**	−0.01	0.08	−0.04	−0.04	0.05	0.03	−0.08	0.02	−0.17**	0.15
	(−3.15)	(−2.38)	(−0.33)	(1.57)	(−0.72)	(−0.55)	(0.72)	(0.29)	(−0.59)	(0.42)	(−2.24)	(1.40)
News	—	—	—	0.14	0.21	0.30*	—	—	—	—	—	—
				(1.29)	(1.60)	(1.87)						
$News_{-1}$	—	—	—	0.01	−0.06	−0.13	—	—	—	—	—	—
				(0.14)	(−0.42)	(−0.81)						
R-bar^2	0.26	0.17	0.00	0.28	0.27	0.01	0.36	0.33	−0.02	0.31	0.22	−0.01
SE regression	0.65	0.70	0.66	0.73	0.90	1.10	0.80	1.10	1.48	0.64	0.83	1.18
F-statistic	42.15	24.54	1.29	15.13	14.18	1.24	7.81	7.19	0.74	11.92	7.69	0.65
Jarque–Bera statistic	22.77	32.14	98.75	0.51	48.32	238.24	0.50	9.04	1.10	1.73	1.73	2.39

Note: All abbreviations are explained in the text; t-statistics are in parentheses. The residuals do not display significant serial correlation.
***Significant at the 1 percent level.
**Significant at the 5 percent level.
*Significant at the 10 percent level.

Table 3. VAR Estimates for Daily Bond Returns

	Precrisis			Asian Crisis			World Crisis			Postcrisis		
	Australia	New Zealand	United States	Australia	New Zealand	United States	Australia	New Zealand	United States	Australia	New Zealand	United States
Constant	0.00	0.00	0.00	0.02	0.00	0.04	0.01	0.01*	−0.07	−0.01	−0.01**	−0.09*
	(0.55)	(−0.43)	(−0.18)	(0.52)	(0.91)	(1.34)	(1.47)	(1.75)	(−0.86)	(−1.15)	(−2.02)	(−1.94)
Australia$_{-1}$	−0.14***	0.06	0.24	−0.02	0.04	−0.12	−0.41***	−0.02	−1.18	−0.25**	−0.02	−0.08
	(−3.31)	(1.40)	(0.80)	(−0.32)	(0.58)	(−0.25)	(−2.74)	(−0.19)	(−0.85)	(−2.50)	(−0.24)	(−0.07)
Australia$_{-2}$	0.00	0.21	0.03	−0.10	0.01	−0.51	−0.13	−0.05	−0.82	0.19**	0.19***	0.62
	(−0.02)	(0.58)	(0.12)	(−1.61)	(0.18)	(−1.18)	(−0.96)	(−0.45)	(−0.65)	(2.02)	(2.63)	(0.61)
NZ$_{-1}$	−0.11**	−0.19***	0.45	0.05	−0.10	0.15	0.14	−0.13	0.34	−0.16	−0.18*	0.13
	(−2.31)	(−4.20)	(1.34)	(0.79)	(−1.52)	(0.34)	(0.79)	(−0.84)	(0.21)	(−1.19)	(−1.75)	(0.08)
NZ$_{-2}$	−0.04	−0.04	0.12	0.01	−0.03	0.01	0.04	0.00	0.32	−0.44***	−0.31***	−1.69
	(−0.76)	(−0.79)	(0.37)	(0.16)	(−0.54)	(0.02)	(0.28)	(0.01)	(0.21)	(−3.72)	(−3.32)	(−1.29)
US$_{-1}$	0.12***	0.08***	−0.04	0.09***	0.07***	0.06	0.06***	0.06***	0.28**	0.14***	0.11***	−0.02
	(19.21)	(14.03)	(−0.87)	(10.67)	(6.96)	(0.99)	(4.53)	(5.42)	(2.27)	(16.96)	(17.17)	(−0.32)
US$_{-2}$	0.01*	0.00	−0.08	−0.01	−0.02	−0.01	0.03	0.03**	0.23	0.04***	0.02*	0.02
	(1.68)	(0.48)	(−1.40)	(−1.02)	(−1.57)	(−0.09)	(1.51)	(2.19)	(1.38)	(2.98)	(1.73)	(0.15)
News	—	—	—	−0.01	0.01	0.00	—	—	—	—	—	—
				(−1.27)	(0.53)	(0.01)						
News$_{-1}$	—	—	—	0.01	0.01	−0.04	—	—	—	—	—	—
				(0.57)	(0.71)	(−0.66)						
R-bar^2	0.39	0.26	0.00	0.29	0.14	−0.02	0.24	0.30	0.03	0.67	0.67	−0.02
SE regression	0.09	0.08	0.60	0.06	0.07	0.45	0.07	0.06	0.65	0.05	0.04	0.56
F-statistic	64.20	36.14	0.72	15.38	6.86	0.44	4.57	5.95	1.30	49.92	50.96	0.47
Jarque-Bera statistic	189.44	32.58	29.98	37.42	103.58	30.18	8.31	1.30	0.64	1.03	1.42	6.02

Note: All abbreviations are explained in the text; *t*-statistics are in parentheses. The residuals do not display significant serial correlation.
***Significant at the 1 percent level.
**Significant at the 5 percent level.
*Significant at the 10 percent level.

The picture for the exchange rates (table 4) is somewhat different in that the contemporaneous news dummies are of the anticipated sign but are insignificant, while the lags of the dummies are significant in both the AUD and NZD equations. The significance of the lagged dummies and not the contemporaneous dummies could possibly be attributed to the timing of the news announcements, or to foreign exchange markets' waiting for the U.S. stock market reaction. The estimated coefficients on the news dummies are positive, implying that bad news in Asia resulted in a depreciation of the AUD/USD and NZD/USD.

Interestingly, the CRB index became more significant in later periods. This suggests that market participants looked more closely at commodity price series, such as the CRB index, when assessing the fundamentals underlying these exchange rates.

4.   COMPARING SPILLOVERS IN CRISES AND AT OTHER TIMES

An important question relating to financial stability is whether the spillover of shocks and volatility is greater when the originating markets are in crisis than in more normal times. At first glance, it might be thought that this is true: Turbulent markets indicate greater uncertainty about the future, and so uncertainty about the effects of news events on third markets is also likely to be greater during these times.

It is not feasible to answer this question using the news-event data described in section 2.3, however. By construction, there were no news events before or after the Asian crisis period (May 1997–August 1998), so we cannot test whether markets responded more to news events in the Asian crisis period than in other periods. Instead, we estimate an expanded version of the VARs presented in section 3.2, with an additional equation in the system to measure movements in Asian financial markets. We present results for returns, rather than volatility (absolute returns), as these were more robust to small specification changes, and allow us to examine the direction and magnitude of the reaction to movements in other markets.

For each market, we present selected impulse responses and variance decompositions, using a recursive-ordering identification scheme with the ordering {Asia, Australia, New Zealand, United States}. In general, alternative orderings made little difference to our results on the effect of the Asian variable on returns in Australia and New Zealand, although the relative ordering of Australia and New Zealand can affect the estimates of their effects on each other. The U.S. market generally had no contemporaneous effect on the Australian and New Zealand markets, even when the system was ordered to permit this. We attribute this result to the time zone differences, with the U.S. trading day starting after the close in Asian, Australian, and New Zealand markets.

To capture movements in Asian financial markets, we use regional indices. For stock markets, we use the Morgan Stanley Capital International (MSCI) Far East Free (excluding Japan) Index. This index is a market-

Table 4. VAR Estimates for Daily Exchange Rate Returns

	Precrisis			Asian Crisis			World Crisis			Postcrisis		
	AUD	NZD	CRB	AUD	NZD	CRB	AUD	NZD	CRB	AUD	NZD	CRB
Constant	0.02	0.03**	0.02	−0.05	−0.08*	−0.05	0.10	0.04	−0.06	0.02	−0.01	0.04
	(0.99)	(2.47)	(1.00)	(−1.17)	(−1.89)	(−1.52)	(1.26)	(0.45)	(−0.78)	(0.39)	(−0.19)	(0.74)
AUD_{-1}	−0.03	0.04	−0.07	0.00	0.07	0.12	0.30*	0.29	0.09	−0.05	−0.08	−0.08
	(−0.70)	(1.31)	(−1.50)	(0.02)	(0.74)	(1.60)	(1.81)	(1.53)	(0.61)	(−0.33)	(−0.61)	(−0.57)
AUD_{-2}	0.00	0.00	0.01	−0.04	−0.05	0.12*	−0.12	0.16	−0.12	0.01	−0.09	−0.14
	(0.06)	(0.10)	(0.22)	(−0.43)	(−0.58)	(1.66)	(−0.72)	(0.86)	(−0.82)	(0.15)	(−0.73)	(−1.09)
NZD_{-1}	0.03	0.00	0.02	0.00	−0.08	0.00	−0.12	−0.10	−0.02	−0.06	0.01	0.12
	(0.57)	(−0.04)	(0.37)	(−0.04)	(−0.80)	(−0.05)	(−0.85)	(−0.62)	(−0.19)	(−0.45)	(0.04)	(0.85)
NZD_{-2}	−0.04	−0.11**	−0.05	−0.10	−0.13	−0.06	0.13	0.05	0.18	0.04	0.04	0.05
	(−0.69)	(−2.49)	(−0.83)	(−1.19)	(−1.43)	(−0.92)	(0.94)	(0.29)	(1.36)	(0.31)	(0.34)	(0.41)
CRB_{-1}	0.06*	0.02	0.05	0.25***	0.27***	0.01	0.56***	0.46***	−0.07	0.42***	0.43***	0.08
	(1.65)	(0.64)	(1.39)	(3.40)	(3.52)	(0.23)	(4.66)	(3.25)	(−0.63)	(4.74)	(5.13)	(0.89)
CRB_{-2}	0.04	0.02	0.00	−0.06	−0.07	−0.07	−0.08	−0.09	0.08	0.05	0.07	−0.04
	(1.08)	(0.57)	(−0.01)	(−0.86)	(−1.03)	(−1.27)	(−0.62)	(−0.58)	(0.66)	(0.56)	(0.83)	(−0.45)
News	—	—	—	0.06	0.02	0.00	—	—	—	—	—	—
				(0.65)	(0.19)	(0.04)						
$News_{-1}$	—	—	—	0.17*	0.17*	−0.07	—	—	—	—	—	—
				(1.85)	(1.77)	(−0.87)						
R-bar²	0.00	0.01	0.00	0.04	0.05	0.01	0.21	0.14	−0.02	0.12	0.14	−0.02
SE regression	0.47	0.36	0.49	0.67	0.68	0.53	0.69	0.80	0.65	0.64	0.62	0.63
F-statistic	0.84	1.82	0.81	2.58	3.08	1.47	4.50	3.15	0.69	4.30	4.85	0.59
Jarque-Bera statistic	86.90	108.37	35.62	37.39	278.11	8.95	0.33	0.30	4.50	1.41	0.53	3.78

Note: All abbreviations are explained in the text; *t*-statistics are in parentheses. The residuals do not display significant serial correlation.

***Significant at the 1 percent level.
**Significant at the 5 percent level.
*Significant at the 10 percent level.

Table 5. Countries Included in Alternative Asia-Region Financial Indices

MSCI Far East Free (Excl. Japan) Index	MSCI Emerging Markets Far East Index	MSCI Emerging Markets Asia Index	EMBI Global Constrained (Asia Subindex)	Troubled Asian Exchange Rate Index
China	China	China	China	
Hong Kong				
		India		
Indonesia	Indonesia	Indonesia		Indonesia
Korea	Korea	Korea	Korea	Korea
Malaysia	Malaysia	Malaysia	Malaysia	Malaysia
		Pakistan		
The Philippines	The Philippines	The Philippines	The Philippines	
Singapore				
		Sri Lanka		
Taiwan	Taiwan	Taiwan		
Thailand	Thailand	Thailand	Thailand	Thailand

Sources: MSCI indices: Morgan Stanley and Bloomberg. EMBI Global: JP Morgan. Exchange rate index compiled by the authors.
Note: MSCI = Morgan Stanley Capital International; EMBI = Emerging Markets Bond Index.

capitalization weighted stock price index covering at least 60 percent of the market capitalization of each industry group. Only the portion of each country's stock market that is freely available to overseas investors is included. We use these "free" series on the basis that contagion reflects movements in markets that foreigners can invest in, rather than those that only domestic investors can access. The countries included are listed in the first column of table 5, the data are presented in figure 4.[8] Although we have elected to use a series that incorporates countries other than those most affected by the crisis (i.e., Indonesia, Korea, Thailand, Malaysia, and the Philippines), this does not appear to distort our results. We obtained very similar results for the impulse responses and variance decompositions using the MSCI Emerging Markets Far East Index, the MSCI Emerging Markets Asia Index, and the first principal component of a data set of stock market returns for the five countries most affected by the Asian crisis.[9]

Analysis of an equivalent VAR system for bond returns is precluded by the lack of long-maturity sovereign debt securities in the crisis-affected countries, equivalent to the benchmark bonds used for Australia, New Zealand, and the United States. Instead, we use the JP Morgan EMBI (Emerging Markets Bond Index) Global Constrained Asia subindex series as a proxy (figure 5). This series is constructed using U.S. dollar–denominated eurobonds for countries without well-developed own markets for sovereign debt.[10] For the exchange rate, we constructed a GDP-weighted fixed-weight exchange rate index based on the spot exchange rates of the four countries listed in the right-most column of table 5 against the U.S. dollar (figure 6). The GDP weights were based on 1996 data from the World Bank

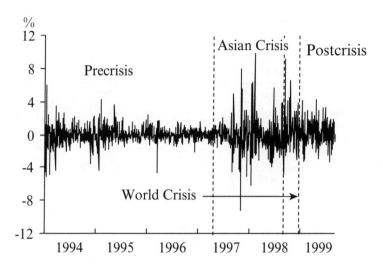

Fig. 4. Morgan Stanley Far East Asia Free Index—daily returns

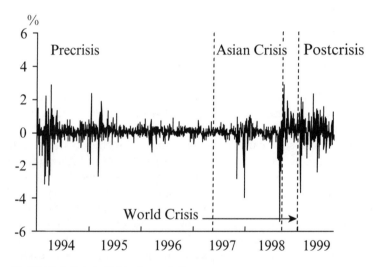

Fig. 5. EMBI Global Asia Subindex—daily returns

(1998), which converts the local-currency GDP levels to U.S. dollars using three-year-average exchange rates. A fall in this index represents depreciations of these countries' currencies against the U.S. dollar.

4.1 Stock Markets

Within each subperiod (precrisis, Asian crisis, world crisis, and postcrisis), our VAR results for stock returns were largely as expected; the detailed estimation results are available from the authors. Much of the variation in

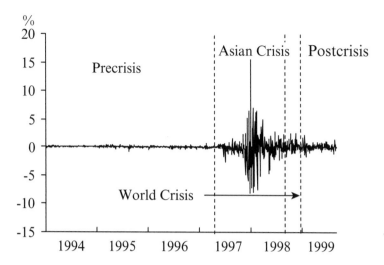

Fig. 6. Troubled Asia Exchange Rate Index—daily returns

Australian and New Zealand returns was driven by overnight developments in U.S. markets. Movements in the Australian and New Zealand
markets did not have an independent effect on U.S. markets. There was
some minor persistence in Australasian markets. The previous day's return
in the Australian market also had a significant positive effect on the New
Zealand market; we attribute this to time zone differences.

The impulse responses shown in figures 7–10, and the variance decompositions in tables 6–9 are based on the recursive identification scheme of
{Asia, Australia, New Zealand, United States}; alternative orderings produced very similar results to those presented here.[11] In particular, even
when the U.S. variable (S&P500) was ordered before the other variables, the
impulse responses of the other variables to an innovation in the S&P500
were still tent-shaped, with the contemporaneous responses being close to
(and almost always insignificantly different from) zero. A similar result
applied for the bond and foreign exchange market results presented in the
following sections.

The variance decompositions for the four periods show that own-
market innovations are the most important, although the S&P500 has a significant impact on the Australian and New Zealand indices in all periods.
The effect of the Asian market variable on Australian and New Zealand
stocks was also fairly important, particularly during the Asian crisis
period. There was some apparent cross-determination between the Australian and New Zealand markets, although this was not robust to different relative orderings. As expected, the S&P500 was virtually entirely
driven by own-market innovations, although the contribution of the Asian
variable in the crisis period was higher than at other times.[12]

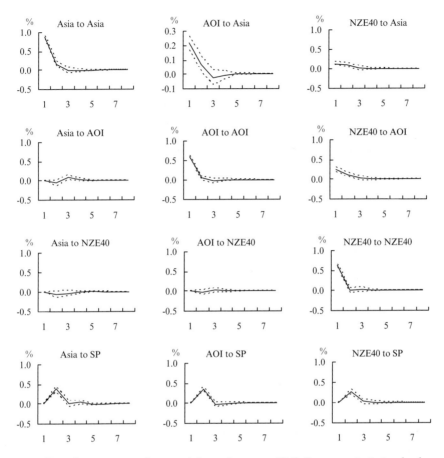

Fig. 7. Impulse responses for precrisis stock returns VAR: Response to 1 standard deviation innovations ± 2 standard error confidence bands
Note: See text for explanation of abbreviations.

When we examine each of the subperiods individually, however, we obtain results that conflict with the usual intuition about the spillover of financial market volatility (i.e., that the transmission of volatility from one market to another should be greater in times of crisis than in more normal times). The implied response of Australian and New Zealand stocks to an innovation from the Asian series was *proportionally smaller* in both the Asian and world crisis periods than in the precrisis period. The impulse response peaked at around 0.2–0.3 percentage points in both the precrisis and Asian crisis periods, even though the size of a 1-standard-deviation innovation in the Asian series was twice as large in the Asian crisis period as in the precrisis period. Moreover, the reaction in the postcrisis period was similar to the reaction in the Asian crisis, and greater than in the world crisis period.

Table 6. Stock Returns Variance Decompositions: Precrisis

Period	Std. Err.	ASIA	AOI	NZSE40	S&P500
Asia: MSCI Far East Free (excluding Japan)					
0	0.879	100.00	0.00	0.00	0.00
1	0.981	83.29	0.43	0.44	15.84
4	0.986	82.42	1.15	0.62	15.81
All Ordinaries Index					
0	0.652	11.22	88.78	0.00	0.00
1	0.757	9.23	66.21	0.27	24.29
4	0.760	9.27	65.82	0.40	24.51
NZSE40					
0	0.698	3.73	13.81	82.47	0.00
1	0.770	5.20	13.71	67.81	13.28
4	0.771	5.22	13.75	67.70	13.33
S&P500					
0	0.653	0.71	0.48	0.19	98.63
1	0.657	0.75	0.66	0.34	98.26
4	0.658	0.79	0.66	0.37	98.18

Note: The second through fifth data columns of the table represent the percentage of error variance in the current period accounted for by current-period innovations to each variable in the model; these four columns should therefore sum to 100. See text for explanation of abbreviations.

4.2   Bond Markets

Figure 12 suggests that returns on the EMBI Global Constrained Index had a small and marginally significant impact on Australian and New Zealand bond returns during the Asian crisis period. However, the greatest reaction of Australian and New Zealand bond returns to the Asian series was in the precrisis period (figure 11).[13] This result may be due to the EMBI series' picking up the effects of the Japanese and European markets on Australian and New Zealand bond yields. Previous work has suggested some role for these other markets, independent of the U.S. market, in explaining bond market movements in Australia (Kortian and O'Regan 1996). Since these markets are omitted from our estimates, it may be that the EMBI series is picking up innovations from those markets during the 1994 bond market sell-off. If the Japanese and European markets had affected Asian markets as well as the Australian and New Zealand markets, then our identification approach will capture this as Australian and New Zealand returns being affected by Asian returns.

There does not appear to be an indirect response to Asia via the U.S. market, suggesting that the Australian and New Zealand bond markets do not fall into the category of periphery markets receiving shocks through a developed central market as suggested by Kaminsky and Reinhart (2003). Overnight developments in U.S. bond markets had a strong effect on Aus-

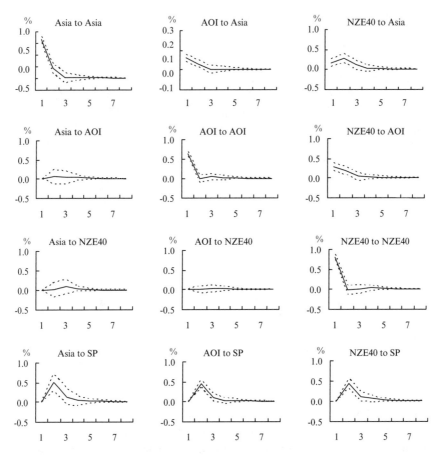

Fig. 8. Impulse responses for Asian crisis stock returns VAR: Response to 1 standard deviation innovations ± 2 standard error confidence bands
Note: See text for explanation of abbreviations

tralian and New Zealand bond returns, accounting for 15–30 percent of their variability in the Asian crisis period, around 40 percent in the world crisis, and around 66 percent in the postcrisis period at the one- to four-day horizon. However, during the Asian crisis (and the world crisis), bond market volatility in Asia, as proxied by EMBI, accounted for an insignificant part of the variation in the U.S. market (less than 1 percent).[14] The corresponding figures for the world crisis and postcrisis bond VAR impulse responses are available in Ellis and Lewis (2001).

There are a number of possible reasons for this smaller response to Asian crisis events by bonds than by stocks. In particular, bond yields are determined primarily by expectations of inflation and (domestic) real interest rates. Therefore, bond returns should be less affected by corporate-sector and trade developments than are other markets; and so the economic-linkages rationale for contagion between asset markets (Lowell, Neu, and

Table 7. Stock Returns Variance Decompositions: Asian Crisis

Period	Std. Err.	ASIA	AOI	NZSE40	S&P500
Asia: MSCI Far East Free (excluding Japan)					
0	1.663	100.00	0.00	0.00	0.00
1	1.789	91.58	0.10	0.01	8.30
4	1.799	90.55	0.22	0.31	8.92
All Ordinaries Index					
0	0.719	18.65	81.35	0.00	0.00
1	0.874	16.28	55.16	0.01	28.56
4	0.884	15.96	54.23	0.24	29.57
NZSE40					
0	0.883	3.58	11.57	84.85	0.00
1	1.049	9.99	11.60	60.09	18.33
4	1.066	10.74	11.48	58.34	19.43
S&P500					
0	1.086	6.50	0.33	1.46	91.71
1	1.092	6.66	0.49	1.56	91.29
4	1.086	6.50	0.33	1.46	91.71

Note: See table 6 note.

Tong 1998) is not as important. This would tend to result in a more muted reaction in bond markets than for stocks and, particularly, exchange rates.

4.3 Exchange Rates

There was a clear reaction of the AUD/USD and NZD/USD rates to movements in Asian markets during the Asian crisis (figure 13). This response was much more obvious than in the other two markets. Exchange-market movements in Asia were significant during the Asian crisis, accounting for just under 8 percent of the variation in the AUD/USD rate, and around 5.5 percent of the NZD/USD at each of the horizons examined (table 11).[15] There was also a significant impact on the NZD/USD rate in the precrisis period. In the other periods, the impulse responses were not more than 2 standard deviations from zero (although nearly so for the AUD/USD in the world crisis). While this might partly reflect the poor fit of the linear model—evidenced by the large error bands in most periods—it makes the contrast with the Asian crisis period even more striking. The corresponding figures for impulse responses from the exchange rate VAR are available in the working paper version of this chapter (Ellis and Lewis 2001).

As might be expected from the results in section 3.2, another feature of these results is the increasing importance over time of the CRB index in explaining daily movements in both the AUD/USD and NZD/USD exchange rates. This is demonstrated in the increasing share of total variance

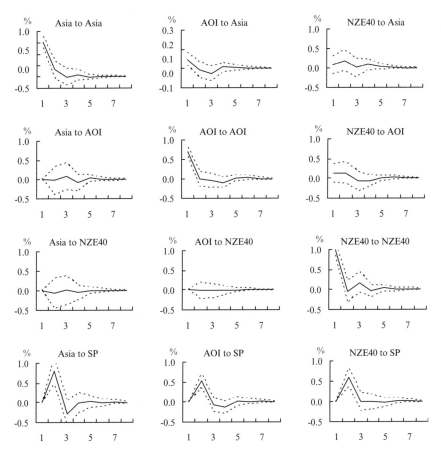

Fig. 9. Impulse responses for world crisis stock returns VAR: Response to 1 standard deviation innovations ± 2 standard error confidence bands
Note: See text for explanation of abbreviations.

accounted for by the CRB index across the subperiods reported in table 11. Since Australia's and New Zealand's exports have tended to become more diverse over time, rather than more concentrated in commodities, this result cannot reflect changing fundamentals. This type of development may be evidence that financial market integration brings to regional markets an increased proportion of less-informed traders who may look to indicator variables with little information content—but high-frequency availability—in forming their views and trading strategies (such as explored in Calvo and Mendoza 1999).

4.4 Interpretation

Our results indicate that responses to crises can vary between asset classes, something also evident in the papers by Baig and Goldfajn (1999) and Ito

Table 8. Stock Returns Variance Decompositions: World Crisis

Period	Std. Err.	ASIA	AOI	NZSE40	S&P500
Asia: MSCI Far East Free (excluding Japan)					
0	1.535	100.00	0.00	0.00	0.00
1	1.769	78.68	0.03	0.13	21.16
4	1.798	76.42	0.49	0.21	22.88
All Ordinaries Index					
0	0.751	10.94	89.06	0.00	0.00
1	0.920	7.41	59.32	0.03	33.25
4	0.951	9.13	56.75	0.10	34.03
NZSE40					
0	1.046	0.53	1.63	97.85	0.00
1	1.232	2.76	2.52	70.71	24.00
4	1.254	3.21	3.06	70.52	23.22
S&P500					
0	1.390	1.73	4.24	0.00	94.02
1	1.408	1.72	5.48	0.36	92.44
4	1.444	2.81	7.48	0.55	89.17

Note: See table 6 note.

and Hashimoto (this volume). There is not a uniform notion of increased uncertainty driving a uniform result: rather, each asset class is influenced by both common and market-specific factors. In addition, there are differences between the results in the Asian crisis and world crisis periods, which may reflect the different nature of shocks hitting Australian and New Zealand financial markets in the two periods. The Asian crisis countries are largely commodity importers and significant trading partners of Australia and New Zealand; the countries in financial distress in the world crisis period—primarily Russia and Brazil—are commodity exporters with little bilateral trade with Australia and New Zealand, although they are competitors in third markets.

The VAR estimates imply that Australian and New Zealand stock and (to a lesser extent) bond markets were *less* affected by movements of a given size in Asian markets during the crises than at other times. That is, spillover from these markets in crisis to unrelated markets appears to be weaker than it is between markets that are already in similar environments. However, these results could partly reflect the type of information captured by a regional market index. Financial market returns depend on common—or "global"—shocks, regional shocks, and country-specific (idiosyncratic) shocks. By using a regional index, we are effectively averaging across country-specific shocks, so that most of the information in the series will reflect regional and global shocks.

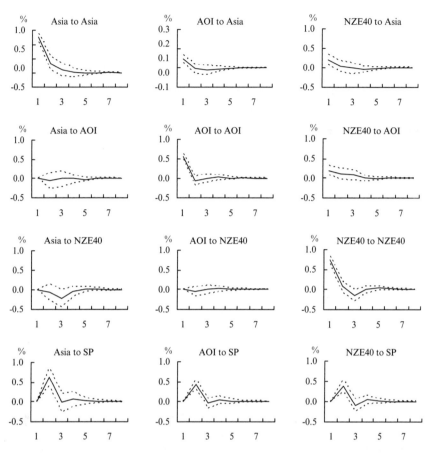

Fig. 10. Impulse responses for postcrisis stock returns VAR: Response to 1 standard deviation innovations ± 2 standard error confidence bands
Note: See text for explanation of abbreviations.

During the crisis periods, however, the Asian market variables incorporated idiosyncratic (country-specific) and regional shocks that were much larger than in noncrisis periods. Although country-specific shocks would ordinarily tend to average out and thus not show up in a regional index, this was clearly not the case during the Asian crisis. These Asia-specific shocks may be less important to Australian and New Zealand markets than the global shocks also captured in the Asian data. Therefore, the estimated coefficients on the stock price indices during the Asian crisis period might have been smaller because the series contained *proportionally less* information relevant to markets in Australia and New Zealand.

By contrast, spillover of financial market volatility to *exchange rates* was greater during the crises than at other times. This difference is an example

Table 9. Stock Returns Variance Decompositions: Postcrisis

Period	Std. Err.	ASIA	AOI	NZSE40	S&P500
Asia: MSCI Far East Free (excluding Japan)					
0	1.255	100.00	0.00	0.00	0.00
1	1.450	80.51	0.14	0.20	19.15
4	1.473	78.52	0.19	2.51	18.79
All Ordinaries Index					
0	0.621	14.28	85.72	0.00	0.00
1	0.767	9.49	56.85	0.48	33.18
4	0.774	10.19	56.01	0.52	33.28
NZSE40					
0	0.808	7.04	6.73	86.22	0.00
1	0.912	5.69	7.03	68.25	19.03
4	0.937	5.71	7.43	67.55	19.31
S&P500					
0	1.147	0.01	0.07	0.35	99.57
1	1.158	0.18	0.09	2.04	97.69
4	1.168	0.77	0.30	2.05	96.87

Note: See table 6 note.

of the tendency for the asset class to matter more in determining spillovers than did the country where the market was located. Indeed, the importance of Asian export markets for Australia and New Zealand may imply that Asia-specific shocks are more important than other shocks for exchange rates.

5. CONCLUSION

This chapter contains several findings on the responses of financial markets in Australia and New Zealand to the events of the Asian crisis. Australia's and New Zealand's stock markets and exchange rates tended to be more volatile on days in which significant news occurred in Asia than was true for other days in the Asian crisis period. Days adjacent to news-event days also tended to be more volatile than other days in this period. This was not the case for the bond markets, which were most volatile in the precrisis period encompassing the global bond market sell-off in 1994.

In general, Australian and New Zealand financial markets were positively correlated with Asian news events. Good news tended to be associated with rising stock prices and appreciating exchange rates, with the reverse being true for news events that we classified as bad. This could be interpreted as the financial markets' response to events in trading-partner countries that could influence export demand and domestic corporate profitability.

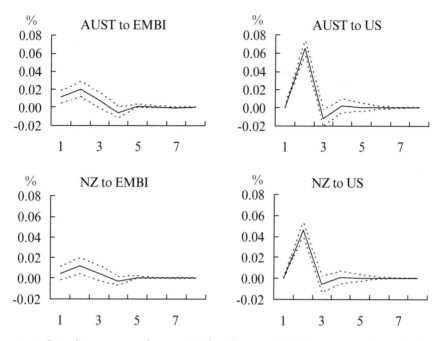

Fig. 11. Impulse responses for precrisis bond returns VAR: Response to 1 standard deviation innovations ± 2 standard error confidence bands

Once we controlled for overnight developments in U.S. markets, however, the Asian news events appeared to have very little independent effect on Australian and New Zealand stock markets. Foreign exchange markets reacted with a one-day lag. It is possible that some of these events occurred after the close of the Auckland and Sydney trading sessions, so that markets here could react only after their U.S. counterparts. Alternatively, financial markets may have processed the information inefficiently, by waiting for the U.S. markets to react; daily movements in U.S. markets are clearly important determinants of daily returns in Australian and New Zealand markets for all three asset classes. Although markets in Australia and New Zealand reacted with a lag to the news dummies, they had a contemporaneous relationship with Asian financial markets. This suggests that the timing explanation might be closer to the truth.

Our results do not suggest that spillover of volatility in stock and bond markets is necessarily greater during crises than in more normal times. The greater volatility observed in Australia and New Zealand in the Asian crisis period was simply due to the original shocks being larger than in other periods, consistent with Forbes and Rigobon's (2002) finding of no contagion, but rather increased interdependence for equity markets. By contrast, volatility spillover in foreign exchange markets did appear greater in the Asian and world crises than at other times. This result suggests that trade linkages influence the investment decisions of market

Table 10. Bond Variance Decompositions

Period	Std. Err.	AUST	NZ	US	EMBI
Precrisis					
Australian bond futures					
0	0.085	98.22	0.00	0.00	1.78
1	0.110	59.73	0.23	35.65	4.39
4	0.111	58.57	0.30	36.10	5.03
New Zealand bond futures					
0	0.081	18.27	81.40	0.00	0.33
1	0.095	13.60	60.79	23.90	1.70
4	0.095	13.52	60.37	24.11	2.00
Asian crisis					
Australian bond futures					
0	0.062	97.53	0.00	0.00	2.47
1	0.075	67.29	0.38	30.26	2.07
4	0.076	67.09	0.41	30.27	2.23
New Zealand bond futures					
0	0.067	15.32	82.05	0.00	2.63
1	0.073	12.83	68.87	15.83	2.47
4	0.074	12.76	68.04	16.66	2.54
World crisis					
Australian bond futures					
0	0.065	100.00	0.00	0.00	0.00
1	0.079	74.59	0.28	23.02	2.12
4	0.081	70.27	0.51	25.75	3.47
New Zealand bond futures					
0	0.057	34.44	64.27	0.00	1.29
1	0.069	23.40	44.42	30.82	1.36
4	0.075	20.24	37.72	39.96	2.08
Postcrisis					
Australian bond futures					
0	0.050	99.16	0.00	0.00	0.84
1	0.090	31.04	0.84	67.55	0.57
4	0.092	30.10	2.33	66.23	1.34
New Zealand bond futures					
0	0.039	33.55	66.45	0.00	0.00
1	0.070	10.41	21.72	67.36	0.51
4	0.071	10.30	22.31	65.31	2.08

Note: See table 6 note.

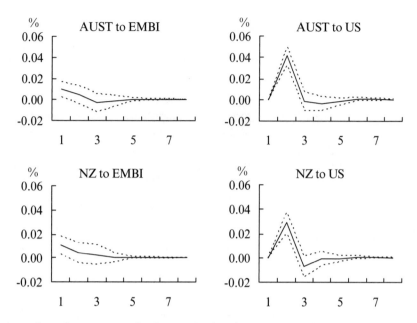

Fig. 12. Impulse responses for Asian crisis bond returns VAR: Response to 1 standard deviation innovations ± 2 standard error confidence bands

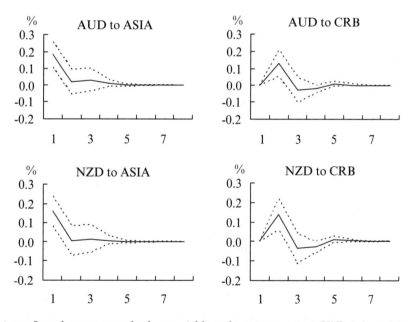

Fig. 13. Impulse responses for four-variable exchange rate returns VAR, Asian crisis: Response to 1 standard deviation innovations ± 2 standard error confidence bands
Note: See text for explanation of abbreviations.

Table 11. Exchange Rate Variance Decompositions

Period	Std. Err.	AUD	NZD	CRB	ASIA
Precrisis					
AUD/USD					
0	0.468	99.60	0.00	0.00	0.40
1	0.469	99.03	0.01	0.56	0.41
4	0.470	98.60	0.18	0.74	0.48
NZD/USD					
0	0.360	21.98	75.80	0.00	2.22
1	0.361	22.21	75.27	0.10	2.43
4	0.363	22.13	75.29	0.17	2.41
Asian crisis					
AUD/USD					
0	0.660	92.23	0.00	0.00	7.77
1	0.673	88.59	0.00	3.85	7.56
4	0.680	87.79	0.50	4.08	7.63
NZD/USD					
0	0.672	54.82	39.37	0.00	5.81
1	0.687	52.46	37.86	4.13	5.56
4	0.697	52.64	37.39	4.50	5.47
World crisis					
AUD/USD					
0	0.646	95.02	0.00	0.00	4.98
1	0.754	70.72	0.62	22.95	5.72
4	0.762	70.34	1.23	22.60	5.82
NZD/USD					
0	0.759	58.14	40.80	0.00	1.05
1	0.821	50.84	35.24	12.35	1.58
4	0.850	52.01	32.95	12.61	2.43
Postcrisis					
AUD/USD					
0	0.608	97.79	0.00	0.00	2.21
1	0.657	84.05	0.03	13.05	2.87
4	0.679	79.40	0.26	12.37	7.96
NZD/USD					
0	0.588	57.72	39.43	0.00	2.85
1	0.640	48.84	33.34	15.18	2.63
4	0.661	46.46	31.55	14.91	7.07

Note: See table 6 note

participants, as well as the global shocks that characterized the world crisis period.

In addition to our findings on responses to events in Asia, the results in this chapter allow us to compare market behavior in Australia and New Zealand at a more general level. Markets for the same assets in the two countries tend to behave more similarly than markets for different assets in the same country. The dynamic responses of bond prices and exchange rates to shocks originating in Asia are similar in the two countries for each asset class, although the linkages between the two classes may have further information to contribute to this story. There were some differences in the stock market responses, with the impulse response for New Zealand being more drawn out in the Asian crisis period. There was a cumulated divergence in the levels of the two countries' stock markets during the Asian crisis, and a small divergence in the levels of their exchange rates during the world crisis and postcrisis periods. However, there is no evidence of a systematic difference in responses to Asian news events or financial market developments.

This exploration of the Australian and New Zealand experience in the East Asian currency crisis clearly illustrates that even countries with strong fundamental linkages to crisis countries, such as trade and geographical proximity, will not necessarily be drawn into crisis volatility. The different asset classes here showed less volatility in the crisis periods than the postcrisis period, and in two of the asset markets U.S.-based shocks were more important sources of volatility than the headline Asian shocks of the time. The observed differences between the countries that suffered transmission from the Asian crisis and those that did not relate at least partly to the underlying structure of the economy—the Australian and New Zealand experience fits well with the conclusions of Sachs, Tornell, and Velasco (1996) that strong fundamentals will render a crisis event a temporary phenomenon, at most. Precisely what the differences are which protect a particular economy is very difficult to ascertain in advance.

Appendix: Chronology of Major Events in the Asian Crisis

Date	Event	Type of News
1997		
15 May	Thailand, after a week of selling pressure and massive intervention in the forward markets, announces wide-ranging capital controls aimed at segmenting the onshore and offshore markets.	Bad
27 June	The Bank of Thailand suspends the operations of sixteen troubled finance companies and orders them to submit merger or consolidation plans.	Bad
2 July	Floating of the Thai baht (baht devalues by 15% in onshore markets; 20% in offshore markets). Pressure spreads to the Philippine peso, Malaysian ringgit, and Indonesian rupiah	Bad

Date	Event	Type of News
11 July	Bangko Sentral ng Pilipinas announces the peso will float in a wider range, abandoning the de facto peg. Bank of Indonesia widens the rupiah trading band from 8% to 12%.	Bad
14 July	Bank Negara Malaysia is reported as abandoning the defence of the ringgit.	Bad
28 July	Thai government requests IMF assistance.	Bad
5 August	Thailand suspends a further forty-two troubled finance companies.	Bad
14 August	Indonesia abandons the rupiah trading band. The rupiah depreciates by 4%.	Bad
20 August	Thailand and the IMF agree on a US$17 billion financial stabilization package.	Good
27 August	Malaysia imposes trading restrictions on the stock market, including an effective ban on short selling.	Bad
29 August	Bank of Indonesia introduces selective credit controls on rupiah trading.	Bad
8 October	Indonesia announces it will seek IMF assistance.	Bad
17 October	Malaysia announces an austerity budget. Authorities stop supporting the New Taiwan dollar, which falls by 6%. Pressure on Hong Kong dollar and equity markets intensifies. Review of Thai emergency funding.	Bad
20–23 October	Financial turbulence in Hong Kong. Hang Seng index falls by 23% in four days. Overnight interest rates rise from 7% to around 250%. S&P downgrades Korea's and Thailand's sovereign ratings.	Bad
27 October	The Dow Jones loses 554 points, following the crash in the Hang Seng. Equity markets in Brazil, Argentina, and Mexico see their biggest single-day losses, as the crisis ripples across the globe.	Bad
28 October	Russian equity prices decline by 23%.	Bad
31 October	Bank resolution package announced in Indonesia, resulting in the closure of sixteen troubled private banks. Leads to a depositor run on others. After intense pressure on the real, the Central Bank of Brazil doubles the central bank intervention rate to 43%.	Bad
5 November	IMF standby credit for Indonesia of US$10.1 billion approved; US$3 billion made available immediately.	Good
10 November	In Thailand, opposition leader Chuan Leekpai takes over as prime minister. In Russia, interest rates are raised by 7 percentage points and authorities announce that the intervention band for the rouble will be widened from ±5% to ±15%.	Bad
17 November	Korea abandons defence of the won.	Bad

Date	Event	Type of News
1997 *(cont'd)*		
18 November	Korean finance minister resigns. Authorities announce a reform package.	Bad
20 November	Daily fluctuation band for the Korean won widened from ±2.25% to ±10%.	Bad
21 November	Korea requests IMF assistance.	Bad
3 December	Korea and the IMF agree on a US$57 billion financial assistance package.	Good
8 December	Thai authorities close fifty-six of the suspended finance companies.	Bad
16 December	Floating of the Korean won.	Bad
23 December	Rating agencies downgrade Korea's sovereign rating to speculative grade. The won falls nearly 2,000 per U.S. dollar.	Bad
24 December	IMF and other lenders announce speeding up of disbursement of financial assistance and that international commercial banks will roll-over short-term debts owed by Korean financial institutions.	Good
30 December	Foreign banks agree to roll-over Korean debt.	Good
1998		
2 January	Indonesia announces plans to merge four out of seven state-owned banks. Malaysia announces plans for mergers of finance companies.	Good
6 January	Indonesian budget introduced; badly received by financial markets.	Bad
13 January	Thailand amends law for foreign investors in banks to be reclassified as domestic companies, allowing them to hold property.	Good
15 January	Indonesia and the IMF announce agreement on revised economic program aimed at strengthening and reinforcing the ongoing IMF-supported program.	Good
16 January	International lenders officially agree to roll-over Korean short-term bank debt.	Good
20 January	Thailand allows full foreign ownership of securities firms.	Good
27 January	Indonesia guarantees commercial bank obligations, allows overseas investments in local banks, and announces a freeze on debt payments.	Good
29 January	Agreement between Korea and its external creditors to exchange US$24 billion of short-term debt for government-guaranteed loans at 2.25–2.75 percentage points over six-month LIBOR.	Good

Date	Event	Type of News
1998 *(cont'd)*		
30 January	Thailand lifts currency restrictions, reunifying the spot market.	Good
9–10 February	Indonesia's plan to create a currency board is opposed by the IMF and several creditor governments, who threaten to withdraw financial assistance.	Bad
13 February	IMF Managing Director Camdessus expresses further concern over Indonesia's move to a currency board. He is of the "strong view" that the time for a currency board in Indonesia has "not yet come" because of preconditions.	Bad
4 March	In a second review of Thailand's economic program, the IMF relaxes certain macroeconomic policy targets and approves disbursement of second tranche.	Good
10 April	Indonesia signs new letter of intent on economic program with IMF.	Good
21 May	Indonesia's president Suharto resigns.	Bad
25 May	The Korean stock market falls to an eleven-year low.	Bad
1 June	The Thai stock market index, continuing its slide from early March, falls to a ten-year low.	Bad
4 June	Indonesian authorities reach an agreement to restructure the external debt of Indonesia's banking and corporate sectors.	Good
10 June	Third Quarterly Review of Thailand's assistance program indicates restructuring on track.	Good
2 July	World Bank approves a US$1 billion loan to Indonesia. Loan is part of US$4.5 billion pledged by the World Bank last year.	Good
8 July	Standard and Poor's affirms its CCC+ rating on the Republic of Indonesia's US$400 million Yankee bond due in 2006, the CCC+ long-term foreign currency, and its B− long-term local currency issuer credit ratings. Outlook is now described as negative.	Bad
10 July	Malaysian stock index hits nine-year low.	Bad
16 July	IMF approves U.S.$1 billion payment; promises another US$6 billion to Indonesia.	Good
24 July	Moody's cuts Malaysia's foreign currency debt rating to Baa2 from A2. Reasons cited are the country's recession, growing debt, and lack of clear policy direction in response to the Asian crisis.	Bad
4 August	The Philippines benchmark stock index slides to its lowest level since April 1993 on continuing loss of confidence in the region.	Bad

Date	Event	Type of News
1998 (cont'd)		
6 August	Malaysia's sovereign risk rating cut to BBB from A by Thomson BankWatch.	Bad
7 August	Singapore stock index reaches a 9.5-year low.	Bad
11 August	Agence France-Presse (AFP) reports that the Indonesian government is in default on some of its sovereign debt. The government denies this.	Bad
13 August	Moody's and Standard and Poor's cut ratings for Russian sovereign debt.	Bad
14 August	Hong Kong government intervenes in the stock market, purchasing an estimated HK$3 billion in stocks and futures, in an attempt to stop the speculation against the currency.	Bad
17 August	Russia allows the rouble to float freely within a corridor between 6.00 and 9.50 to the USD and makes some other changes to Russian financial markets. Standard and Poor's cuts Russia's long-term foreign currency debt rating to CCC from B−.	Bad
25 August	IMF Executive Board approves extended funding arrangement for Indonesia.	Good
31 August	Standard and Poor's downgrades Hong Kong's sovereign credit rating to A, with a negative outlook. The rating agency also cites a decline in Hong Kong's financial strength because of the Asian crisis.	Bad

Sources: BIS (1998, table VII.6, p. 131) and IMF (1998, box 2.12, p. 49).

NOTES

1. Although this classification is somewhat arbitrary, it did not seem to be crucial to our results.

2. The bonds data are for the "next" contract to be delivered, which is a very close substitute for the underlying spot instrument (i.e., physical ten-year bonds). The markets in these instruments on the futures exchanges are deep and liquid and provide reliable price readings. These markets are generally considered to be more liquid than those for the corresponding physical securities.

3. This rather arbitrary dating is not the only way to define periods of crisis. Eichengreen, Rose, and Wyplosz (1995, 1996) define a crisis period by the occurrence of extreme values of an index of "exchange market pressure," defined as a weighted average of movements in exchange rates, interest rates, and international reserves, relative to interest rate and reserves changes in a numeraire country; see also the review of crisis dating in Jacobs, Kuper, and Lestano (this volume).

4. In contrast, Forbes and Rigobon (2002) define the precrisis period as 1 January 1996 to 16 October 1997, and Dungey et al. (this volume) define the precrisis period as 1 January 1997 to 16 October 1997 in examining equity markets.

5. Over the whole period, the average absolute daily percent change in Australian stocks was 0.6 percent, compared to 0.7 percent for New Zealand. However, in the period since October 1997, average volatility has increased to 0.7 percent and 0.9 percent, respectively.

6. The U.S. market's day t occurs after the close of Asian, Australian, and New Zealand day t, but before their day $t + 1$. This also applies to the timing of the CRB series; we therefore include only lags of the CRB index, not its contemporaneous value, in the equations for explaining returns on Australasian exchange rates.

7. The estimated coefficients on the lagged U.S. bond futures are substantially less than 1, despite the yields on the underlying securities moving closely together, because of differences in the quoting conventions used in the markets trading futures contracts. This does not affect those coefficients' significance or the values of the other coefficients.

8. Detailed documentation for the MSCI indices are available from Morgan Stanley's Web site (http://www.msci.com).

9. These results are available from the authors.

10. The EMBI Global Constrained Index is a market-capitalization-weighted index, and includes emerging-market issues by sovereign and quasi-sovereign entities denominated in U.S. dollars. It considers only those issues with a current face value amount outstanding of US$500 million or more, with at least 2.5 years until maturity. More detailed information on the construction of EMBI Global is available on JP Morgan's Web site.

11. There are $4 \times 3 \times 2 \times 1 = 24$ possible orderings for a four-variable VAR; if Australia and New Zealand are treated as a bloc (i.e., kept together but with potentially different ordering within the bloc) there are twelve. The results for the other orderings are available from the authors.

12. We have omitted the responses of the S&P500 to other variables from the impulse response graphs, as they are very close to zero.

13. In both precrisis and Asian crisis periods, the point estimate is around 0.01, although the size of a 1 standard deviation EMBI shock in the Asian crisis period was somewhat larger.

14. In this section and the section presenting results for the bilateral exchange rates, we omit the impulse responses and variance decompositions for the U.S. and Asian variables from the graphs and tables. These results are available from the authors.

15. The large fraction of NZD/USD variability accounted for by the AUD/USD rate is an artifact of our recursive-ordering identification scheme, and may reflect that the Australian dollar and New Zealand dollar tend to be traded as a bloc.

REFERENCES

Almeida, A., C. Goodhart, and R. Payne, 1998, The Effects of Macroeconomic News on High Frequency Exchange Rate Behavior, *Journal of Financial and Quantitative Analysis* 33, 383–408.

Baig, T., and I. Goldfajn, 1998, Financial Market Contagion in the Asian Crisis, *International Monetary Fund Working Paper* 98/155.

———, 1999, Financial Market Contagion in the Asian Crisis, *International Monetary Fund Staff Papers* 46, 167–195.

Bank for International Settlements, 1998, Financial Intermediation and the Asian Crisis, *BIS 68th Annual Report*, 117–141.

Calvo, G. A., and E. G. Mendoza, 1999, Regional Contagion and the Globalization of Securities Markets, *National Bureau of Economic Research Working Paper* 7153.

Campbell, F., and E. Lewis, 1998, What Moves Yields in Australia? *Reserve Bank of Australia Research Discussion Paper* 9808.

Dornbusch, R., Y. C. Park, and S. Claessens, 2000, Contagion: Understanding How It Spreads, *World Bank Research Observer* 15, 177–197.

Dungey, M., and V. L. Martin, 2001, Contagion in the East Asian Currency Crisis, in J. R. Behrman, M. Dutta, S. Husted, P. Sumalee, C. Suthipand, and P. Wiboonchutikula, eds., *Restructuring Asian Economics for the New Millennium* (Elsevier Science, Amsterdam).

Eichengreen, B., A. K. Rose, and C. Wyplosz, 1995, Exchange Market Mayhem: The Antecedents and Aftermath of Speculative Attacks, *Economic Policy: A European Forum* 21, 249–296.

———, 1996, Contagious Currency Crises: First Tests, *Scandinavian Journal of Economics* 98, 463–484.

Ellis, L., and E. Lewis, 2001, The Response of Financial Markets in Australia and New Zealand to News about the Asian Crisis, *Reserve Bank of Australia Research Discussion Paper* 2001-3.

Engle, R. F., T. Ito, and W. L. Lin, 1990, Meteor-Showers or Heat Waves: Heteroskedastic Intradaily Volatility in the Foreign-Exchange Market, *Econometrica* 58, 525–542.

Fleming, M., and J. A. Lopez, 1999, Heat Waves, Meteor Showers, and Trading Volume: An Analysis of Volatility Spillovers in the U.S. Treasury Market, *Federal Reserve Bank of San Francisco Working Papers in Applied Economic Theory* 99-09.

Fleming, M. J., and E. M. Remolona, 1997, What Moves the Bond Market? *Federal Reserve Bank of New York Economic Policy Review* 3, 31–50.

Forbes, K. J., and R. Rigobon, 2002, No Contagion, Only Interdependence: Measuring Stock Market Comovements, *Journal of Finance* 57, 2223–2261.

International Monetary Fund, 1998, The Asian Crisis: Capital Markets Dynamics and Spillover (Chapter II), *World Economic and Financial Surveys; International Capital Markets; Developments, Prospects, and Key Policy Issues* September.

Kaminsky, G. L., and C. M. Reinhart, 2003, The Center and the Periphery: The Globalization of Financial Turmoil, *National Bureau of Economic Research Working Paper* 9479.

Kaminsky, G. L., and S. L. Schmukler, 1999, What Triggers Market Jitters? A Chronicle of the Asian Crisis, *Journal of International Money and Finance* 18, 537–560.

Kim, S.-J., 1996, Inflation News in Australia: Its Effects on Exchange Rates and Interest Rates, *Applied Financial Economics* 6.

———, 1999, The Short-Term Dynamics of Bond Futures Market Response to New Information: Australian Evidence, *The University of New South Wales School of Banking and Finance Working Papers* 1999-03.

Kim, S.-J., and J. Sheen, 2000, International Linkages and Macroeconomic News Effects on Interest Rate Volatility: Australia and the U.S., *Pacific Basin Finance Journal* 8, 85–113.

Kortian, T., and J. O'Regan, 1996, Australian Financial Market Volatility: An Exploration of Cross-Country and Cross-Market Linkages, *Reserve Bank of Australia Research Discussion Paper* 9609.

Lane, T., A. Ghosh, J. Hamann, S. Phillips, M. Schultze-Ghattas, and T. Tsikata, 1999, IMF-Supported Programs in Indonesia, Korea and Thailand, *International Monetary Fund Occasional Paper* 178.

Lowell, J., C. R. Neu, and D. Tong, 1998, Financial Crises and Contagion in Emerging Market Countries, *RAND Working Paper* MR-962.

Masson, P. R., 1999, Contagion: Monsoonal Effects, Spillovers and Jumps between Multiple Equilibria, in A. Pierre-Richard, M. Miller, D. Vines, and A. Weber, eds., *The Asian Financial Crisis: Causes, Contagion and Consequences* (Cambridge University Press, Cambridge).

Pericoli, M., and M. Sbracia, 2003, A Primer on Financial Contagion, *Journal of Economic Surveys* 17, 571–608.

Roubini, N., 1999, Chronology of the Asian Currency Crisis and Its Global Contagion, *http://www.stern.nyu.edu/~nroubini/asia*

Sachs, J. D., A. Tornell, and A. Velasco, 1996, Financial Crises in Emerging Markets: The Lessons from 1995, *Brookings Papers on Economic Activity* 2, 147–215.

Summers, P. M., 2001, Forecasting Australia's Economic Performance during the Asian Crisis, *International Journal of Forecasting* 17, 499–515.

World Bank, 1998, *World Bank Atlas* (World Bank Group, Washington, DC).

7

The Normal, the Fat-Tailed, and the Contagious

Modeling Changes in Emerging-Market Bond Spreads with Endogenous Liquidity

Paul R. Masson, Shubha Chakravarty, and Tim Gulden

1. INTRODUCTION

Despite extensive study of capital flows to developing countries, it is safe to assert that there remain a number of issues about which there is not yet a clear consensus among economists.[1] Three important issues stand out. First, though there are many models of balance of payments crises, there is little agreement in particular cases on the dominant cause. Specifically, are crises the results of poor economic fundamentals, or are they self-fulfilling, triggered by a rush for the exits by investors?[2] Are the relevant economic fundamentals excessive monetary expansion, government deficits, or financial-sector problems? Second, does a crisis in one country trigger one in another? As is the case for a financial crisis in a single country, here also it is necessary to identify the relevant set of fundamentals, since there are numerous linkages that would explain the co-movement in financial vari-

4

Masson, Brookings Institution and University of Toronto, Paul.Masson@Rotman.Utoronto.ca; Chakravarty, Brookings Institution and Columbia University, shubha_c@yahoo.com; Gulden, Brookings Institution and University of Maryland, tgulden@umd.edu. This chapter is a revised and abridged version of the paper presented at a conference on "International Financial Contagion: Theories and Evidence" in Cambridge, UK (30–31 May 2003). It has benefited from comments received there and at a seminar at Brookings. We are grateful to Heather Milkiewicz for research assistance, to Adrian de la Garza for providing the emerging-market spread data, and to Rob Axtell, Martin Evans, and Carol Graham for comments and encouragement; Ben Klenow provided a valuable alternative source for excess kurtosis in the model. We would also like to acknowledge our debt to Elizabeth Littlefield and Michael Mauboussin for sharing their knowledge of how the market works. Jon Parker provided help with ASCAPE programming.

ables across countries. This leads to the third issue: what are the causes of co-movement—macroeconomic fundamentals, or instead financial contagion operating through various channels, including shifts in investor attitudes, balance-sheet effects, or regional portfolio rebalancing triggered by a crisis in one country? In other words, is co-movement excessive?

In this chapter, we do not test statistically among the various channels that have been advanced in the literature, but rather simulate a simple model of balance of payments crises, focusing on both interacting expectations and varying liquidity as important features affecting emerging-market bonds. We posit a simple model of currency crises (which admits of both fundamental and self-fulfilling triggers of crises) where investors hold both emerging-market and developed-country assets. Thus, portfolio rebalancing could, in principle, lead to co-movement in asset prices. We depart from the assumption made in most models of contagion, namely, the assumption that there is a representative agent forming rational expectations. Instead, investors form expectations on the basis both of their past experience and of imitation of other (more successful) investors. These assumptions are sufficient to produce interesting dynamics, quite independent of the fundamentals, and we study their implications for triggering crises and causing contagion. This work is in the tradition of (multi-)agent-based models, which have been widely applied in a number of disciplines; some of that work is briefly surveyed below.

Our aim is also to see whether such a model can replicate in more detail the properties of the distributions of interest rates on emerging-market bonds. While there is a considerable literature on the structure of returns in various developed-country financial markets (e.g., Mandelbrot 1963; Mantegna and Stanley 1995; and Bouchaud and Potters 2000), emerging-market bonds have received less attention. In a companion paper (Masson 2003), daily data for JP Morgan's Emerging Market Bond Indices Global (EMBIG)[3] were analyzed for the twenty or so countries for which data were available. The following properties were identified on the basis of statistical analysis of the distributions of daily changes in spreads relative to U.S. Treasury securities. First, the distribution is very much not normally distributed, but rather exhibits fat tails, indicating that extreme events are much more likely than for the normal. This is a stylized fact that is significant, because it may allow one to distinguish among models of financial crises and contagion. Second, changes in spreads are serially correlated, indicating a possible departure from market efficiency. This applies to almost all emerging-market bonds, and typically the first-order serial correlation coefficient is positive, and significant. Third, there is evidence of contagion, defined as excessive co-movement: changes in spreads (and hence asset returns) are considerably more correlated across countries than are macroeconomic fundamentals defined to include trade between countries.

Agent-based computational approaches have advanced understanding of what causes heavy-tailed price movements. Lux and Marchesi (1999) demonstrated that multi-agent models can produce heavy-tailed distributions without assuming similarly distributed movements in fundamentals. Farmer and Joshi (2002) showed that market structure plays a large part in determining market behavior, and Farmer et al. (2004) showed that liquidity can drive the production of heavy-tailed price movements. MacKenzie (2003) investigated empirically the social structure of emerging-market investment decisions, providing support for the theory that imitation may be a major mechanism in producing heavy-tailed returns and excessive comovement between markets with uncorrelated fundamentals.

While this area of research is often associated with collaborations between economists and physicists, evolutionary biology has become increasingly influential in understanding market dynamics. Gandolfi, Gandolfi, and Barash (2002) provides a survey of these linkages. Farmer (2002) demonstrates that useful parallels can be drawn between multi-agent financial market models and standard models in population biology, where survival depends on "fitness." Blume and Easley (2002) examine fitness dynamics in a market setting, demonstrating that market selection favors profit-maximizing firms, but leads to systems that are much less stable than standard profit-maximizing models would predict.

In this chapter, we simulate various parameterizations of a model of investment in emerging markets in order to see what features are necessary to replicate these stylized facts. This model is an extension of the single-country model in Arifovic and Masson (2004). It combines a simple balance of payments crisis model with hypotheses concerning the formation of expectations by investors. In particular, we assume that investors form and update their expectations on the basis of the success (or otherwise) of their investment strategies. If the latter are successful (in the sense of giving a better return than some randomly chosen comparator), then the investor retains the expectation and strategy; otherwise, the investor adopts the comparator's strategy. In addition, investors at times experiment by randomly choosing a new rule. Thus, the investors in the model do not have information about economic fundamentals (the evolution of the trade balance and foreign exchange reserves), but adapt their strategies on the basis of past results. This has the potential of producing bandwagon effects— that is, serial correlation of changes of asset holdings and spreads, as expectations of excess returns for a particular asset become self-fulfilling, reinforcing that asset's attractiveness. Finally, both economic fundamentals and investor behavior contribute to triggering crises, which occur when a country's reserves go to zero, forcing it to default; this can occur as a result of a bad shock to the trade balance or because a sufficient number of investors withdraw their capital (a "sudden stop," in Calvo's words[4]). The model, when implemented for a single emerging-market bond, has some success in producing an alternation of booms and crashes in emerging markets, similar to actual data (see Arifovic and Masson).

The model also succeeds in producing serial correlation of changes in spreads, as is present in the actual data. It is clear that the "bounded rationality" of investors means that past success in investing reinforces strategies in a way that produces serially correlated changes in returns. To the extent that imitation occurs also, there will be herding (i.e., reinforcement of strategies across investors). In Arifovic and Masson (2004), that herding is the cause of booms and crashes in investment in emerging markets.

However, the model in Arifovic and Masson (2004) does not include more than one emerging-market bond, and several are needed to model contagion across markets. Moreover, that model assumes that all liabilities are short-term, so that the liquidity of a secondary market does not come into play. It turns out that a simple extension of the model to two emerging-market bonds with market-clearing prices is not able to replicate two of the stylized facts mentioned above: the basic model could not produce fat-tailed distributions, nor did co-movement in interest rate spreads for pairs of emerging-market countries emerge when the fundamentals were not themselves correlated. However, an extension of the model to include lack of liquidity is able to reproduce these two properties of the actual data, excess kurtosis and excessive co-movements across countries. We present below simulations of various parameterizations of the basic model without varying liquidity; while the first two moments of the distribution can easily be reproduced, the fourth moment is much smaller than in the real-world data, indicating that the simulated distribution has much thinner tails than the actual one. Indeed, simulated changes are in some cases even more thin-tailed than the normal. Furthermore, correlations in emerging-market spreads are small, even when the fundamentals are assumed to be highly correlated. Instead, the model would predict small negative correlations, as portfolio shifts out of one asset, would, other things equal, produce inflows into the others. It is clear that herding behavior, which is consistent with positive serial correlation in returns on individual country bonds, need not produce contagion, which requires some cross-country linkage based on economic fundamentals, correlated expectations, shifts in attitudes to risk, or portfolio rebalancing affecting the whole asset class.

The complete model includes a market in emerging-market bonds in which liquidity is provided by a market maker. Following the literature, market makers' bid-ask spreads are assumed to vary positively with the volatility of asset prices, not only in that security but also in others, while the market maker's midmarket price varies inversely with the size of the inventory held of that security. The changing degree of liquidity in the market provides a possible explanation of extreme movements of interest rates. Market practitioners point to the fact that at times of crisis, the market "dries up," as everyone attempts to get out at the same time. Moreover, market makers, who typically deal in a number of different securities, react to losses in one market by increasing their bid-ask spreads for the other bonds in which they deal. Thus, lack of liquidity may spill over to other emerging-market bonds.

This version of the model is capable of producing the excessive kurtosis and excess co-movement that is present in the actual data. While it is not the only possible explanation—and we discuss an alternative model that is capable of producing the excess kurtosis and contagion—it explores a plausible channel that has so far received little attention in the literature. We think that it deserves further exploration, both on the side of modeling as well as in detailed study of the way the trading in emerging-market bonds works. The microstructure of trading in emerging-market bonds seems to be a promising area for future research, and one that has so far received little attention, unlike the foreign exchange market (see, e.g., Evans and Lyons 2002).

The plan of the chapter is as follows. The next section describes the basic model, which draws on Arifovic and Masson 2004. Section 3 details the statistical properties of the distribution of simulated emerging-market spreads using various parameterizations of the model with a single emerging-market bond; for none of them does excess kurtosis approach that in the actual data. Section 4 simulates the same model with two emerging-market bonds, noting that despite herding behavior (resulting from investors imitating other successful investors), there is no correlation of spreads across countries. Section 5 introduces a more general model with two-period emerging-market bonds, which can be traded in the period before they mature. This model is shown, when liquidity as provided by a market maker is endogenous, to produce excess kurtosis and excessive co-movement. Section 6 concludes.

2.   A MODEL OF EMERGING-MARKET CRISES

We proceed to describe a canonical balance of payments crisis model, and in the next section examine to what extent it can replicate the actual data. In this model, all capital flows are assumed to take the form of purchases or sales of the debt of the emerging-market government. The model links the ability of a country to service its debts to the existence of non-negative reserves: once reserves hit zero, a default is triggered, leading to losses by investors. The evolution of the balance of payments (i.e., the sum of the trade balance, minus interest payments abroad, plus net capital inflows) is the key to the ability of a country to repay its borrowings, and the interest on them.

Foreign investors choose from a very simple menu of investments: in the one-emerging-market case (to be generalized to several, below), they form expectations of the probability of a default on emerging-market debt, and choose to invest either in the safe (U.S. Treasury) security, paying a known and constant return r^*, or the emerging-market bond, paying r_t. The amount that they invest this period in the emerging-market bond, summed across all investors, is denoted D_t.

A default occurs at t if reserves would have gone negative. The basic balance of payments equation in the model is

$$R_t = R_{t-1} + D_t - (1 + r_{t-1})D_{t-1} + T_t, \tag{1}$$

where R_t are reserves and T_t is the trade balance.[5] The trade balance is a stochastic process that in this model constitutes the economic fundamental.

Investors form expectations of the probability of default. Let investor i's estimated probability be π_t^i and expected size of the default be δ_t^i. We assume that the market interest rate is set to be equal to the U.S. rate plus the average of all n investors' expectations.[6] More exactly, the market rate plus unity is a geometric average over unity plus the expected probability times the size of devaluation, times unity plus the U.S. rate:

$$1 + r_t = (1 + r^*)\left(\prod_{i=1}^{n}(1 + \pi_t^i \delta_t^i)\right)^{1/n} \qquad (2)$$

This formulation allows us to determine both the interest rate, which reflects average expectations, and the quantity of capital flowing to emerging markets, which reflects the skewness of the expectations of default. To illustrate this, assume that risk aversion is zero, so that an investor puts all his or her money in either the safe asset or the emerging-market bond, whichever pays the higher expected return. If an investor then has a more optimistic assessment of the probability (and size) of default than the average embodied in r_t, all money will be placed in emerging-market bonds (negative holdings of either asset are ruled out). If the investor is less optimistic, then all wealth will be put into the safe asset. In these circumstances, the skewness of the distribution of expectations across investors will determine the amount that is invested in emerging markets: positive skewness of the distribution of devaluation expectations will indicate that more than half of investors are to the left of the average (hence more optimistic), so that investment in emerging markets will be higher than in the case of negative skewness (see Arifovic and Masson 2004).

Investors are assumed not to observe the economic fundamental (the trade balance) or reserves. While an extreme assumption, it reflects a reality noted by observers of this market, namely, the ignorance of many investors in emerging-market bonds (who then "woke up" to the flaws of the Asian Tiger economies after the crises occurred—see Goldstein 1998). Starting from some distribution of initial priors, expectations are updated on the basis of past investment returns, with an element of imitation and experimentation. In particular, if investor i puts a proportion x_t^i into the emerging-market bond (and the rest into the safe asset), by analogy with evolutionary biology (Blume and Easley 2002; Gandolfi, Gandolfi, and Barash 2002; Bowles and Hammerstein 2003) one can define "fitness" as

$$\mu_t^i \equiv (1 - x_t^i)(1 + r^*) + \frac{x_t^i(1 + r_t)}{(1 + \delta_t)} - 1,$$

where δ_t is the actual default size (or zero, if no default) in period t. The variable μ_t^i is in fact the realized rate of return on investor i's portfolio. Each investor is assumed to observe the expectations and fitness of another investor, chosen at random.[7] Investor i, in updating the expected probability and size of default (π_t^i, δ_t^i), will compare the fitness of his or her own expectations with those of a randomly chosen comparator (where the probability of being picked depends on relative fitness—i.e., more successful rules are more likely to be imitated[8]); if the latter's fitness is greater, then the comparator's expectations will be adopted; if less than or equal, then the investor's own will be retained. In addition, with some probability p_{ex} the investor would simply discard their expected probability of default π_t^i and pick a new one randomly, drawn from a uniform distribution on the interval $[0, \pi^{max}]$, and similarly for the size of default, if it is endogenous. However, in the simulations below we assume for simplicity that the size of default is fixed and known, because, for instance, a default triggers fixed costs that are independent of the amount of the shortfall of reserves. So, in this case, both expected and actual default size (if one occurs) are known and equal to $\bar{\delta}$. We will henceforth assume this to be the case.

Investors' wealth is endogenous and evolves over time, depending on investor strategy and the rate of return:

$$W_t^i = (1 + \mu_{t-1}^i)W_{t-1}^i - \bar{r}W_{t-1}^i \tag{3}$$

where the last term is consumption out of wealth (at a constant, exogenous rate $\bar{r}$). The model is completed by a stochastic process for the trade balance. This specifies the trade balance as an AR[1] model:

$$T_t = \alpha + \beta T_{t-1} + u_t \tag{4}$$

where $u_t \sim N(0, \sigma^2)$. Estimates based on annual data for various countries are found in Masson (1999). An isomorphic model would replace the balance of payments equation by the government's budget constraint, impose an upper bound on debt (provoking default if reached), and replace the trade equation with a stochastic process on the primary (non-interest) government deficit. Such a model would give qualitatively similar results.

The simplest version of the model is as described above. However, there are two further complications that need to be explained: (a) portfolio selection when investors are risk averse, and (b) conversion of the model from an annual frequency to the monthly or daily frequency that matches our empirical data for emerging-market spreads. These complications are briefly discussed here; details are given in the appendices.

To account for risk aversion, we assume that investors maximize expected utility. Substituting into the first-order conditions a second-order Taylor's expansion of the utility function, we obtain the familiar mean-variance model of choice between a riskless asset and one or several risky assets. For the case of just one emerging-market bond, the resulting expression for the proportion of the portfolio held in the emerging-market bond will be given by

$$x_t^i = \frac{b^i\left(r_t - \dfrac{1+r}{1+\bar{\delta}}\pi_t^i\bar{\delta} - r^*\right)}{\pi_t^i(1 - \pi_t^i)\bar{\delta}^2}. \tag{5}$$

The expression in the denominator is the variance of the return on the risky asset, while the numerator (multiplied by a parameter b^i that is inversely proportional to a measure of risk aversion) is the expected yield differential in favor of the risky asset, if positive.

If $0 < x_t^i < 1$, then the proportion accounted for by the emerging-market bond in i's portfolio is given by equation (5); if not, then $x_t^i = 0$ or $x_t^i = 1$. In the limiting case of zero risk aversion ($b^i \to \infty$), investors merely select the asset yielding the highest expected return (given the constraints $0 \leq x_t^i \leq 1$). The general case is discussed in Appendix A.

For the model to be useful it needs to integrate high-frequency financial markets with lower frequency economic fundamentals. Appendix B discusses the approach taken, namely to convert equation (4) to a monthly or daily autoregression on the assumption that the true stochastic process in fact operates at the higher frequency. In addition, adjustments have to be made to make stocks and flows consistent. Interest rates have to be scaled appropriately, as does the probability of default. At a daily frequency, it makes little sense to update expectations on the basis of one-period returns; thus, we specify a memory horizon $h \geq 1$ over which past returns are averaged when comparing fitness with a comparator.[9] Finally, we take account of the possibility that not all investors are active at a daily frequency; we specify a probability p_{inv} that an investor will update expectations and alter his or her portfolio in any given period.

3.   RESULTS OF A SIMPLE MODEL WITH ONE EMERGING-MARKET BOND AND A SAFE ASSET

The model is essentially that of Arifovic and Masson (2004), calibrated to the reserves and external debt of Argentina in 1996, and using a stochastic equation for the trade balance that is estimated with historical data.[10] As in Arifovic and Masson, the model produces a succession of booms and crashes. However, as we will see, it does not produce a distribution for the changes in spreads that has tails as fat as those in the actual data.

The model was first converted to a daily frequency, using the method described in Appendix B. This produced the following equation for the trade balance (as a percentage of GDP as are the other variables):

$$T_t = 0.23282 + 0.99867T_{t-1} + \varepsilon_t \tag{6}$$

where $\sigma_\varepsilon = 0.73198$ is the standard deviation of shocks to the trade balance, calculated as a percentage of GDP, so that the typical trade balance shock corresponds to roughly three-quarters of a percent of GDP. A crisis is triggered if the country's reserves would otherwise go below a certain threshold, here assumed to be zero. A crisis is best interpreted as a (possibly partial) default[11] on contracted debt in a proportion $0 \leq \bar{\delta}/(1 + \bar{\delta}) \leq 1$ that prevents reserves from going negative. It is assumed that $\bar{\delta} = 1$, so that a default reduces the value of debt by half.

We first summarize in table 1 the properties of the actual data on emerging-market spreads for the periods of data availability between 1994 and 2002, for the emerging-market countries for which JP Morgan

Table 1. Summary Statistics for the Distribution of Actual Changes in Emerging-Market
        Spreads, All Countries (Spread Data in Percentage Points)

Summary Statistics	Daily	Monthly
Mean	0.00214	−0.0219
Standard deviation	0.4832	0.5585
Skewness	−0.305	−5.70
Excess Kurtosis	86.06	82.34
Largest	11.54	4.09
Smallest	−10.70	−8.46
Jarque-Bera test for normality	8,592,384	8,015,985
Number of observations	27,842	1,297

Note: Countries are Argentina, Bulgaria, Brazil, Colombia, Ecuador, Korea, Morocco, Mexico, Nigeria, Panama, Peru, the Philippines, Poland, Qatar, Russia, Turkey, Ukraine, Venezuela, and South Africa. Daily data spanned 31 December 1993 to 19 July 2002, or shorter periods when a country's data was not available for the whole period.

collected data (the countries and time periods are detailed in Masson 2003, which also presents a more detailed analysis). Both the daily and monthly (month-end to month-end) changes exhibit a large amount of excess kurtosis in comparison to the normal (whose kurtosis is 3.0). Interestingly, the distribution is nearly symmetric, and the mean change is close to zero. As well as skewness and kurtosis, the table reports the Jarque-Bera test statistic of the null hypothesis of normality, based on those two moments,[12] and the maximum and minimum change in the spread.

The distribution of simulated daily changes in emerging-market spreads over the U.S. Treasury bill rate is given in table 2, for simulation runs of length 28,000 days (of which the first 100 were dropped to minimize the effects of initial conditions). It can be seen that unlike the actual data for changes in spreads, the simulations reported in the first four lines do not produce fat tails. In fact, the distribution has thin tails, not fat tails, since the kurtosis is less than the value of 3 that characterizes the normal. Skewness, although small, is consistently positive. As a result, normality is rejected at a very small p-value, using the Jarque-Bera test. It is also the case that the simulations tend to produce serial correlation in changes in spreads (not reported); since this stylized fact is easy to replicate, we do not dwell on it further.

Table 2 explores whether the absence of fat tails is robust to changing the model's parameters. The table presents statistics for simulations with alternative values for risk aversion, the probability of experimentation, the probability of investing in a given period, the maximum value for the probability of default, the standard deviation of shocks to the trade balance, and the endogeneity of wealth. Increasing the value of π^{max} from 0.1 to 0.5 causes dramatic increases in the dispersion of changes in spreads, while introducing risk aversion also has that effect, but more moderately. In contrast, decreasing the probability of experimentation, not surprisingly, lowers volatility. Other changes reported in table 2 have relatively modest impacts. In particular, a striking result is that multiplying by 10 the standard

Table 2. One Emerging Market Monthly Model: Simulated Effects of Daily Changes in Parameters on the Distribution of Changes in Emerging-Market Spreads, in Percentage Points (27,900 Observations)

Memory Length	Parameter Values					Wealth Endogenous	Distribution Statistics					
	P_{ex}	P_{inv}	π^{max}	b^{max}	σ_ε		Range	Mean[a]	Std. Dev.	Skewness	Kurtosis	Jarque-Bera
1. 1	0.333	0.9	0.1	∞	0.730	N	(−1.26, 1.59)	0.0004	0.364	0.049	−0.119	27.6
2. 1	0.333	0.9	0.1	∞	0.730	N	(−1.25, 1.52)	0.0006	0.366	0.045	−0.117	25.3
3. 5	0.333	0.9	0.1	∞	0.730	N	(−1.25, 1.45)	0.0005	0.348	0.016	−0.053	4.5
4. 5	0.333	0.9	0.5	∞	0.730	N	(−7.86, 6.68)	−0.0020	1.731	0.018	−0.031	2.6
5. 5	0.333	0.9	0.5	5	0.730	N	(−6.32, 6.62)	0.0060	1.539	0.052	0.032	13.8
6. 5	0.333	0.9	0.5	5	0.730	Y	(−6.37, 7.18)	−0.0015	1.537	0.070	0.033	24.1
7. 5	0.333	0.9	0.5	5	7.320	Y	(−5.96, 5.42)	−0.0005	1.328	0.005	0.042	2.2
8. 5	0.167	0.5	0.1	5	0.730	Y	(−7.10, 6.42)	0.0081	1.520	0.067	0.176	56.9
9. 5	0.167	0.5	0.1	1	0.730	Y	(−8.07, 7.67)	0.0119	1.723	0.029	0.081	11.5
10. 5	0.167	0.5	0.1	100	0.730	Y	(−6.24, 6.97)	0.0048	1.426	0.145	0.179	135.0

Note: See text for explanation of variables.
[a]Multiplied by 10,000.

deviation of shocks to the trade balance (row 6) scarcely affects the distribution of the change in spreads. Thus, the fluctuations in the model—capital flows into and out of emerging markets that provoke occasional crashes and spikes in spreads—result here from shifting expectations rather than economic fundamentals (see also Arifovic and Masson 2004).

None of the above changes has a great effect on skewness or excess kurtosis, though the latter is positive in some cases. The Jarque-Bera test sometimes, but not always, rejects normality, as before (the critical value at the 1% level is 9.21). Thus, though these changes affect the range and variance of the distribution of changes in spreads, in all cases the distribution does not exhibit significantly fat tails. The model as it stands does not seem able to replicate this stylized fact, one that is strongly present in the actual data. Our results contrast with the view expressed by Cont and Bouchaud (2000) to the effect that herd behavior (which we have present in our model in the form of imitation) is sufficient to produce fat tails in returns.

4. SIMULATING A MODEL WITH SEVERAL EMERGING-MARKET BONDS

We then proceed to simulate a model in which there is more than one emerging-market bond, in order to consider contagion phenomena. It is an important stylized fact that actual returns on emerging-market debt seem to be highly correlated—perhaps more so than would be dictated by economic fundamentals, and an extensive literature discusses why crises might occur together in several emerging-market countries. In the data (see Masson 2003), changes in emerging-market spreads are indeed highly correlated—though this may not be the same as the co-occurrence of crises.[13] This is a feature that we would hope our model with several emerging market countries could reproduce.

As detailed in Appendix A, in this case investors need to formulate estimates of the covariance of defaults among emerging-market countries when allocating their portfolios. We take the correlation between them (or correlation matrix, in the case of more than two risky assets), but not the variances, as given; that is, investors do not update their priors concerning the extent that returns move together. One would expect that the perceived correlation would be a key parameter for explaining the existence of contagion.

The simulations were performed with a model with only two emerging-market countries, each of them with parameters identical to the case of one emerging market described above, with uncorrelated shocks to the trade balance. Because the added complexity of the model slowed execution time, and in order to approximate more closely the typical time horizons of investors, we simulated at a monthly, not daily, frequency. Time aggregation will tend to reduce excess kurtosis, but in the actual data it is still present at a monthly frequency (see table 1).

An interesting issue is whether it is investors' beliefs that emerging-market bonds are similar that induces contemporaneous crises. A variant

Table 3. Two Emerging Markets: Simulated Distribution of Monthly Changes in Spreads, in Percentage Points (900 Observations)

Perceived Correlation of Defaults	−1.0	−0.5	0.0	0.5	1.0
Country 1					
Mean	−0.0004	−0.0003	−0.0002	−0.0002	−0.0004
Standard deviation	1.893	1.648	1.691	1.664	1.642
Skewness	−0.0000	−0.0038	0.0208	0.0119	0.0349
Excess Kurtosis	0.2133	0.0954	0.0978	0.0851	0.1571
Country 2					
Mean	−0.0002	0.0001	−0.0000	−0.0002	−0.0000
Standard deviation	1.898	1.650	1.679	1.652	1.642
Skewness	−0.0110	0.0462	0.0366	0.0048	0.0291
Excess Kurtosis	0.3432	0.1458	0.0856	0.0758	0.1409
Correlation of simulated changes in spreads	−0.0083	−0.0833	−0.0929	−0.1021	0.0066

of this argument has been used to explain the East Asian crisis, namely the "wake up call hypothesis" (Goldstein 1998): a crisis in one country (Thailand) made investors realize that there were fundamental problems in neighboring countries with similar institutions—or investors may have been misled into thinking there were, even though this was not the case. If the latter, true economic fundamentals might be uncorrelated, though investors treated them as being correlated. Investors might either overestimate the degree of correlation, or think that other investors' portfolio shifts would produce correlation where none existed. Such behavior might conceivably produce a self-fulfilling, rational expectations equilibrium, in which there was contagion across emerging-market bonds.

Table 3 gives the effect of varying the perceived correlation in the defaults by the two banks.[14] This determines the expected degree of covariance of their returns; all investors assume the same (unchanging) correlation, though investors continue to formulate different expectations of the probability of default. While it is unrealistic to suppose investors all perceive the same correlation, this polar case is considered to see whether a case can be made for self-fulfilling correlations as a source of contagion. The table reports on simulations where that correlation is fixed at a value that goes from −1.0 to +1.0. To repeat, the covariance of the two countries' macroeconomic fundamentals in these simulations is actually zero: innovations to the two emerging markets' trade accounts in their balance of payments are in fact uncorrelated.

The striking result is that for most of the values of the perceived correlation coefficient—even when it is positive—the correlation of returns is negative. Thus, there seems to be no self-fulfilling element to expectations here: even if investors believe that crises will occur simultaneously in the two emerging markets, this does not provoke co-movement of their spreads relative to U.S. Treasuries. Thus, this conjectured co-movement is not sufficient to explain any contagion phenomenon, quite to the contrary.

The explanation for the negative co-movement in spreads is simple: since the two assets are substitutes in an investor's portfolio, there is a tendency to increase holdings of one when the other asset is viewed as having a greater chance to default. This portfolio substitution effect dominates any effect resulting from treating the two assets as somehow members of the same risk class. Indeed, the effect of conjecturing a negative correlation among their returns makes investors want to hold both assets, since doing so reduces overall portfolio risk. The reason for this can be seen in equation (A4) of Appendix A. A more negative correlation, other things equal, increases demands for the two securities. Paradoxically, this may thus produce positive correlation in their defaults, not the negative one that was conjectured, since by varying holdings in tandem investors will provoke contemporaneous booms and crises. The converse applies when investors conjecture positive correlations. However, these effects again are very small on the joint distribution of emerging-market spreads, producing only very slight differences in their correlations. Moreover, differences in the latter are not systematically related to the perceived correlations of default.[15]

In sum, the simple model with two emerging markets does not fit the stylized facts better than the model with one market, since in addition to producing kurtosis that is little different from that for the normal for each of the simulations in table 3, it does not provide an explanation for contagion. Thus, the model needs to be either replaced or extended in order to provide an adequate depiction of regularities in emerging-market debt. In the next section we consider an extension that models the varying liquidity of the market through the introduction of a market maker who varies the bid-ask spread as a function of the market's volatility and the market maker's own inventory position.

5.   ENDOGENOUS LIQUIDITY: INTRODUCING A SECONDARY MARKET AND A MARKET MAKER

Conversations with market professionals suggest that emerging-market bonds suffer from periods of pervasive illiquidity, and that this applies across a range of countries rather than being localized in just a single country facing difficulties in its balance of payments.[16] We therefore expand the model by introducing a secondary market in emerging-market debt; bonds are now assumed to have two periods to maturity (except the U.S. asset, which takes the form of cash). Investors purchase debt from emerging-market governments when they are issued (the primary market), with rates of interest determined as described above. However, if investors want to sell before maturity, or to buy a bond with only one period remaining until maturity, they need to deal in the secondary market with a market maker who quotes a buy and a sell price, which differ by the bid-ask spread, and whose average price reflects the size of the market maker's inventory of the security.

There is an extensive literature modeling the behavior of market makers.[17] Market makers are usually assumed to avoid taking speculative positions, making their income by trading, not investing. Therefore, the size of their inventory of securities has an important role in influencing the size of their bid-ask spread (O'Hara and Oldfield 1986). Shen and Starr (2002) develop a model of optimal market maker behavior in which the spread depends positively on the security price's volatility, the volatility of order flow, and the market maker's net inventory position. We follow them in making liquidity (which is inversely related to the size of bid-ask spreads) depend on the market maker's costs, which rise with increasing volatility. We extend their model by including more than one security. We also assume (as do Shen and Starr) that threat of entry leads to zero profits in the long run. Thus, the model mimics competitive behavior (though for simplicity we include only a single market maker in the model). However, the Shen-Starr model takes the evolution of prices over time as exogenous. This is not useful for our purposes, since market makers deal sequentially with many investors and could acquire unbounded inventory positions unless they adjusted the price. Instead, market makers in our model make decisions both on the price level and on the bid-ask spread; we assume that these decisions are separable.

We proceed to describe the investor's decision tree and the role of the market maker.

5.1   Investor

Instead of three assets—the riskless U.S. bond and two emerging-market bonds—we now have five, since investors hold emerging-market bonds with remaining terms to maturity of one and two periods. However, the two maturities of bond issued by a given country are viewed as perfect substitutes, since the probability of default is the same in both periods and the investor does not face stochastic consumption shocks, so is indifferent to the term to maturity.[18] Thus, at the beginning of each period, each investor calculates optimal holdings (x_0, x_1, x_2) of U.S., emerging-market 1, and emerging-market 2 bonds, respectively, as described in Appendix A. After having redeemed maturing bonds, the investor has holdings (ω_1, ω_2) of emerging-market bonds, which are compared with desired holdings. Let $\Delta_j = x_j - \omega_j$ (we omit here the index i that characterizes the investor).

If $\Delta_j > 0$, the investor buys Δ one-period bonds from the market maker or new two-period bonds directly from the emerging-market country, depending on whether

$$\frac{(1 + r_{j,-1})^2}{p_j^b} > 1 + r_j.$$

That is, the investor chooses the bond with the highest return (since bonds pay two periods' interest at maturity, the market maker's selling price on a one-period bond p_j^b has to reflect accrued interest).

If $\Delta_j < 0$, then the investor sells $-\Delta_j$ to the market maker, unless

$$\frac{(1 + r_{j,-1})^2}{p_j^s} < 1 + r^*.$$

That is, the investor liquidates excess holdings unless the market maker's price is so low that the return to holding on to them is greater than the return from investing in the safe asset. Since the investor may be risk averse and demand a premium for holding risky assets (which is already embodied in the desired allocation between the safe asset and the two risky asset classes), this rule of thumb sets a conservative lower bound to the price an investor will accept.

5.2   Market Maker

The market maker is assumed to be a middleman who covers costs but takes no speculative position, aiming only to minimize exposure, long or short. Assuming that there are the same quadratic costs to deviating from zero holdings in either bond (as in Shen and Starr 2002), the market maker's bid-ask spread could depend on the volatilities in the two markets. We parameterize the weight given to the own-volatility and the other bond's volatility using the ξ parameter; we allow for various possibilities. In the base-case simulations reported below, we assume equal weights on the two volatilities; but, as we shall see below, allowing no volatility spillovers produces similar simulation results.

We calculate volatilities as exponentially weighted averages of the absolute value of the change in the rate in the primary market; a fixed window with equal weights would be an alternative, but one that requires storing a larger volume of past data. The constant A is chosen to roughly enforce the zero long-run profit constraint, as would occur under competition among market makers, even though for convenience we model only a single market maker; any excess profits are remitted to the emerging-market governments in equal shares (and hence augment their reserves). Thus, the market maker could be thought of as an agent of the emerging-market governments. The bid-ask spread is set at the beginning of each period. Within each period, the market maker deals sequentially with investors who want to transact, quoting a buy or a sell price. The market maker (who does not initially hold an inventory of bonds) is not prevented from going short, but adjusts the price as a result of transactions in order not to accumulate too-large long or short positions. Thus,

$$\text{spread}_t = A + B\left[(1 - \xi)\,\text{vol}_{1t} + \xi\,\text{vol}_{2t}\right]$$

$$\text{vol}_{jt} = (1 - \gamma)\sum_{k=1}^{\infty}\gamma^{k-1}\left|\Delta r_{j,t-k}\right|$$

$$\text{price}_{jt} = (1 + r_{j,t-1})e^{-\theta X_{jt}}$$

where A, B, ξ, γ, and θ are positive parameters, vol_{jt} is the volatility of rate j, Δr_{jt} is the one-period change in the primary market interest rate set on bond j, and X_{jt} is the market maker's net holdings of security j. In the limit

$\gamma \to 0$ volatility depends only on the absolute value of the change in the rate in the most recent period; $\gamma = 1$ weights all past periods the same. When $\xi = 0$, only the security's own volatility influences the spread; when $\xi = 1/2$ (the benchmark case), the two securities' volatilities have an equal effect.

We also study the cases where liquidity is not an issue (i.e., bid-ask spreads are zero), and where, on the contrary, there is no liquidity in the secondary market (i.e., investors have to hold their bonds for the full two periods until maturity). These two cases are nested in the model: in the first case, by $A = B = 0$; in the case of no liquidity, by A large enough that investors choose never to transact. In the first case we also increase the value of θ and term it "market clearing," even though because of the sequential nature of transactions the market maker does not play the role of a Walrasian auctioneer who first polls all investors for their excess demand schedules and then finds a market-clearing price.

The spread is fixed at the beginning of the period, while the market maker's price varies within the period, depending at each point on the inventory position that has resulted in transactions with investors. Thus the market maker buys at p_{jt}^b and sells at p_{jt}^s, where the prices are given by

$$p_{jt}^b = \text{price}_{jt} \, (1 - \text{spread}_t)$$

$$p_{jt}^s = \text{price}_{jt} \, (1 + \text{spread}_t)$$

The market maker's holdings evolve through transactions with each investor. After dealing with investor i,

$$X_{jt}^{(i)} = X_{jt}^{(i-1)} - \Delta_{jt}^{(i)} \, \text{price}_{jt}^{(i)} \, [1 + \text{sign}(\Delta_{jt}^{(i)}) \, \text{spread}_t]$$

The latter term depends on whether the transaction is a buy or a sell—that is, on the sign of the investor's excess demand. In fact, the simulations randomize the order in which investors transact with the market maker so that investors $i - 1, i, i + 1 \ldots$ vary from period to period. At the end of each period of buying and selling with all the investors who want to transact, the market maker either covers a short position by buying one-period bonds from the emerging-market country, or holds a long position until it matures in the following period.

First, we consider the two polar cases, perfect market clearing (zero bid-ask spreads) and no liquidity (infinite bid-ask spreads), as well as an intermediate parameterization with endogenous liquidity in which investors can, for a price, transact in the secondary market. Summary statistics for both primary and secondary markets—that is, the interest rate on new issues and their equivalent on one-period-old bonds that correspond to transactions with the market maker—are reported in table 4, where all the simulations were run over 1,800 periods (months). The same seed was used across cases, so that the results are comparable and are not due to the random numbers chosen.[19] The first 500 simulated periods were ignored in each case—a longer period than before because this model seemed more sensitive to initial conditions.

Table 4. Effect of Endogenous Liquidity versus No Liquidity and Market Clearing: Summary Statistics for Monthly Changes in Emerging-Market Spreads, Primary and Secondary Markets, in Percentage Points

| | No Liquidity | | | | Market Clearing | | | | Endogenous Liquidity | | | |
| | Secondary Market | | Primary Market | | Secondary Market | | Primary Market | | Secondary Market | | Primary Market | |
	Country 1	Country 2	Country 1	Country 2	Country 1	Country 2	Country 1	Country 2	Country 1	Country 2	Country 1	Country 2
Mean	n.a.	n.a.	0.002	−0.002	0.000	0.000	0.000	0.000	−0.001	0.000	0.000	−0.001
Standard deviation	n.a.	n.a.	1.456	1.517	6.631	14.506	0.543	0.646	1.047	1.195	0.449	0.445
Skewness	n.a.	n.a.	0.380	0.630	0.103	0.100	0.014	6.204	−0.009	0.264	−0.478	−0.442
Excess Kurtosis	n.a.	n.a.	3.983	4.085	17.078	12.119	15.058	133.242	4.758	13.476	3.233	4.200
Jarque-Bera	n.a.	n.a.	891	990	15,800	7,958	12,282	969,984	1,226	9,852	616	994
Largest	n.a.	n.a.	8.02	8.84	48.27	96.53	5.40	13.13	4.35	10.08	2.09	2.31
Smallest	n.a.	n.a.	−6.07	−8.40	−47.04	−95.21	−4.56	−3.58	−4.79	−7.91	−2.72	−3.03
Correlation	n.a.		−0.423		0.430		0.565		0.121		0.592	

There is a stark difference in the results for the three cases. The no-liquidity case (the left panel) gives tails that are greater than the normal, but modestly so: kurtosis is around 4. Changes in spreads for the two emerging-market countries are negatively correlated, as in the results described above. In contrast, both the market clearing case and the intermediate endogenous-liquidity case, in which liquidity is provided by the market maker but varies endogenously depending on historical volatility, produce considerably fatter tails than the normal.[20] Though it would be expected that the secondary market would exhibit the larger kurtosis, excess kurtosis applies to both the primary and secondary markets, though the determination of interest rates in the primary market has formally not been changed. Instead, it seems that transactions in the secondary market, by affecting the amounts held of primary securities, increase the likelihood of large changes in primary interest rates. Though not reported, it is the case that there is always positive correlation, for a given emerging-market country, between the change in spreads in primary and secondary markets. It is even true in the market-clearing case that for one of the countries, kurtosis is greater in the primary than the secondary market, but this seems to be an artifact due to the specific seed used. The market-clearing case also exhibits great instability of interest rates, as shown by the very large standard deviations and ranges of fluctuation in secondary markets. Finally, the correlation between the two countries' changes in spreads, instead of being negative (the no liquidity case), is now strongly positive.

In order to elucidate the factors contributing to the excess kurtosis and positive correlation, we simulate the model with different parameters for market-maker and investor behavior, with the results reported in table 5 (the values taken by these parameters in table 4 are given in brackets).

We first explore whether making spreads depend on the other country's volatility ($\xi > 0$) is crucial to the positive correlation discovered in table 4. The first panel reports results with $\xi = 0$. It is still the case that there is positive correlation in changes in the two emerging-market spreads. Thus, an active secondary market is a feature that contributes to the observed co-movement in emerging-market interest rates, whether there are volatility spillovers or not. In these simulations, the economic fundamentals are non-stochastic and uncorrelated, so there is no reason for co-movement in changes in their interest rates. As we saw above, investors' portfolio behavior was insufficient to produce co-movement (and in fact produced negative correlation), but the introduction of a liquid secondary market is able to do so.

In addition, we revisit the issue of how investors' expectations formation might influence the results, by varying key parameters relative to the basic market-maker case. To summarize the formation of expectations of the probability of default, each investor either compares beliefs to those of one or several randomly chosen comparators (two in table 4)—where an investor is more likely to be chosen as a comparator the higher is their

Table 5. Effect of Key Parameters on Simulations with Market Maker: Summary Statistics for Monthly Changes in Emerging-Market Spreads, in Percentage Points

	Zeta = 0 (0.5)				Number of Comparators = 5 (2)				Number of Comparators = 1 (2)			
	Secondary Market		Primary Market		Secondary Market		Primary Market		Secondary Market		Primary Market	
	Country 1	Country 2	Country 1	Country 2	Country 1	Country 2	Country 1	Country 2	Country 1	Country 2	Country 1	Country 2
Mean	0.001	0.002	0.000	0.000	0.008	0.008	0.008	0.008	0.000	0.000	0.000	0.000
Standard deviation	0.922	2.071	0.603	0.669	1.479	2.527	0.913	0.908	0.627	0.962	0.433	0.397
Skewness	0.377	0.498	0.641	0.015	0.753	0.025	0.549	0.588	1.267	0.302	2.150	1.003
Excess Kurtosis	5.3115	11.070	16.471	9.748	8.651	20.448	10.667	16.245	40.639	17.111	32.780	11.962
Jarque-Bera	1,559	6,692	14,784	5,147	4,177	22,648	6,229	14,370	89,805	15,879	59,205	7,969
Largest	5.11	17.67	5.32	5.42	10.29	23.04	6.69	7.19	8.09	7.64	6.05	4.10
Smallest	-4.55	-12.31	-4.73	-3.94	-8.14	-23.68	-6.00	-7.08	-7.04	-6.91	-2.48	-1.60
Correlation	0.149		0.039		0.132		0.276		0.232		0.585	

	Investor Memory = 12 Months (2)				Maximum Probability of Default = 0.5 (0.2)				Probability of Experimentation = 0.333 (0.05)			
	Secondary Market		Primary Market		Secondary Market		Primary Market		Secondary Market		Primary Market	
	Country 1	Country 2	Country 1	Country 2	Country 1	Country 2	Country 1	Country 2	Country 1	Country 2	Country 1	Country 2
Mean	-0.002	0.002	0.001	0.003	-0.001	-0.011	0.004	-0.007	0.001	0.001	0.002	-0.001
Standard deviation	3.514	3.711	1.095	0.955	7.672	7.300	3.687	3.833	8.923	7.478	1.511	1.483
Skewness	0.077	0.047	1.231	0.608	-0.098	-0.010	1.190	0.699	0.030	-0.032	0.796	0.732
Excess Kurtosis	52.337	33.515	10.243	7.839	19.722	14.664	9.170	4.794	5.454	8.889	2.013	1.107
Jarque-Bera	148,373	60,843	6,011	3,409	21,071	11,648	4,862	1,351	1,611	4,280	357	182
Largest	36.96	42.67	8.21	6.34	59.63	56.98	27.23	23.76	42.52	41.14	6.98	6.08
Smallest	-38.99	-42.16	-6.32	-4.83	-69.45	-61.29	-18.37	-18.37	-44.72	-41.45	-4.76	-3.85
Correlation	-0.081		-0.255		-0.130		-0.119		-0.194		-0.582	

fitness—or, with probability p_{ex} (0.05), experiments by randomly choosing a new chosen strategy. Fitness is calculated over a particular horizon for past returns, which we call "investor memory"; in the simulations of table 4, investor memory is set at two months. Expectations of the default probability are assumed bounded; that bound is the "maximum probability of default" (0.2), labelled π^{max} in earlier simulations.

In table 5, we see whether changing each of these parameters in turn significantly affects the distribution of returns; the other parameters in each case are set to their values in the endogenous-liquidity case of table 4.[21] We summarize the results as follows. First, the number of comparators matters for kurtosis but not in a monotonic way. It seems that having both fewer (1) and more (5) comparators (relative to 2) increases the possibility of large and sudden shifts of opinion, producing occasional larger interest rate movements. Second, longer investor memory (12 rather than 2 months) also increases kurtosis, but reverses the positive correlation. Third, increasing the upper bound on the expected probability of default π^{max} (to 0.5) increases the variance of the distribution (not surprisingly, since expectations now take values over a wider range) but does not significantly affect kurtosis. More surprisingly, however, the correlation properties of the changes in the two emerging-market countries' returns change from positive to negative. It appears that allowing for higher interest rates (associated with greater expected probability of default) qualitatively affects outcomes. Fourth, increasing the probability of experimentation (to 0.333) substantially reduces kurtosis in the primary market. In this case, there is not enough imitation causing the herd behavior that is an important source of financial crises (and large changes in interest rates). Also interesting is that more experimentation reverses the positive correlation that emerged in the market-maker model.

Despite its apparent simplicity, the model is complicated enough that changes in parameters produce nontrivial consequences that cannot be easily be inferred. Clearly, further investigation is needed to map out the regions in the parameter space where the phenomena of interest, excess kurtosis and positive correlation of changes in emerging-market returns, occur. It is also true that other information structures are possible and relevant (see, e.g., Watts 1999), and are worth exploring in the context of our model. For instance, there could be a group of trend setters (e.g., Goldman Sachs, Tiger Fund, or other large investment banks or hedge funds) whose strategies are widely watched and imitated. Or it could be that imitation is regional, with traders in New York, London, and Tokyo constituting separate groups. Exploring these possible networks among traders may be a subject of our future research, which we would hope to make precise by interviews with actual market participants. It may also be worth considering different access to information; market makers (and big investment banks generally, regardless of whether they make a market in a particular security) are widely believed to benefit from superior knowledge relative to other investors (in part because of their contacts with emerging-market countries and their role as underwriters). Agent-based models are particularly useful for studying such interactions (see, e.g., Epstein and Axtell 1996).

We would nevertheless conclude on the basis of our preliminary results that the introduction of a market maker and changing liquidity makes a significant step toward reproducing the stylized facts describing the actual data for emerging-market spreads. There are two crucial linkages here that help to reproduce some of the features of the actual data on emerging-market spreads, and would be present in any reasonable model of liquidity provision and portfolio selection. The first linkage results from the assumption that the market maker's bid-ask spread increases with volatility. However, having the market maker respond to volatility in one market by raising bid-ask spreads in the other market as well is not a necessary feature to produce the co-movements we see in the simulations—similar properties emerge when $\xi = 0$. Second, investors choose to retain their holdings in emerging-market debt when liquidity is too low—that is, when the prices at which they can sell are too unattractive (relative to holding on to their bonds). In any model of optimal portfolio selection, there will be prices at which investors will refuse to transact in the secondary market, and hence their initial holdings will matter. When expectations shift suddenly in the same direction, low liquidity will mean that prices need to adjust a lot in order to make it possible for investors to trade and get closer to their desired portfolio positions. Being locked into their holdings may cause them to incur large losses if there is a subsequent default, and this will then change the dynamic of their expectations formation and their desired bond holdings next period. The endogeneity of spreads is also important in causing serially correlated effects. Iori (2002) finds that if thresholds defining a no-trading range are constant over time (or zero), then volatility clustering does not occur in her model.

6. CONCLUDING COMMENTS

We have identified various important features of the data for interest rates on emerging-market debt and formulated a model, which, after being extended to include endogenous liquidity, is able to replicate some of those features—in particular, fat tails in the distribution of the changes in spreads (against U.S. Treasury securities) and positive correlation between changes in emerging-market interest rates (even though the economic fundamentals are assumed uncorrelated in the simulation model). The analysis is necessarily exploratory and suggestive, rather than definitive. Nothing proves that some other model, even a reasonably parsimonious one like the one presented here, may not replicate the stylized facts as well as, or better than, this one.[22] And despite its simplicity, there needs to be more exploration of the effects of changing parameters or structure in order to understand the essential factors at work. We have identified the networks involved in imitation as a promising avenue to explore. Our model, like other models of heterogeneous agents, has interesting interactions between cross-sectional variability and time series volatility. Moreover, frictions that inhibit continuous rearranging of portfolios produce non-convexities with interesting distributional implications.[23] We hope to understand better in future work the key aspects of heterogeneity that produced the observed time series properties.

Other financial models have also produced returns with fat tails—for instance, through assuming that there are two types of traders, noise traders and fundamentalists, whose numbers vary in some fashion (see, e.g., Lux 1998 and Lux and Marchesi 1999). Most of the analysis to date has been applied to equity, foreign exchange, or developed country bond markets, all of which are deep and liquid. Studying the emerging debt markets is valuable in itself, not least because sharp movements in rates are associated with fears of (and the occurrence of) large defaults and currency devaluations. But, in addition, periods of illiquidity in these markets are much more of an issue than for advanced country financial markets, and contagion across markets has generated more concern also. Indeed, Rigobon (2002) finds that the upgrade of Mexico by rating agencies increased the universe of potential investors, and significantly decreased co-movements with other emerging markets. He therefore ascribes an important role to liquidity factors in explaining contagion. We hope to obtain market-participant data that confirms the link between volatility and illiquidity. In any case, the results of our chapter suggest that endogenous liquidity can, in and of itself, produce some of these features, and hence warrants further research in the context of emerging-market fluctuations.

APPENDIX A: INVESTOR PORTFOLIO SELECTION WITH RISK AVERSION

We consider here the case with one riskless asset and two risky assets; it generalizes easily to the case of several risky assets. Portfolio return R is given by

$$R^i = x_0^i r^* + x_1^i \left(\frac{1 + r_1}{1 + \delta_1} - 1 \right) + x_2^i \left(\frac{1 + r_2}{1 + d_2} - 1 \right), \tag{A1}$$

where r^*, r_1, and r_2 are the interest rates on the riskless (U.S.) asset, and on emerging-market bonds 1 and 2, respectively. Realized default proportions are denoted δ_1, δ_2 on assets 1 and 2, respectively. Portfolio proportions x_j^i sum to 1 for each investor i, so we can also write the portfolio return as

$$R^i = r^* + x_1^i \left(\frac{1 + r_1}{1 + \delta_1} - 1 - r^* \right) + x_2^i \left(\frac{1 + r_2}{1 + \delta_2} - 1 - r^* \right). \tag{A2}$$

By assumption, the investor maximizes a utility function $U^i(R^i)$ with respect to x_1^i, x_2^i, given expectations of default $\delta_j^i = E^i(\delta_j)$. The first-order conditions are

$$E^i\left[U'^i(R)\left(\frac{1+r_1}{1+\delta_1}-1-r^*\right)\right]=0$$

$$E^i\left[U'^i(R)\left(\frac{1+r_2}{1+\delta_2}-1-r^*\right)\right]=0$$

We expand U^i in a second-order Taylor's expansion around the expected return

$$\bar{R}^i \equiv E^i(R^i) = r^* + x_1^i(\mu_1 - r^*) + x_2^i(\mu_2 - r^*)$$

where $\mu_j^i \equiv E^i[(1+r_j)/(1+\delta_j)-1]$:

$$U'^i(\bar{R})(\mu_1^i - r^*) + U''^i(\bar{R}^i)(x_1^i \, var_1^i + x_2^i \, cov_{12}^i) = 0$$
$$U'^i(\bar{R})(\mu_2^i - r^*) + U''^i(\bar{R}^i)(x_1^i \, cov_{12}^i + x_1^i \, var_2^i) = 0 \qquad (A3)$$

and

$$var_j^i \equiv E^i\left(\frac{1+r_j}{1+\delta_j}-\mu_j^i\right)^2$$

$$cov_{12}^i \equiv E^i\left[\left(\frac{1+r_1}{1+\delta_1}-\mu_1^i\right)\left(\frac{1+r_2}{1+\delta_2}-\mu_2^i\right)\right].$$

Writing

$$V^i \equiv \begin{bmatrix} var_1^i & cov_{12}^i \\ cov_{12}^i & var_2^i \end{bmatrix}, x^i \equiv \begin{bmatrix} x_1^i \\ x_2^i \end{bmatrix}, \mu^i \equiv \begin{bmatrix} \mu_1^i \\ \mu_2^i \end{bmatrix}$$

and letting

$$b^i \equiv -\frac{U'^i(\bar{R}^i)}{U''^i(\bar{R}^i)}$$

the first-order conditions can be solved to yield

$$x^i = b^i V^{i-1}(\mu^i - r^*). \qquad (A4)$$

As is well known from portfolio theory, the composition of the risky asset portfolio will not depend on the degree of risk aversion (the inverse of b^i)—that is, the portfolio proportions captured by ratio x_1^i/x_2^i will be independent of b^i. However, the proportion of the total portfolio held in the safe asset will depend inversely on b^i. In the limit as $b^i \to 0$, $x^i \to 0$ and all wealth is held in the safe asset. In the simulations, b^i varies across investors, and is initialized by drawing from a uniform distribution in a prespecified range.

The expected return on each bond depends on the expected default. Default size is assumed known and exogenous (and $\bar{\delta} = 1$, which implies that default reduces the value of the bond by half), so the key variable is each investor's estimate of the probability of default on bond j, π_j^i, which varies from investor to investor. So $E^i(\delta_j) = \pi_j^i \bar{\delta}$, and the expected return for a given investor can be written

$$\mu_j^i = \pi_j^i\left(\frac{1+r_j}{1+\bar{\delta}} - 1\right) + (1 - \pi_j^i)r_j = r_j - \frac{1+r_j}{1+\bar{\delta}}\pi_j^i\bar{\delta},$$

its variance

$$var_j^i = E^i\left(\frac{1+r_j}{1+\delta_j} - 1 - \mu_j^i\right)^2 = \pi_j^i\left(\frac{1+r_j}{1+\bar{\delta}} - 1 - \mu_j^i\right)^2 + (1 - \pi_j^i)(r_j - \mu_j^i)^2,$$

and the covariance between bonds 1 and 2

$$cov_{12}^i = E^i\left[\left(\frac{1+r_1}{1+\delta_1} - 1 - \mu_1^i\right)\left(\frac{1+r_2}{1+\delta_2} - 1 - \mu_2^i\right)\right] = \rho_{12}^i\sqrt{var_1^i\,var_2^i},$$

where ρ_{12}^i is the investor i's estimate of the correlation between the two assets' returns. In the simulations, this correlation is a fixed parameter that is assumed to describe the expectations of all investors.

APPENDIX B: CURRENCY CRASH MODELS AT DIFFERENT FREQUENCIES

Instead of equation (1), the flows T_t need to be divided by n, where n is either 12 (monthly) or 365 (daily):

$$R_t = R_{t-1} + D_t - (1 + r_{t-1})D_{t-1} + \frac{T_t}{n} \tag{A5}$$

All interest rates need to be converted from annual to a monthly or daily frequency:

$$1 + r_t^{(n)} = (1 + r_t)^{1/n}$$

where r_t on the RHS stands for the annual data, $r_t^{(n)}$ on the LHS stands for the monthly or daily data. As for the probability of a default, let π_t^i be the probability over the coming year, and $\pi_t^{i(n)}$ for a fraction $1/n$ of the year. Assuming that the probability of a default in each of the months or days is independent of the others, then

$$1 + \pi_t^{i(n)} = (1 + \pi_t^i)^{1/n}.$$

Another problem is the trade-balance equation, however, because the lagged endogenous variable now refers to the previous *month's* value, not the previous year's. Persistence should be greater at higher frequency, and so should be the coefficient on the lagged endogenous variable. Suppose that the true adjustment takes place at the higher frequency, as in the following equation:

$$T_t = a + bT_{t-1} + \varepsilon_t \tag{A6}$$

If we go to a lower frequency (e.g., the time period is twice as long),

$$T_t = a + b(a + bT_{t-2} + \varepsilon_{t-1}) + \varepsilon_t$$
$$= a(1 + b) + b^2T_{t-2} + b\varepsilon_{t-1} + \varepsilon_t.$$

More generally, if the time period is n times as long as the initial (high-frequency) data, then

$$T_t = a(1 + b + \ldots + b^{n-1}) + b^n T_{t-n} + \varepsilon_t + b\varepsilon_{t-1} + \ldots + b^{n-1}\varepsilon_{t-n+1}$$

$$= a\frac{1 - b^n}{1 - b} + b^n T_{t-n} + \varepsilon_t + b\varepsilon_{t-1} + \ldots + b^{n-1}\varepsilon_{t-n+1}$$

It is this equation that is assumed to have resulted in the coefficient estimates from annual data, say,

$$T_s = \alpha + \beta T_{s-1} + u_s$$

where s is indexed by years. If we infer back from the lower frequency data we can calculate what the coefficients in (A6) should be from:

$$a\frac{1 - b^n}{1 - b} = \alpha, \quad b^n = \beta$$

Similarly, the variance of the shocks to the trade balance needs to be adjusted downward using

$$\sigma_\varepsilon^2 = \frac{1 - b}{1 - b^n}\sigma_u^2.$$

NOTES

1. A sampling of the recent literature is contained in Claessens and Forbes (2001).

2. See for instance, the debate between Obstfeld, on the one hand, and Krugman and Garber, on the other, about the causes of the Mexican crisis of 1994–95 (see Krugman 1996). Krugman, however, changed his position following the Asian crisis, now admitting that there were self-fulfilling elements.

3. See JP Morgan Securities, Inc. (1999) for the methodology of EMBIG.

4. See Calvo (1998).

5. Reserves could also be assumed to earn interest, but since the U.S. rate is assumed constant this complication adds little to the model.

6. The basic model thus assumes risk neutrality. When investors are risk averse, a risk premium that reflects the average across investors is embodied in the market return on the emerging-market bond.

7. Other information structures are of course possible; for instance, only particularly visible investors (like hedge funds) known to have expertise could serve as comparators. We discuss this possibility in the concluding section.

8. As in Arifovic and Masson (2004), if returns are negative, the underlying expectations are not imitated.

9. Sections 4 and 5 report on simulations at a monthly frequency, however.

10. See Masson (1999).

11. However, it can also be interpreted as a devaluation that lowers the foreign currency value of debt contracted in domestic currency. See Masson (1999).

12. It is distributed as a chi-square with 2 degrees of freedom.

13. In particular, our simulations of the market-maker model described below produce high correlations of changes in spreads, but not the co-occurrence of defaults.

14. We simulated 1,000 months (corresponding roughly to the pooled sample of actual data), but dropped the first 100 observations.

15. An alternative, which we have not tried, is to make investors' expectations of the probabilities of default in the two emerging markets move in tandem. This would, by construction, force their interest rates to move together.

16. One definition of liquidity is the narrowness of the bid-ask spread; another is based on the volume of transactions (see Duffie and Singleton 2003). Unfortunately, data for neither measure are publicly available on a consistent basis for emerging-market bonds. In future work, we hope to obtain proprietary data from market participants on spreads, as well as quantitative data on the volume of transactions.

17. LeBaron (2001) discusses alternative market structures for agent-based financial models, including models with market makers, while Farmer and Joshi (2002) study the interaction of investors with different trading strategies in a model with market makers.

18. However, the actual occurrence of default may differ since, if reserves go to zero, the borrower defaults on bonds that mature in that period, while they may (if reserves are positive by then) not default on second-period bonds.

19. In addition, here the simulations for simplicity impose a zero U.S. interest rate and a zero rate of consumption on the part of investors; the trade balances for both emerging-market countries are also zero. As a result, the sum of the net worth of emerging-market governments and investors is a constant (market makers' net worth is also constant, since they remit profits to governments).

20. All of the market maker simulations use a value of $\theta = 0.0001$. The market-clearing case increases this parameter by an order of magnitude, to $\theta = 0.001$.

21. These simulations are done using the same random seed as in table 4, but in order to examine sensitivity to random draws we redid simulations with ten different realizations of the random variables. These simulations are available from the authors.

22. For example, Ben Klemens (personal communication, 3 November 2003) has produced excess kurtosis in the distribution of spreads by modifying this model such that each investor revises expectations of default in light of market consensus as revealed in the secondary market price. The rationale for such a model is described in Klemens (2003).

23. There is an analogy here with the literature on income inequality and growth (see Galor and Zeira 1993).

REFERENCES

Arifovic, J., and P. R. Masson, 2004, Heterogeneity and Evolution of Expectations in a Model of Currency Crisis, *Nonlinear Dynamics, Psychology, and Life Sciences* 8, 231–258.

Blume, L. E., and D. Easley, 2002, Optimality and Natural Selection in Markets, *Journal of Economic Theory* 107, 95–135.

Bouchaud, J.-P., and M. Potters, 2000, *Theory of Financial Risks: From Statistical Physics to Risk Management* (Cambridge University Press, Cambridge).

Bowles, S., and P. Hammerstein, 2003, Does Market Theory Apply to Biology? in P. Hammerstein, ed., *Genetic and Cultural Evolution of Cooperation* (MIT Press, Cambridge).

Calvo, G. A., 1998, Capital Flows and Capital-Market Crises: The Simple Economics of Sudden Stops, *Journal of Applied Economics* 1, 35–54.

Claessens, S., and K. J. Forbes, 2001, *International Financial Contagion* (Kluwer Academic, Boston).

Cont, R., and J.-P. Bouchaud, 2000, Herd Behavior and Aggregate Fluctuations in Financial Markets, *Macroeconomic Dynamics* 4, 170–196.

Duffie, D., and K. J. Singleton, 2003. *Credit Risk: Pricing, Measurement, and Management* (Princeton University Press, Princeton, NJ).

Epstein, J. M., and R. L. Axtell, 1996. *Growing Artificial Societies, Social Science from the Bottom Up* (Brookings Institution Press, Washington, DC).

Evans, M. D. D., and R. K. Lyons, 2002, Informational Integration and Fx Trading, *Journal of International Money and Finance* 21, 807–831.

Farmer, J. D., 2002, Market Force, Ecology and Evolution, *Industrial and Corporate Change* 11, 895–953.

Farmer, J. D., L. Gillemot, F. Lillo, S. Mike, and A. Sen, 2004, What Really Causes Large Price Changes? *Quantitative Finance* 4, 383–397.

Farmer, J. D., and S. Joshi, 2002, The Price Dynamics of Common Trading Strategies, *Journal of Economic Behavior and Organization* 49, 149–171.

Galor, O., and J. Zeira, 1993, Income-Distribution and Macroeconomics, *Review of Economic Studies* 60, 35–52.

Gandolfi, A. E., A. S. Gandolfi, and D. P. Barash, 2002, *Economics as an Evolutionary Science: From Utility to Fitness* (Transaction, New Brunswick, NJ).

Goldstein, M., 1998, The Asian Financial Crisis: Causes, Cures, and Systemic Implications, in *Policy Analyses in International Economics* (Institute for International Economics, Washington, DC).

Iori, G., 2002, A Microsimulation of Traders Activity in the Stock Market: The Role of Heterogeneity, Agents' Interactions and Trade Frictions, *Journal of Economic Behavior and Organization* 49, 269–285.

J.P. Morgan Securities, Inc., 1999, *Introducing the J.P. Morgan Emerging Markets Bond Index Global (EMBI Global)* (J.P. Morgan Securities, Inc., Emerging Market Research, New York).

Klemens, B., 2003, Preferences with a Social Component, Department of Humanities and Social Sciences (California Institute of Technology, Ph.D. dissertation, Pasadena, CA).

Krugman, P., 1996, Are Currency Crises Self-Fulfilling? *National Bureau of Economic Research Macroeconomics Annual* 345–378.

LeBaron, B., 2001, A Builder's Guide to Agent-Based Financial Markets, *Quantitative Finance* 1, 254–261.

Lux, T., 1998, The Socio-Economic Dynamics of Speculative Markets: Interacting Agents, Chaos, and the Fat Tails of Return Distributions, *Journal of Economic Behavior and Organization* 33, 143–165.

Lux, T., and M. Marchesi, 1999, Scaling and Criticality in a Stochastic Multi-Agent Model of a Financial Market, *Nature* 397, 498–500.

MacKenzie, D., 2003, Long-Term Capital Management and the Sociology of Arbitrage, *Economy and Society* 32, 349–380.

Mandelbrot, B. B., 1963, The Variation of Certain Speculative Prices, *Journal of Business* 36, 394–419.

Mantegna, R. N., and H. E. Stanley, 1995, Scaling Behavior in the Dynamics of an Economic Index, *Nature* 376, 46–49.

Masson, P. R., 1999, Contagion: Macroeconomic Models with Multiple Equilibria, *Journal of International Money and Finance* 18, 587–602.

———, 2003, Empirical Regularities in Emerging Market Bond Spreads, *unpublished manuscript*.

O'Hara, M., and G. S. Oldfield, 1986, The Microeconomics of Market Making, *Journal of Financial and Quantitative Analysis* 21, 361–376.

Rigobon, R., 2002, The Curse of Non-Investment Grade Countries, *Journal of Development Economics* 69, 423–449.

Shen, P., and R. M. Starr, 2002, Market-Makers' Supply and Pricing of Financial Market Liquidity, *Economics Letters* 76, 53–58.

Watts, D. J., 1999, *Small Worlds: The Dynamics of Networks between Order and Randomness* (Princeton University Press, Princeton, NJ).

8

Political Contagion in Currency Crises

Allan Drazen

1. INTRODUCTION

The possibility of contagion in currency crises across countries is highly topical, to say the least. Though the phenomenon is widely discussed and is supported by solid empirical evidence,[1] construction of convincing theoretical models of contagion is still in its infancy. Moreover, in existing models of contagion, political aspects of the decision whether or not to defend a currency against attack, central to the "new generation" crisis models, do not play an important role. This chapter argues that political factors of two sorts may be key to understanding some examples of apparent contagion, most importantly the European Monetary System (EMS) crisis of 1992–93. First, the political nature of the decision to devalue, combined with incomplete information about government objectives in making this decision, is often crucial to the appearance of speculative pressures. Second, when one of a country's principal objectives in maintaining a fixed exchange rate is (explicit or implicit) political integration with its "neighbors," a devaluation by one of those neighbors will increase speculative pressures on the country. This argument is especially relevant to the EMS but is not limited to it.

In section 2 models of speculative attack are summarized to make clear the political nature of the devaluation decision. In section 3, existing models of contagion are summarized, as is the concept of political contagion introduced in this chapter. In section 4 a very simple model is presented, along with a discussion of how it may be easily extended to a multiperiod framework. Section 5 suggests why, on the basis of varied types of evi-

Drazen: University of Tel Aviv, University of Maryland, College Park and NBER, E-mail: drazen@post.tau.ac.il. Reprinted from *Currency Crises*, 2000. P. K. Krugman (ed.) with permission from NBER and the University of Chicago Press. The author thanks Paul Masson, Carmen Reinhardt, conference participants, and seminar participants at the Hebrew University of Jerusalem for helpful comments, as well as Esteban Vesperoni for able research assistance.

dence, political contagion may have been important in the 1992–93 EMS crisis. Section 6 presents conclusions.

2. MODELS OF SPECULATIVE ATTACK

In Krugman's seminal 1979 paper on exchange rate collapse, an inconsistency in fundamentals induces a steady loss in reserves, ending in an abandonment of fixed rates. For example, the government is running a deficit and is financing it by printing money. The rate of monetary expansion is inconsistent with the fixed exchange rate in the long run; in the short run, individuals do not want to hold the higher level of domestic currency and exchange it for foreign-currency–denominated assets. The peg rate must be abandoned when reserves hit a minimum level, which is common knowledge to all market participants. However, the peg collapses not at the date implied by simply extrapolating the steady decline of reserves but in a speculative attack at some earlier date, namely, the first date at which optimal investor behavior implies such an attack will succeed.

Krugman's model of the inevitable abandonment of an unsustainable peg was a major step in understanding how currencies collapse, and it has been extended in a number of directions. It has been criticized, however, because its description of the decision to abandon a fixed exchange rate is clearly unrealistic in some cases. In the Krugman model policymakers are passive, sticking with current mutually inconsistent policies and abandoning the fixed rate reflexively when the critical minimum level of reserves is reached. They neither take an aggressive role in defending the current exchange rate policy, nor do they adjust their commonly known policy objectives in light of external economic and political developments.

Though it may be accurate in some instances to argue that a devaluation reflects the technical infeasibility of continuing current policy, a more accurate characterization of the behavior of policymakers in many cases is that the decision about whether to devalue reflects the balancing of conflicting objectives. Deteriorating fundamentals are an important part of the story, but the decision to devalue is taken not because it is literally unavoidable but because of the importance of other objectives given external developments. Hence, devaluation is a *political* decision in that maintaining the peg is technically feasible (especially when a central bank can borrow reserves) but is seen by the government as no longer optimal in light of the costs of doing so and the importance of other objectives.

Krugman (1996) and others have applied the term "new crisis model" to models of currency crises that give a central role to government optimization and that characterize the devaluation decision in terms of a choice between conflicting objectives. As Krugman puts in characterizing the new crisis model, "A government—no longer a simple mechanism like that in the classical model, but rather an agent trying to minimize a loss function—must decide whether or not to defend an exogenously specified exchange rate parity" Krugman (1996: 350). To the extent that weighing conflicting objectives is key to deciding how to respond to respond to speculative pressures, political considerations are central to the new crisis model. Examples of this approach include Obstfeld (1995), Drazen and Masson (1994), Masson (1995), Ozkan and Sutherland (1995), Obstfeld (1996), and Bensaid and Jeanne (1997).[2]

In these models, however, the treatment of speculators is far less meticulous than the treatment of policymakers: the latter are modeled as solving an explicit, well-formulated optimization problem; the former act optimally, but the optimization problem is generally either left implicit or is quite simplified. The problem of formulating devaluation expectations is stressed, but the information structure under which this takes place is quite simple. In Obstfeld (1995, 1996), for example, speculator behavior is summarized by their expectations of a devaluation, rationally conditioned on the government's optimal response to a single underlying shock and on the common-knowledge distribution of that shock. Drazen and Masson (1994), and Masson (1995) add uncertainty about the policymaker's objectives (the policymaker's "type"), and consider how it will interact with uncertainty about fundamentals.

A more realistic model of optimal speculator behavior should have them solving a more complicated, dynamic signal extraction problem in which there are several types of shocks. Bensaid and Jeanne (1997) is more satisfactory in this respect, with the probability of devaluation being derived via Bayesian updating of the policymaker's type. Drazen (2000) considers a dynamic model that allows for several types of shocks where the rational expectations of devaluation are formed by Bayesian updating based on the history of policies and the current shock. In that model what is crucial in forming expectations of devaluation is not simply what policies were previously observed but also the circumstances in which they were observed. Not surprisingly, the information-based model of contagion presented here will be based on that model, though in a simplified form.

3. CONTAGIOUS CURRENCY CRISES

"Contagion" appears to be the latest buzzword in foreign currency markets and in asset markets more generally. However, carefully reasoned explanations of the causes of contagion, or even of what constitutes contagion, are as rare as discussions of the phenomenon are common.[3] I will apply the term to currency crises to refer to the phenomenon whereby a currency crisis itself in one country makes a currency crisis (or currency weakness) in another country more likely. The emphasis is meant to differentiate true contagion from a common shock (other than a currency crisis) that affects countries differentially because of their differential susceptibility to infection. When differential vulnerability to an unobserved common shock reflects unobserved characteristics, we may get what looks like true contagion because a crisis in one country will be followed by a crisis in another, with no apparent explanation other than the original crisis itself. This is an identification problem well known in epidemiology. Following the very clear discussion in Masson (1999), we call these "monsoonal effects."[4]

Masson makes a further distinction, arguing that contagion should be applied only to the case "where a crisis in one country may conceivably trigger a crisis elsewhere for reasons *unexplained* by macroeconomic fundamentals" (1999, 2; emphasis added). When a crisis in one country affects the fundamentals in another country (e.g., because a devaluation reduces the competitiveness of other countries and thus makes them more likely to devalue), he uses the term "spillover." I will use the term "contagion" more generally.

3.1 Three General Models of Contagion

A well-developed general model of contagion is that of information "cascades," in which asymmetrically informed investors acquire information sequentially by observing the actions of others who precede them. (See, e.g., Bikhchandani, Hirshleifer and Welch 1992.) Agent 2 on the basis of own information may prefer action A to action B, but agent 2 observes agent 1 choosing B. Agent 2 thus infers that agent 1 has information favoring B, and this may push agent 2 to choose B as well. Agent 3, observing two previous choices of B, may also conclude that B is optimal, although private information alone would imply choosing A. And so on. The general informational cascade model may be more relevant for differentially informed investors in a given market than for contagion across foreign exchange markets. Two basic assumptions for an information cascade would not appear to be satisfied in foreign exchange markets: the cascade model relies on significant differences in private information across agents, but it is far from clear that there are such informational differences across large investors for major currencies; and the cascade model relies on significant transaction costs in order to generate sequential behavior, but foreign exchange markets are not characterized by such high transaction costs. Moreover, in discussions of the applicability of cascades to contagious currency crises, it is not clear what is the relevant information transferred *across* currency markets.

Less formally, the idea of information externalities has been applied to foreign exchange markets as follows. It is argued that with uncertainty about policymakers' commitments to defending fixed exchange rates, the collapse of the exchange rate in one country may provide information that another country in similar macroeconomic circumstances is more likely to abandon its fixed parity. Though the argument is often heard, the logic is often incomplete. One could justify it in terms of a common unobserved shock that affects countries differentially due to different macroeconomic circumstances, but this is a monsoonal effect, rather than true contagion. As a contagion story, one must make clear what *new* information that is *relevant* to the second currency is being provided by the collapse of the first currency. Since devaluation in the first country provides no new information either about macroeconomic conditions per se (but see the arguments about spillovers below) or about the policy-making process in the second country (but see the discussion of political contagion in section 3.2) a less direct mechanism of contagion may be present.

More specifically, the argument that the collapse of the exchange rate in one country implies that another country in similar macroeconomic circumstances is more likely to abandon its fixed parity may be *probabilistic* or statistical. Market participants envision a collapse scenario which could occur under certain circumstances but assign it a low probability until it actually occurs in such circumstances. They then raise the probability of its occurring in similar circumstances elsewhere, perhaps increasing their speculation against those other countries. Hence, a crisis in one country, previously assigned low probability, may raise the probability of devaluation elsewhere. This is not herding to a currently faddish theory of contagion (a phenomenon which may itself be present), but statistical updating on the basis of drawing another observation favorable to a theory.

Another type of contagion model is a "spillover" model (to use Masson's terminology), focusing on trade linkages. This has been modeled formally by Gerlach and Smets (1995) and Eichengreen, Rose, and Wyplosz (1996). An attack-induced devaluation in one country enhances its competitiveness, leading to trade deficits and declining reserves for its trading partners, making their currencies more vulnerable.[5] If one looks simply at bilateral trade linkages, the idea may be relevant for some cases (as in the effect of the floating of the Finnish markka on 8 September 1992 on speculation against the Swedish krona, as discussed by Gerlach and Smets 1995), but it does not appear to be a general explanation. The magnitudes seem wrong because "contagious" attacks hit currencies where the bilateral trade volumes just are not large enough. However, this bilateral view is probably too limited, for we should consider multilateral linkages, whereby two countries compete against one another in the same third-country market. Theoretically, this appears relevant for Asian countries with significant exports to Japan or the United States. However, the trade magnitudes are probably still too small to explain contagion beginning in Thailand, even when both bilateral trade and third-market trade are included.

An analogous argument is that spillovers occur via financial markets, as third-country investors liquidate their positions in one country to cover crisis-induced losses in another. It is far harder to assess empirically how important this was in the recent Asian crisis. In any case, this vehicle for contagion seems of little relevance for the Exchange Rate Mechanism (ERM) crisis of 1992–93.

A third line of argument is that contagion is linked to the possibility of multiple equilibria and self-fulfilling speculative attacks. Masson (1999), in fact, argues that only models of this sort are capable of producing true contagion, reflecting his view (see above) that contagion, by definition, refers to the simultaneous occurrence of currency crises not linked to macroeconomic fundamentals. In his model, a crisis is the result of a deterioration of the current account, reflecting in turn extremely high debt service. Interest rates include a devaluation premium, so that the expectation of a devaluation can be self-fulfilling. Masson's argument concentrates on the simultaneity of a number of such episodes, rather than a causal link between them. Similarly, Eichengreen and Wyplosz (1993) suggest that high unemployment leads market participants to anticipate a future loosening of monetary policy, inducing speculation against the currency. The costs of defending the currency rise, due in part to the induced upward pressure on interest rates, so that a country may in fact devalue where it would not have in the absence of speculative pressure. Hence the expectation of monetary loosening becomes self-fulfilling. This argument, as will be discussed in section 5 below, is close to but not identical to the one presented here.

3.2 Political Contagion

In the previous subsection, we summarized three general models of contagious currency crises. Each type of model is structured along the lines of the second-generation models of crisis, which stress the balancing of conflicting objectives in the devaluation decision, leading us to characterize these models as "political." The objectives themselves, however, are basically economic, and the nature of the contagion is thus economic as well. In this chapter, I want to introduce a fourth type of contagion that is inherently political, in that the objectives that give rise to contagion are primarily political. Contagion will be intrinsically political, for in the absence of the political objective, devaluation in one country would not affect speculative pressure on another country's currency.

First, what does one mean by "primarily political" objectives in economic policy? Economic decisions are often made on the basis of largely political goals. Income distribution programs are a good case in point: transfers are made with the aim of maximizing votes for the incumbent party. The objective of a decision is clearly primarily political when it supports a political objective which is in conflict with an economic objectives. Hence, holding the exchange rate fixed for the purpose of enhanced political integration at significant economic cost is a primarily political decision. As many have argued, this characterization describes the impetus toward fixed exchange rates in the move toward Economic and Monetary Union (EMU). (Feldstein (1997) argues quite strongly on the primarily political nature of decisions surrounding EMU.)

More generally, the point that the decision to keep a fixed parity may be primarily political can be put as follows. One component of increased political-economic integration with other countries is often the maintenance of a fixed exchange rate with respect to their currencies. This may reflect the desire to form some sort of explicit currency area or trading bloc, as, for example, in the case of the EMU. Or it may be less explicit, in the sense that "cooperative behavior" means refraining from competitive devaluations. Hence, one may think of membership in a "club,"[6] whether explicit or implicit, where the benefits of membership are heavily political and the condition for membership is the maintenance of a fixed exchange rate. (We consider in section 5 the specific institutional details which describe the EMU as such a club.)

The concept of political contagion in speculative attacks follows as an implication of the desire for political integration where maintenance of a fixed exchange rate is a membership condition on each potential member of the integrated unit. One must make one further assumption, namely, that the value of membership in the arrangement depends positively on who else is or may be a member. Hence, if a country learns that other potential members of the arrangement place less weight on meeting the conditions required to join, and hence, are less likely to participate, it will find less advantage in joining as well. It will therefore assign a lower value to maintaining a fixed exchange rate, especially when doing so requires sacrificing domestic goals.

To complete the argument, suppose that speculators are uncertain about a country's commitment to a fixed rate because they are uncertain of the weight the country's policymakers put on conflicting objectives. Speculators know, however, that the desire for integration subject to the no-devaluation membership condition is an important objective. Rational behavior on their part will then imply that a successful attack on one currency (or perhaps even speculative pressure on the currency), revealing a weaker commitment than previously believed, creates an externality in the form of a lower commitment of all other potential members. These countries will therefore be more vulnerable to attack.[7] We term this contagious effect *membership contagion*.

4. A MODEL OF MEMBERSHIP CONTAGION

In this section we present a simple model of membership contagion and discuss the underlying concept in greater detail in section 4.3. The possibility of a contagious currency crisis depends on incomplete information about government intentions, allowing revelation of information about the intentions of other countries to affect the probability of a devaluation. This probability is derived under rational expectations, where it is shown how this probability depends on history, on the country's current circumstances, and on the actions of other countries.

To make things as simple as possible, we consider a single-period model, based on the more general multiperiod model presented in Drazen (2000). The more general model allows for an explicit discussion of how rational devaluation probabilities evolve over time as a function of a country's current circumstances and the history of policy—specifically, how information from the history of policy and the circumstances in which those policy decisions were made affects the current information set. Here this updating of the past will be implicit, but it will be clear how the model is easily extended to a dynamic framework.

The sequence of events in the model is as follows. A country which has maintained a fixed exchange rate experiences a stochastic shock η, which is observed by both the government and speculators. Speculators then choose a level of speculation against the currency, given η and the probability they assign to a devaluation (of known size) at the end of the period. Specifically, speculators borrow domestic currency to be repaid at the end of the period and use it to buy foreign currency reserves. Since maintaining the fixed parity requires that reserves remain above some critical level, speculative demand for reserves determines a minimum interest rate i which must be maintained if the government is to defend the fixed parity. On the basis of η and i, the government then decides whether to defend the fixed exchange rate (denoted by choice of policy F) by holding the interest rate at i or to abandon the parity and devalue (policy D) consistent with a lower interest rate. At the end of the period speculators sell their reserves back to the government and pay off their borrowing. Though speculators use a range of information in deciding whether to attack a currency, we consider basically three types of shocks here: a country-specific factor that is unobservable to speculators (the country's unobservable "type"), a country-specific shock that is observable to both the government and speculators; and, to model contagion, a cross-country observable shock.[8] New information relevant to speculators will generally fall into one of these categories.

4.1   Speculator Behavior

As already indicated, key to speculator behavior is their borrowing of domestic currency in order to buy foreign currency reserves. Speculators are assumed to be atomistic, but the total cost of borrowing is assumed to be an increasing, convex function of the quantity borrowed.[9] This assumption allows us to maintain the simplicity of working with a parametric interest rate, rather than an interest rate schedule, but at the same time to prevent speculators from taking infinite speculative positions. Under these assumptions, one can easily show that total demand for reserves by profit-maximizing speculators is increasing in the probability p that speculators assign to a devaluation and decreasing in the cost of borrowing funds (see Drazen 2000). For simplicity, we make the further reasonable assumption that the cost of borrowing funds is such that demand for borrowing goes to zero as i approaches infinity and goes to zero as p goes to zero.

Suppose that maintaining the fixed exchange rate requires foreign currency reserves to be above some minimum level. For given devaluation expectations, defending the fixed rate then requires keeping the interest rate high enough that total demand for reserves is no greater than this minimum level. (Speculators' beliefs about the probability of a devaluation are fully summarized by p, where we discuss below how rational beliefs are formed, conditional on available information.) This determines the lowest interest rate consistent with maintaining the fixed parity (the "minimum required interest rate"), which given our assumptions is an increasing, continuous function of p, namely, $i(p)$.

4.2   The Government's Choice Problem

We now turn to the decision problem of a social-welfare-maximizing government that has an announced commitment to a fixed exchange rate. If the government is to maintain the fixed parity (policy F), it must raise the interest rate to the level $i(p)$ consistent with maintaining sufficient foreign currency reserves, with the associated welfare loss due to the detrimental effect of high interest rates on the domestic economy. Four areas of negative impact are generally mentioned: negative impact on economic activity, especially when the economy is seen as depressed; negative impact on mortgage interest rates, especially when these rates are directly indexed to money market rates and defense of the exchange rate requires holding market rates high for significant periods (as in the case of the United Kingdom); impact of interest rates on increasing the budget deficit; and possible destabilization of the banking system. We represent these losses by a function $H(i, \eta)$, where H is an increasing and concave function in both the domestic interest rate i and the shock η and $H(\cdot) = 0$ if the government chooses to devalue rather than defend the fixed parity. The shock η is observed by both the government and speculators. It is meant to represent any currently observed factor known to affect the value the government may assign to maintaining a fixed exchange rate, such as changes in the level of foreign currency reserves or changes in domestic unemployment rates.

Not defending the fixed parity and devaluing has both benefits and costs. Since our interest is in the latter, we assume the benefits are subsumed in the function H. Whereas the benefits of devaluation are generally purely economic, the cost of not defending a fixed exchange rate are more political in nature in that they are costs associated with reneging on a commitment. In a multiperiod model loss of reputation would be foremost among these. Membership effects, as discussed in section 3.2, present another example of this sort of cost when devaluing creates a bar to participation in a cooperative arrangement. Two aspects of this cost are important for our modeling of contagion: first, that the cost the government assigns to devaluing is asymmetric information, known to the government but not fully known to speculators; and, second, that this cost depends, among other things, on (at least partially) known information about the commitment of other countries to cooperative arrangement, or club, of the sort discussed in section 3.2 above.[10] We consider them in turn, both in some detail.

The first aspect, asymmetric information about a government's intentions, is modeled as an element x which affects the loss from a devaluation, where x is known with certainty only to the policymaker himself (the policymaker's "type"). Speculators, on the other hand, know only the distribution of possible types as summarized by a distribution $G(x)$, defined over $[\underline{x}, \bar{x}]$. The information summarized by the distribution and its supports could reflect learning about the government on the basis of past observation of its policies and of the circumstances in which these policies were undertaken, as will be discussed below.

The second aspect is summarized by a parameter Z, an index of the value to the country of being in the club. Z could be simply the number of other countries that satisfy the membership criteria, or it could be a weighted sum, with weights depending on the importance for the home country of a given country's participation. More generally, Z could encompass the probability of the club arrangement coming into being, as a function of the behavior of other countries. We present a fuller discussion of the determinants of Z in the next subsection. The loss ζ from a devaluation will equal xZ if the policymaker devalues and will equal zero otherwise.

The trade-off that a social-welfare-maximizing policymaker faces if the currency is attacked—maintaining the fixed exchange rate against maintaining low interest rates—may then be represent by the loss function:

$$L = H(i, \eta) + \zeta(xZ), \tag{1}$$

where the second term is zero if the government defends the fixed exchange rate, while the first term is zero if it does not.[11]

The government's policy choice, given the realization η and the interest rate $i(p)$ required to maintain the fixed exchange rate consistent with speculator's beliefs, as summarized by p, will be summarized by a cutoff type $\hat{x}$ of policymaker who is just indifferent between devaluing and not devaluing. All types with $x < \hat{x}$ will devalue; all types with $x \geq \hat{x}$ will maintain the fixed parity. To see why, first derive the cutoff $\hat{x}$ by equating the value of L in equation (1) under policy F (so that $L = H$) and policy D (so that $L = \zeta$), so that:

$$\hat{x} = \frac{H(i[p], \eta)}{Z}$$

$$= \hat{x}(p, \eta, Z). \tag{2}$$

The cutoff $\hat{x} = \hat{x}(p, \eta, Z)$ is continuous and increasing in p and η and continuous and decreasing in Z. For a type with $x \geq \hat{x}$, $xZ \geq H$, so that it will be optimal to defend the fixed parity rather than devalue; for a type with $x < \hat{x}$, $xZ < H$, so that it will be optimal to devalue. Hence, the cutoff rule fully characterizes a government's optimal behavior, and the probability of a devaluation depends on $\hat{x}(p, \eta, Z)$, given x and $G(x)$. For future use it is useful to denote by $\underline{\eta}$ the value of η such that $\hat{x} = \underline{x}$, for given p and Z. That is, $\underline{\eta}$ is the value of η such that even the government type with the lowest cost of devaluation finds it optimal to maintain a fixed exchange rate, so that the probability of a devaluation is zero.

The nature of the optimal policy should be intuitive. Other things equal, the higher is speculation against the currency (summarized by p), the more likely a government is to find it optimal to devalue, rather than keep interest rates high. (That is, an increase in $\hat{x}$ means that the probability that x lies below $\hat{x}$ increases.) The realization of an exogenous shock η will affect the government's incentive to devalue, and, as we shall see, the equilibrium level of speculation itself. Finally, the fewer countries that are potential members of the association (or the less important are the other qualifying countries, or the less likely for the association to come into being), the lower is Z and the higher is $\hat{x}$, so the higher is the probability of a devaluation.

The determination of $\hat{x}$, and its implications for possible policy choices, also indicates how updating would take place in a multiperiod model. Suppose $\hat{x}$ is above $\underline{x}$ in period $t - 1$, as it will be for sufficiently high η, and the government chooses to defend the currency. This policy choice implies that the government's x is above $\hat{x}$, so that the lower support of the distribution at the beginning of t will be $\hat{x} > \underline{x}$, the lower support in $t - 1$. This is simply Bayesian updating, with the implied updating of the distribution of $G(x)$. If the realization of the current shock η was sufficiently low that $\hat{x} \leq \underline{x}$, all possible types would defend the fixed rate and the observation of policy F would provide no information, so the lower support of the distribution at the beginning of $t + 1$ would remain $\underline{x}$. Hence, the current lower support $\underline{x}$, and the associated distribution $G(x)$, summarizes what has been learned about the government's type prior to the current period on the basis of past observation of its policies and of the circumstances in which these policies were undertaken. The dynamics of speculative attacks based on such learning is the main focus of Drazen (2000), and this inference problem is one of the two key features distinguishing the multiperiod model presented in that paper from the single-period example presented here. (The other is the government's intertemporal optimization problem when it knows speculators are solving such an inference problem.[12] Although we solve only a static problem, this discussion, combined with the discussion of the government's multiperiod objective in footnote 11, indicate how the model can be easily made dynamic.

4.3   Determinants of the Value of Membership

The heart of the model of membership contagion is the parameter Z, indicating the value of membership in a club, which depends on who else is, or is not, in the club. The extent of membership contagion will then depend on the specification of the club for which no-devaluation is the key membership criterion. As already indicated, this club may be a formal arrangement, such as an explicit common currency area or a trading bloc, or a far less explicit arrangement. To the extent that governments see such clubs as important, the political nature of the decision about whether or not to devalue may be seen in part as the decision about which club to join, the club of devaluers or the club of nondevaluers. Furthermore, if one views such clubs broadly, the club may be defined by politicians at the time devaluation decisions are being debated, rather than simply preexisting or previously agreed upon arrangements. Hence, the concept of membership effects, and the possibility of contagion that arises from it, should be seen as including, but more broad, than simply explicit currency or trading arrangements.

The easiest case is that of explicitly defined clubs with no-devaluation as an explicit membership criterion, as is the case of the EMU as discussed in section 5. The link, however, from the no-devaluation membership criterion to contagion may be simple and direct, or it may be more subtle. The simplest link is where a devaluation disqualifies one country from joining the club for at least some period of time, and where the value to other potential members depends positively on that country's being a member. A less direct link is one in which devaluation by one country does not literally disqualify it over the relevant time horizon but makes its participation, or perhaps the existence of the arrangement itself, discretely less likely, thus lowering the value of membership to other potential members, making them more likely to devalue. This may be a more accurate description of the possible causal link from eventual membership in the EMU and the contagious currency crises in the EMS in 1992–93. An unanticipated devaluation by one potential member will reveal lower commitment to fixed exchange rates than previously believed, not only to speculators, but also to other potential members. This raises the probability they assign to that country's devaluing in the future and thus lowers the probability they assign to its meeting the membership criterion when it becomes effective.

In the context of an explicit currency union such as the EMU with a specific membership criterion of no-devaluation over a given horizon, there may be an even more subtle form of membership contagion. A devaluation by a country that other potential members view as important may lead to a weakening of the membership rules themselves. Suppose there is a desire to maximize the likelihood that the EMU will come into being with, say, Italy as a member. Italian abandonment of the fixed parity in a way that might disqualify it because of failure to meet the membership criterion may lead to the no-devaluation rule being weakened, though not scrapped entirely. The weaker criterion would make other countries more likely to devalue, as this would no longer disqualify them as previously. If several countries cannot "clear the bar," one might anticipate the bar to be lowered, so that others that could have will put less effort into maintaining fixed rates. One should be careful, however, in distinguishing between the argument that contagion may result from a devaluation-induced weakening of a no-devaluation criterion and the far stronger argument that a country that devalued believed ex ante this would have no membership consequences. There is no real evidence that ERM countries that abandoned their fixed parities in 1992–93 did so with the anticipation that the criteria would be changed in such a way that this would have no political costs, nor that a devaluation by a potential EMU member left the probability of EMU unchanged.

A related, though less formal, argument is that once a major player devalues and deviates from a previously solid arrangement, other players suddenly realize, "It can be done!" This is a variant of the argument in section 3.1 whereby contagion across countries in similar macroeconomic circumstances may reflect a probabilistic calculation, whereby seeing the phenomenon once significantly raises the probability that market participants assign to its occurring elsewhere. Replacing "probability" by "possibility" and replacing "market participant" by "government" shows how the analogy can be made. It has been argued (see, e.g., Eichengreen and Jeanne 2000) that Britain's leaving the gold standard in 1931 may have had contagious effects on other countries for this reason.

What about less explicit clubs? More specifically, what sort of less explicit clubs might generate membership effects? And how might membership be defined? On a regional basis, politicians may attach weight to being "lumped together" in the eyes of international investors with neighbors whose economic performance is especially good, while differentiating themselves from countries in the same region whose performance is seen as poor. To the extent there is a correlation between perceived performance and exchange rate regime, more specifically, fixed exchange rates, one obtains no-devaluation clubs. Such a club effect may be relevant for Asia or Latin America.[13] One possibility for membership contagion then comes the argument in the previous two paragraphs, by which a devaluation by one club member weakens the membership criterion and makes other members more likely to devalue. That is, if one "success story" that previously maintained fixed rates suddenly devalues under specific circumstances, governments may perceive that avoiding devaluations under all circumstances is no longer a criterion in the eyes of investors to be part of the favored group. Of course, when devaluation itself is seen as revealing weakness, a "reverse contagion" may result. If devaluations by its neighbors are seen as revealing economic problems which may have a regional component, a country's commitment to fixed exchange rates may be strengthened because it wants to make clear it that still belongs the no-devaluation club. The strength with which China and Hong Kong defended their exchange rates in the recent Asian turmoil would appear to reflect reverse membership contagion.

4.4   Speculator Inference and Rational Devaluation Beliefs

In section 4.2 we derived the optimal behavior of speculators on the basis of their beliefs about the probability of a devaluation p. On the basis of speculator behavior, we derived optimal behavior of the government in deciding whether to defend the fixed exchange rate. To close the model, we must ensure that the beliefs of speculators are consistent with government optimal behavior, that is, that they are rational. Hence, we must calculate the true probability of devaluation based on the beliefs p and equate them.

Given the cutoff nature of the government's optimal decision problem, the probability of a devaluation should reflect beliefs over government types. These beliefs are fully summarized by the set $[\underline{x}, \bar{x}]$ and the conditional cumulative distribution associated with this set, $G(x)$. The actual probability of a devaluation, call it π, can then be calculated using $G(x)$ and the cutoff type $\hat{x}$, namely, as $G(\hat{x})$ for states where $\hat{x} > \underline{x}$ (i.e., for $\eta > \underline{\eta}$, as defined above) and zero otherwise. With the actual probability of devaluation π so defined, we may relate it to the perceived probability p using the definition of $\hat{x} = \hat{x}(p, \eta, Z)$ in equation (2). Since our focus is not on the role of history as summarized by $\underline{x}$, we will suppress the dependence of π on $\underline{x}$ and concentrate on the roles of η and Z. The rational equilibrium devaluation probability, for given values of η and Z, is then:

$$\begin{aligned}
\pi &= G(\hat{x}(p, \eta, Z)) && \text{for } \eta > \underline{\eta}(Z),\\
&= 0 && \text{for } \eta \leq \underline{\eta}(Z),
\end{aligned} \tag{3}$$

where $\underline{\eta}(Z)$ is defined by equation (2) for $\hat{x}(0, \eta, Z) = \underline{x}$. Equation (3) will always be satisfied for $\pi = 0$, as $\hat{x}(0, \eta, Z) < \underline{x}$. There will be at least one interior solution for sufficiently high η, given Z (i.e., $\eta > \underline{\eta}(Z)$), or for sufficiently low Z, given η. Given the characteristics of $\hat{x}(p, \eta, Z)$ from equation (2) and the definition of $\pi(\eta, Z)$ in equation (3), it is clear that the equilibrium level of speculation π is increasing in η and decreasing in Z. The solution $\pi(\eta, Z)$ is central to our analysis of the dynamics of contagious speculative attacks.

The model admits the various types of contagion discussed above. An *information cascade* depends on what information is being transmitted; membership contagion discussed below will provide an example. Contagion via *spillover of fundamentals* can be represented by a change in fundamentals in another country inducing an increase in η, and hence in π. Contagion arising from *multiple equilibria* follows from the possibility of multiple solutions to equation (3). There will always be a solution $\pi = 0$, namely where speculators believe there is no probability of a devaluation and do not speculate against the currency (due to the interest cost of borrowing), so that the government finds it costless to defend the currency. There may also be multiple interior solutions. (In this case, we take the highest value of π which satisfies the first part of equation (3) as the interior solution for the discussion of other types of contagion, so that equation (3) will have one positive and one zero solution.)

Our focus is on *political contagion* in speculative attacks, more specifically, the possibility of *membership contagion*, as discussed in section 4.3. This would be characterized by the positive dependence of π on Z, the (possibly weighted) index of other potential members of the club. (A crucial assumption is that Z is known to both speculators and the government, as is the fact that $\zeta(xZ)$ is increasing in Z.) Hence, as long as no-devaluation is a membership criterion and a devaluation provides new information about Z, one obtains true contagion: a successful speculative attack on one potential member country will increase the probability of attack on other potential members.

5. MEMBERSHIP CONTAGION IN THE 1992–93 EMS CRISIS

We now ask whether there is any evidence relating speculative attacks in the 1992–93 EMS crisis to membership contagion. (As argued above, the concept is also applicable to the desire for membership in less formal cooperative arrangements, but we focus here on the EMS.) We present not formal econometric tests but evidence of more in the nature of "case studies," culled from other sources, suggesting that the concept may in fact be relevant. This will concern the answer to two questions: First, is there evidence that a devaluation in one country affected the probability of a devaluation in other countries? Second, if the answer to the first question is positive, is there evidence that this contagion may reflect membership effects?

On the first question, there seems to be general agreement that Britain's abandonment of its defense of the pound sterling in September 1992 did put pressure on some other European currencies. One can see this using the Eichengreen-Rose-Wyplosz index of crisis. More simply, looking at forward rates (measured as deutsche mark per unit of domestic currency), one can see a sharp fall in the rates for the Italian lira, the Spanish peseta, and the Irish punt, and a less sharp fall for the Danish krona and the French franc on September 14, 1992.[14] The Swedish abandonment of its defense of the krona in November appears to have had similar contagious implications.

The far harder question is whether membership effects were involved. This may be itself divided into two questions. First, as far as immediate causation, does a devaluation by one potential member lower the perceived probability of EMU? Second, does a lower probability of EMU actually taking place lower the political resolve of potential members to defend their fixed parity?

The first question is largely one of institutional detail, though not entirely, as the discussion in section 4.3 should make clear. As is well known, one of the convergence criteria required to qualify for EMU is that a country maintain exchange rate stability: it must keep its currency within their EMS fluctuation bands "without severe tensions" for at least two years before joining the monetary union. A devaluation, even one time, outside the EMS bands may thus prevent a country from joining the EMU. This formal membership criterion could then lower the perceived probability of EMU either directly, if the devaluation occurred within two years of when the criterion would be relevant, or indirectly, whereby a devaluation at some point lowers the perceived probability of a wide EMU coming into being in the more distant future. This second linkage, more relevant when discussing the connection between the EMS crisis of 1992–93 and later implementation of EMU, is discussed in section 4.3. Given the uncertainty about whether some countries would be able to meet the no-devaluation-for-two-years criterion when it becomes binding, a current devaluation would lower the perceived probability of EMU coming into effect.

One caveat concerns the previously discussed possibility that the failure of a large country to meet the convergence criteria might create the expectation that the criteria themselves would be changed so much that the devaluation has no effect on perceptions about the likelihood of EMU. As discussed above, there appears to be no evidence for this extreme view. When Italy and the United Kingdom withdrew in September 1992, the perception was quite the opposite; namely, raising serious questions about the future of EMU. Hence, in terms of the model, the EMU convergence criteria imply that a devaluation by one potential EMU country will lower Z for all other potential EMU members.[15]

Will the reduced possibility of EMU lower the "political resolve" of countries that have maintained the fixed parity and make them more likely to devalue? There is much to suggest that this may be the case. First, there seems no doubt that the desire to play a role, preferably an important one in the EMU, was a factor in decisions not to devalue. For example, in his discussion of monetary policy in the EMS during this period, Mélitz (1995) asks why many countries (especially France) followed Germany's lead in adopting tight monetary policy though they were going through recessions. Given France's lower inflation than Germany's and its high unemployment, there is no reason a devaluation would have led markets to question France's monetary discipline. To explain the policy choice, Mélitz argues that "the French official behavior can best be explained on the basis of long-run political goals. By maintaining the policy of the *franc fort*, the French authorities wished to promote the aim of monetary union and, in addition, assure themselves an important place, along Germany's side, in future European monetary control" (1995, p. 26).

An even stronger statement of how new information about the political "will" in one country affects currency values in other countries can be found in Eichengreen and Wyplosz (1993). Speaking about the relation between speculative pressures and the prospects for EMU, they write:

> Until the summer of 1992, anticipations of a smooth transition to monetary union had stabilized expectations and hence the operation of the EMS. At that point, the protracted process of negotiation and ratification allowed doubts to surface about whether the treaty would ever come into effect. This altered the costs and benefits of the policies of austerity required of countries seeking to qualify for European monetary union, leading the markets to anticipate that those policies would ultimately be abandoned. (1993, p. 52)

They go on to argue that this may have played a role in the Fall 1992 crisis. They suggest, as I have, that in making policy decisions, these governments traded off the costs of high unemployment against the benefits associated with qualifying for monetary union. Were the benefits of the latter reduced, the government's calculations would be affected. They write:

> An implication of this trade-off is that the stability of exchange rates should be correlated with the prospects for European monetary union. This was clearly the case in 1992. The weakness of the lira dated from the day the negative outcome of the Danish referendum was known. The lira, the British pound, the Danish krona, and the French franc all fell on June 3, the first day after the referendum. The Danish nej was a surprise; it had not been forecast by the opinion polls. Initially, reports stated that legal experts saw no way the Maastricht treaty, or even parts of it, could be approved and enacted by only eleven EC members. Doubts were compounded by press reports that confusion about the treaty's viability would stoke German concerns about the wisdom of pressing ahead with European monetary union. Italian businessmen voiced fears that Danish rejection would undermine Italy's resolve to comply with the convergence criteria laid down at Maastricht.[16]

The Eichengreen-Wyplosz argument is clearly close to the argument about membership contagion presented here, though it is not a contagion story per se, whereby weakness in *one* currency weakens *another* via the political decision-making mechanism. It is more accurately characterized as a nondevaluation, common shock—the negative outcome of the Danish referendum and, more generally, of the process of protracted negotiations mentioned in the first quote—hitting *all* currencies before any one of them is attacked. But the arguments are similar, each stressing how what are termed here membership effects can weaken the currencies of potential members in a club. The argument in this chapter takes the Eichengreen-Wyplosz argument one step further, showing how membership effects can induce contagion in currency crises.

6. CONCLUSIONS

The argument here was not meant to suggest that membership contagion explains the EMS crisis of 1992–93 to the exclusion of other factors. German monetary policy had "monsoonal" effects, and spillovers of competitiveness clearly played a role in some of the EMS devaluations, as they have in other contagious currency crises. The purpose of the chapter was to highlight a political mechanism for contagion that may have played a role in recent currency crises but has received no careful discussion in the literature. The discussion in section 5 should make clear the importance of external political events on currency crises in general and the possibility of contagious membership effects in particular. Moreover, such effects need not be limited to explicit monetary unions. The next step is to find stronger evidence of such membership effects, in both explicit and implicit cooperative arrangements. It will not be easy, but it may be quite worthwhile.

NOTES

1. See, e.g., Eichengreen and Wyplosz (1993), Gerlach and Smets (1995), and, especially, Eichengreen, Rose, and Wyplosz (1996).

2. A model based on an optimizing government is not identical to one with multiple equilibria and the resultant possibility of self-fulfilling crises. A new crisis model can have a unique equilibrium, as in Drazen and Masson (1994), whereas a nonoptimizing model can have multiple equilibria, as discussed by Krugman (1996).

3. E.g., the most common reason by far that market traders gave for devaluation contagion within the EMS in the Eichengreen and Wyplosz (1993, 98) survey was that "markets 'tasted blood' (realized that there were profits to be made)."

4. Masson focuses on shocks from industrial countries affecting Asian emerging markets, hence the terminology. We will use the term a bit more generally.

5. An alternative argument is that changes in the price levels of trading partners reduce demand for money, leading to a depletion of reserves.

6. I use the term "club" for lack of another term that is concise rather than cumbersome. One should note, however, that the role of clubs in providing public goods is not central to the argument here.

7. This contagion argument should be distinguished from the earlier argument about the spillover of competitive pressures via real exchange rate effects in implicit trading arrangements. The previous argument concerned the trade effect of a lower real exchange rate following a nominal devaluation, which induces a trading competitor to devalue. Here, the argument focusses on the contagious nature of "breaking the rules," *independent* of any effects on the real exchange rate.

8. In a multiperiod version of the model, the country-specific unobservable "type" would be time invariant, while the observable country-specific shock would be time varying.

9. In a multiperiod model, assuming that speculators can adjust their position period by period allows one to retain the feature that in deriving their optimal position, risk-neutral speculators would need only to consider the probability of devaluation in the current period, and would not need to form expectations of the probability of devaluation in future periods. See Drazen (2000).

10. There is no contradiction between saying that the country's commitment to the fixed rate is not fully known and the commitment of other countries to a cooperative arrangement, which may itself depend on their maintaining fixed rates, is at least *partially* known. If this point is not clear here, it will be below.

11. In a multiperiod framework the government would minimize a discounted loss function in which each term would take the form of equation (1), where the cost $\zeta(xZ)$ would be interpreted as a one-time cost. Optimization would be forward looking, in that the implications of policy of F or D in any period for future tradeoffs would be considered. See Drazen (2000).

12. A very similar multiperiod inference problem, as applied to the information conveyed by a policy of capital account liberalization, is presented in Bartolini and Drazen (1997).

13. It seems quite relevant for France as well in the early part of the EMS period. In contrast to the strongly expansionary policies that the socialist government followed after coming to power in May 1981, there was an important change in behavior in June 1982, reinforced in March 1983, when France shifted to far tighter fiscal and monetary policies, the *politique de rigueur*. The purpose of this change in policy, which had a serious cost in terms of significantly higher unemployment, was to convince investors of a change in underlying government objectives. France made this change credible by accepting high unemployment without devaluing. There were no realignments for a three-year period, despite unemployment rising above 10 percent. For a fuller discussion, see Drazen and Masson (1994).

14. The model would predict that not all currencies would be equally affected by contagion. For strong currencies with $\pi = 0$ originally, the increase in Z would still leave $\hat{x} < x$, so that equilibrium $\pi(\eta, Z)$ will still equal zero, and no change in speculative pressures will be observed. For other currencies, however, a successful speculative attack elsewhere will increase already speculative pressures or will introduce them if absent (i.e., where the increase in z pushes $\hat{x}$ above x, so that π rises from zero to $G(\hat{x}(p, \eta, Z)) > 0$).

15. Moreover, as discussed in section 4.3, the perception that membership criteria would be significantly changed could lead to membership contagion via a different linkage.

16. Eichengreen and Wyplosz (1993, 85–86). For references on these, especially quotes in the Financial Times, June 4 and June 23, 1992 on Italy, see note 43 of Eichengreen and Wyplosz (1993).

REFERENCES

Bartolini, L., and A. Drazen, 1997, When Liberal Policies Reflect External Shocks, What Do We Learn?, *Journal of International Economics* 42, 249–273.

Bensaid, B., and O. Jeanne, 1997, The Instability of Fixed Exchange Rate Systems When Raising the Nominal Interest Rate Is Costly, *European Economic Review* 41, 1461–1478.

Bikhchandani, S., D. Hirshleifer, and I. Welch, 1992, A Theory of Fads, Fashions, Customs, and Cultural Change as Informational Cascades, *Journal of Political Economy* 100, 992–1026.

Drazen, A., 2000, Interest-Rate and Borrowing Defense against Speculative Attack, *Carnegie-Rochester Conference Series on Public Policy* 53, 303–348.

Drazen, A., and P. R. Masson, 1994, Credibility of Policies Versus Credibility of Policy-Makers, *Quarterly Journal of Economics* 109, 735–754.

Eichengreen, B., A. K. Rose, and C. Wyplosz, 1996, Contagious Currency Crises: First Tests, *Scandinavian Journal of Economics* 98, 463–484.

Eichengreen, B., and C. Wyplosz, 1993, The Unstable EMS, *Brookings Papers on Economic Activity* 1, 51–143.

Feldstein, M., 1997, The Political Economy of the European Economic and Monetary Union: Political Sources of an Economic Liability, *Journal of Economic Perspectives* 11, 23–42.

Gerlach, S., and F. Smets, 1995, Contagious Speculative Attacks, *European Journal of Political Economy* 11, 45–63.

Krugman, P., 1979, Model of Balance-of-Payments Crises, *Journal of Money Credit and Banking* 11, 311–325.

———, 1996, Are Currency Crises Self-Fulfilling?, *National Bureau of Economic Research Macroeconomics Annual* 345–378.

Masson, P. R., 1995, Gaining and Losing EMS Credibility—The Case of the United Kingdom, *Economic Journal* 105, 571–582.

———, 1999, Contagion: Monsoonal Effects, Spillovers and Jumps between Multiple Equilibria, in P.-R. Agénor, M. Miller, D. Vines, and A. Weber, eds., *The Asian Financial Crisis: Causes, Contagion and Consequences* (Cambridge University Press, Cambridge, New York, and Melbourne).

Mélitz, J., 1995, Comment, in C. Bordes, E. Girardin, and J. Mélitz, eds., *European Currency Crises and After* (Manchester University Press; distributed in the U.S. by St. Martin's Press, Manchester).

Obstfeld, M., 1995, The Logic of Currency Crises, in B. Eichengreen, J. Frieden, and J. von Hagen, eds., *Monetary and Fiscal Policy in an Integrated Europe* (Springer, Heidelberg).

———, 1996, Models of Currency Crises with Self-Fulfilling Features, *European Economic Review* 40, 1037–1047.

Ozkan, F. G., and A. Sutherland, 1995, Policy Measures to Avoid a Currency Crisis, *Economic Journal* 105, 510–519.

Index